The Uncertain Revolution

The Uncertain Revolution

Washington & the Continental Army at Morristown

JOHN T. CUNNINGHAM

CORMORANT
PUBLISHING
An imprint of Down The Shore Publishing

West Creek, New Jersey

Copyright © 2007 John T. Cunningham. All rights reserved.

Material in this book may not be used, transmitted, uploaded or reproduced, in whole or in part in any form or by any means, digital, electronic or mechanical, including photocopying, video, audio or other recording, or by any information, storage and retrieval system without written permission, except in the case of brief quotations embodied in critical articles and reviews. For permissions or information, contact the publisher at the address below. Images published herein are also protected by separate copyright, which is retained by the credited owner. Copyrighted material is used here by special arrangement, with the permission of and licensed by the copyright holder.

An imprint of Down The Shore Publishing

Box 100, West Creek, NJ 08092
www.down-the-shore.com

DOWN THE SHORE
PUBLISHING

The words "Down The Shore" and the Down The Shore Publishing logos are registered U.S. Trademarks.

Manufactured in the United States of America.
2 4 6 8 10 9 7 5 3 1
First printing, 2007

Publication of this book was made possible, in part, by generous support from Norman B. Tomlinson, Jr.

Book design by Leslee Ganss

Library of Congress Cataloging-in-Publication Data

Cunningham, John T.

The uncertain revolution : Washington and the Continental Army at Morristown / John T. Cunningham.

p. cm.

Includes bibliographical references and index.

ISBN-13: 978-1-59322-028-0 (hardcover)

ISBN-10: 1-59322-028-6 (hardcover)

1. Washington, George, 1732-1799--Headquarters--New Jersey--Morristown. 2. United States. Continental Army--Military life. 3. Morristown (N.J.)--History, Military--18th century. 4. Watchung Mountains (N.J.)--History, Military--18th century. 5. New Jersey--History--Revolution, 1775-1783--Campaigns. 6. United States--History--Revolution, 1775-1783--Campaigns. 7. Morristown Region (N.J.)--History, Local. 8. Watchung Mountains (N.J.)--History, Local. 9. Morristown National Historical Park (N.J.)--History. I. Title.

F144.M9C86 2007

973.3'33--dc22

2007020470

*To Eric Olsen and Tom Winslow,
park rangers/historians at Morristown National
Historical Park, whose encouragement and
continuing support made this book possible.*

TABLE *of* CONTENTS

The Palladian-style front door of the Ford Mansion, where George Washington spent his second winter in Morristown.

A PERSONAL PERSPECTIVE

This is a book that has been taking shape in my mind since childhood. I grew up in a New Jersey village called Brookside, about four miles west of Morristown and about three miles northeast (as the crow flies) of Jockey Hollow.

My sense of Jockey Hollow was stirred when a boy named Charlie joined our fourth grade class in the two-room Brookside Grammar School. He told us of his bedroom, where "some girl" during "some war" had hidden her horse to keep it away from some enemy or other. Charlie insisted hoof prints could be seen in the floor.

The next Saturday morning, I walked the three miles to Charlie's house and knocked on the family's huge back door. His mother bade me enter what today likely would be called a very large all-purpose room. It featured an imposing fireplace, seven or eight-feet wide. She told me that they cooked meals in the fireplace, ate meals and played games on a big oak table in front of the fire, and did homework by its light. It seemed to me a wonderful way of life.

Charlie hustled me to the bedroom door as soon as possible. I peered into the room, big enough for at least a horse and a bed. Charlie pointed to what he called "horse prints" on the floor. I couldn't see them but I took his word.

Soon after, the National Park Service acquired Charlie's house and hundreds of surrounding acres as the nucleus of American's first national historical park. I learned the house belonged to the Wick Family during the American Revolution and the "girl" of Charlie's tale was Temperance ("Tempe") Wick.

Sadly (in my opinion), I also learned that while Tempe had a horse, there was absolutely no evidence that a horse had ever been hidden inside the house. Charlie's story was not true, however traditional and accepted it has become. It is the park's most enduring legend.

When I was in high school, I visited the Ford Mansion in Morristown for the first time — on my own volition. No teacher prepared me for either the Jockey Hollow encampment or the magnificent Ford Mansion, or the fact that erupting volcanoes of 125 million years ago were a central reason for Morristown's major role in the American Revolution.

I have been in the Ford Mansion many times as an adult on journalistic assignments linked to Washington's occupancy in the winter of 1779-80. On one such visit I saw a very large metal (bronze, as I recall it) model of two parallel mountain ridges interrupted by a deep gap. The model, about three feet wide, was of the "gap in the Short Hills," a vivid exposition of the formation and its value as a defensive site.

Quite recently, I inquired about the bronze "map" (for want of a better name). It has been stored in an unknown place and temporarily mislaid, I was told. Yet it remains firmly fixed in memory as one of the most significant teaching devices I have ever seen.

The ridges, the gap and the significance of this geological wonder are briefly explained in the Introduction. I am convinced that no geographic (and geological) entity was more important in ultimately winning the war than the Watchung Mountains.

I remain thankful to Charlie for introducing me to the girl with the horse, however fictional; it gave me a sentimental attachment to Jockey Hollow. I also will forever be thankful to the park ranger who long ago showed me the bronze model that gave me an insight into why the natural fortress became so vital in winning the war.

The Tempe Wick myth is part of this book, as are the stories of Molly Pitcher and Fort Nonsense. Tempe did live in the Wick house and owned a favorite horse, there is an eyewitness account of a woman tending a cannon at the Battle of Monmouth and the fort called "Nonsense" was a very important part of the Morristown story. A visiting historian-folklorist bestowed the nonsensical name on the fort, years after the Revolution had passed.

Far more important to this book is the "gap map." It never left my mind. Each time I looked at it, and each time I passed through the gap (until modern Route 24 all but nullified it), the conviction grew that the gap — and the mountain ridges it pierced — were keys to America's ultimate victory in the American Revolution.

It is a story that must be told.

John T. Cunningham
Florham Park, New Jersey

Five scenes from Washington's years in Morristown are featured in this eight panel bronze door of the Theodore N. Vail mansion on South Street in Morristown. Three are presented in this book on pages 45, 123 and 255.

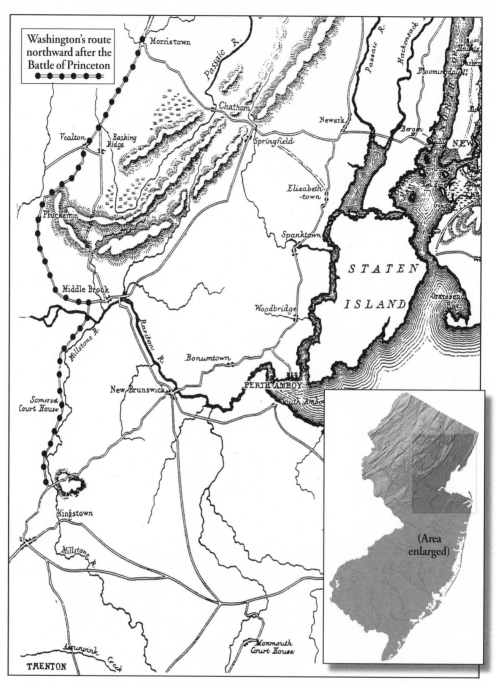

Washington's route
northward after the
Battle of Princeton

*After the Battle of Princeton, Washington headed north to Somerset Court House (now Millstone)
on the Millstone River, to Pluckamin around the western edge of the Watchung Mountains,
to Vealton (Bernardsville), and then north to Morristown.*

A MIGHTY FORTRESS

V ictory in the American Revolution was insured more by a series of fiery, volcanic eruptions 150 million years ago than by the military genius of George Washington or the valor of his often uncertain soldiers. The eruptions sent several waves of molten lava streaming across barren land to form what are now New Jersey's Watchung Mountains, the American Revolution's most formidable natural bulwark.

The two outer Watchung ridges, like the outer walls of a tremendous fortress, rise as high as 879 feet above sea level, just north of what is now Paterson. Elsewhere along the top of the basaltic formation the ridges are between 450 and 600 feet high. Considering that sea level is less than eight miles from the outer ridge, the rise of the formation is precipitous, and in places, cliff-like.

Geological time also saw an ancient ancestor of today's Passaic River carve out a deep gap in the ridges, midway on a straight line between Morristown and the lower tip of New York. The location of the gap is uncanny, considering the role it was destined to play in American history.

There were lesser gaps to the south, but none offered an easy or convenient passage through the ridges. The major gap, usually known as the Springfield Gap, could be defended easily by sharpshooters or light artillery posted on the top of either side of the opening. The British made only two anemic efforts to pass through the opening, in the autumn of 1777 and at the end of the Battle of Springfield on June 23, 1780. Both were quickly repulsed.

Immediately behind the gap were widespread, irregular marshlands, forming what might be considered an "inside moat." The most important fen, known even in colonial days as the Great Swamp, was fearsome to anyone on foot. (Today this is part of the Great Swamp National Wildlife Refuge.)

It should be evident that the emerging United States could only be conquered by whichever side controlled or neutralized New York and Philadelphia. The corridor and roads linking the cities ran for a considerable distance within easy view of the Watchungs. The countryside as far away as Sandy Hook could be monitored from heights in the southern part of the mountains.

The Watchung ridges were a perfect refuge and vantage point as long as the British command maintained its headquarters in New York. The British left only once during the war, in 1777, when General William Howe took his army to Philadelphia for the winter. Washington immediately broke camp to follow the enemy south, eventually wintering at Valley Forge.

Historians disagree on why Washington took his army north after the electrifying triumphs at Trenton and Princeton at the end of 1776 and the beginning of 1777. It is true that he had little other recourse, but his many civilian years as a surveyor and his reliance on map makers surely made him aware of the strategic value of the Watchung Mountains. He did not command by whim.

The mountain ridges offered the safety and security Washington needed for winter quarters, which he established within or close to the formation. He set up winter camps twice in Morristown and a third time on one of the Watchung's southern slopes, about fifteen miles due south of Morristown.

Then, for the winter of 1780-81, while he spent the winter in New Windsor, New York, Washington sent 2,500 men, a substantial force — about half his main army — back to Morristown for yet another winter. No other area of the infant United States, from Savannah to Boston, came close to the Watchungs in constant military importance.

Washington's obvious strategy throughout the war was to avoid extended direct open field conflict with the enemy. Even the Battles of Trenton and Princeton, for all their brilliance, were "hit and run" affairs. The cautious tactics shielded the precious troops and earned Washington the unseemly sobriquet of "the master of defeat and retreat."

The commander's armies were at least elusive and often evanescent, particularly in winter when many men drifted away from camp The three major winter camps behind the Watchungs were replete with suffering, despair, desertion, thievery, indifference and open mutiny.

Soldiers at Middlebrook faced an indifferent public; farmers sold produce mainly to those offering the highest profits – and if that meant the British, so be it. The American troops were starving, freezing, barefoot, and angry.

The winter of 1779-80 at Morristown tested the army in nearly every conceivable way. The fifth snow of the season was falling on December 1, when the first soldiers reached Morristown and marched south about three miles to begin building log huts for themselves in Jockey Hollow.

Twenty-eight snows fell that winter, and a blizzard in early January 1780 left drifts more than four feet high on the roads. A regimental clothier wrote that some troops were "as naked as Lazarus" and Washington wrote that with respect to supplies, the situation of the army was "beyond description."

Continental money was virtually worthless. Desertions were numerous. Washington had to order farmers to sell food to the army at fair prices or face having grain and beef cattle seized by armed soldiers. Serious mutinies erupted at Jockey Hollow in Morristown in the spring of 1780 and on New Year's Day in 1781.

The desperation of woefully abused American soldiers is a basic theme of this book — and nowhere was the suffering or congressional indifference worse than during the horrific winter of 1779-80 at Morristown.

Congress became so annoyed by Washington's endless stream of letters describing the evils of that winter that it sent a committee to study the situation, with instructions to cut the numbers of troops and reduce the army budget much as possible. It just couldn't believe that things were as bad as the general painted them.

Ten days after it arrived in Morristown, the committee sent one of its members galloping to Philadelphia with a report meant to shatter the complacency of congress. In short, the committee said conditions at Jockey Hollow were far worse than Washington had been reporting.

The construction of present day Route 24 to connect interstate routes 78 and 287, via the original gap, has all but obliterated any evidence of this once-vital passageway. Huge amounts of fill have brought the highway's pavement close to the top of the gap. While the road is steep, it hides the old formations that baffled British and Hessian forces throughout the war.

A century and a half, and millions of dollars later, huge machines blasted new gaps through the Watchungs — near Paterson, on Eagle Rock Avenue, along Route 280 at West Orange, and the cuts which speed Route 78 traffic through the column-like formations common to basaltic ridges.

It is hard for the modern visitor to imagine the Watchungs as a defensive barrier. In the late 1700s, behind those towering walls, through swamps and across a broad river, the American army endured for longer periods than anywhere else in America. Despite desperate suffering in the ranks, Washington's army survived in their mountain stronghold, and rose again and again to find victory.

Washington's familiar position astride his steed is captured in this heroic bronze equestrian statue that stands directly across the street from the front of the general's 1779-80 winter headquarters in Morristown.

Chapter One

OPTING *for* SECURITY

eneral George Washington, his top advisers and what remained of the American
army stood in the cold winds east of Princeton on January 3, 1777, a few minutes
after American troops had finished an amazing ten days of triumph by smashing
the British army in Princeton. A quick survive-or-perish decision had to be made: where
would they take this ragged, hungry, weary army to give it a chance to survive?

Washington and most of his generals thirsted to strike northeastward a dozen miles or
so over the nearly level ground that led to New Brunswick. Such boldness could capture
the British stronghold, with the possible bonus of £70,000 in English gold rumored to be
cached in the Raritan River town. It was believed that only a small garrison had been left to
guard the town when British General Charles Cornwallis had raced his army to Trenton in
the hope of overwhelming Washington.

New Brunswick was a tempting target. Major James Wilkerson of Philadelphia later
recalled that "pressed as we were for time, it was the desire of the commander in chief, and
the inclination of every other officer" to attack the British position. Wilkerson said the
overwhelming lament was "Oh, that we had 500 fresh men to beat up their quarters!"

There were no fresh men. The exhausted troops had dropped to the ground as soon as
the halt was called. Neither was there time for a debate. The frustrated, embarrassed English
army was racing in from the west, "in an infernal sweat," as General Henry Knox, the one-
time Boston bookseller and now head of an emerging American artillery regiment, recalled
it. The British commander, Lord Cornwallis, completely outwitted and outfought by Washington, was (again according to Knox) "running, puffing, and blowing and swearing."

Cornwallis and his regrouped forces now blocked off any return to the encampment
across the Delaware River. The British also could easily isolate and destroy the exhausted

After the stunning victory at Princeton on January 3, 1777, Washington had to move quickly to escape the oncoming British. A short consultation led to the decision to seek safety in Morristown.

Continental army if an attempt were made to move southward over level ground.

Clearly in the minds of the American officers was the fear that even if the Americans could occupy New Brunswick, the war might end with Washington's force under siege on the banks of the Raritan River, unable to make a tactical move and with winter supplies cut off. Cornwallis certainly would have pressed the battle-worn Continentals if they headed for New Brunswick; other British forces from New York could have closed the circle.

Only one safe, open road beckoned: northward through the Millstone River valley to the New Jersey hills. It is not clear — and probably never will be — exactly why Washington chose to spend the winter at Morristown. However, Wilkerson said "it had previously been determined by the general, on advice of General St. Clair, after the plan of visiting New Brunswick was abandoned, to take quarters at Morristown."

Many historians argue that the turn to the north was made in lieu of any other option. However, sufficient evidence exists to indicate that Washington sensed what advantages might be found in Morristown for his depleted forces. He had not brought his overmatched army this far by gambling on whims.

For one thing he knew of Colonel Jacob Ford, Jr., wealthy young iron master and intrepid leader of the strong Morris County militia. Ford and his family lived in Mor-

Washington's Map Maker

Two years of moving armies through uncharted American wilderness so acutely underscored the need for accurate maps that George Washington wrote Congress on July 19, 1777: "A good geographer to survey the roads and take sketches of the country where the army is to act would be extremely useful."

The letter was not a philosophical exercise. The general told Congress that the man for the job was Robert Erskine, manager of the Ringwood iron mine. Washington had met him only three weeks before.

Washington notified Erskine on July 28 that Congress had commissioned him "Geographer and Surveyor General of the American Army." The general urged an acceptance: "There can be no time when your services will be more necessary than the present."

Three days later, Erskine accepted, and sent Washington a detailed plan of how he proposed to map the war zones. He needed help: "The more hands are employed in it, the sooner it may be accomplished."

Within three years Erskine furnished Washington with more than 200 fine maps. They covered much of Connecticut, New York and New Jersey, the very heart of the war effort. Most of the maps are now preserved in the New York Historical Society.

Erskine had been a loyal British subject and lived in England for the first forty-two years of his life. Born in Scotland, he had received a perfunctory education as an engineer. Soon after his twenty-fifth birthday he was threatened with debtor's prison when a partner in their small British company absconded with the firm's funds. Two years later Erskine invented a successful water pump that made enough to pay the bills. The invention also earned him membership in Great Britain's prestigious Royal Society.

He came to New Jersey in 1771 to manage the English-owned American Company iron works at Ringwood. Gathering war clouds troubled Erskine. He warned his employer in England that revolution could not be turned aside. When war finally came, Erskine threw his lot in with the Americans.

Erskine was working on his last map on September 18, 1780, when he was stricken with a severe cold and a sore throat. Two weeks later he died at Ringwood. He lies in a simple tomb near the ironworks, seldom noticed except by historians who use his maps.

ristown's newest and most-costly home on the eastern edge of the village. Ford brought another plus to the table: he was the son-in-law of prominent Morristown Presbyterian Pastor Timothy Johnes. Presbyterians dominated the area for miles around Morristown; where there were Presbyterians, there would be powerful support for the American cause.

Washington undoubtedly would have known of the steep, rugged Watchung Mountains to the east, midway between Morristown and the British headquarters in New York. If nothing else, he would have remembered the mountain ridges to the west that paralleled his route for many miles as he fled southward through New Jersey in the fading days of November and December 1777.

More important, from his own work as a surveyor in his youth, Washington appreciated the value of cartographers and their knowledge of terrain. His mapmakers most certainly knew of previous detailed maps of northern New Jersey, including one drawn in 1769 by English mapmaker William Faden (whose updated map of New Jersey published in 1778 is a classic). Faden's maps showed, however vaguely, the steep mountains rising west of Newark.

If Faden in London knew of the mountains, Washington's mapmakers who roamed the hills surely knew the thirty-mile-long geological phenomenon better. Known as the Watchung Mountains, they were located about twelve miles west of the lower tip of Manhattan. Morristown lay another fifteen miles west.

Washington led his army north from Princeton, following the road along the Millstone River as it flowed northward. In the late afternoon of January 3, he halted his long column of marchers at Somerset Court House (now Millstone). Their gear had been left behind in the lightning strike at Princeton; the exhausted men had no alternative other than sleeping on the ground without blankets.

Washington and his officers were quartered in the John Van Dorn house and outbuildings. The several hundred British prisoners taken at Princeton spent the night locked up in the well-guarded county courthouse and the adjacent jail.

Marching resumed the next morning at first light, following the road that led to Weston and the Raritan River. The troops crossed the Raritan River on VanVeghtan's bridge at Finderne. Just ahead, the slopes of the snow-dusted Watchung Mountains rose sharply and trailed northeastward until they disappeared in a purple haze. The marchers veered left along the foothills road, then turned north again toward Pluckemin, about a dozen miles from Somerset Court House.

The weary column halted at Pluckemin on January 4 and remained there on January 5, permitting the men the only extended rest they had enjoyed in nearly two weeks. The halt provided an opportunity to bury British Captain William Leslie, who had been wounded at Princeton. He had died in a captured supply wagon that carried him north,

Hessian soldiers who plundered and pillaged as they marched across New Jersey turned many undecided residents into fervent patriots.

and was buried in Pluckemin. Later, the burial was remembered in a stone erected in his memory by renowned Colonial Doctor Benjamin Rush, a friend of Leslie's father. It is still in place.

On January 6, the army resumed its march, heading through Vealton (or Vealtown, now Bernardsville). North of Vealton, as the army closed in on Morristown, the narrow dirt road widened slightly at the base of prominent Kemble Mountain, which rose about 500 feet above the road and continued all the way north to the edge of Morristown. As the army approached the settlement, the marching column first saw the 120-foot-tall steeple of the Presbyterian Church on the east side of the town's New England-like green.

The exhausted yet exuberant Continental Army burst triumphantly across the green just before sunset on January 6, 1777. They kept pace to the slow beating of drums and the sounding of a few shrill fifes. These were America's heroes of the moment, the men who had turned the war around with their amazing defeat of a Hessian force in Trenton only twelve days before, followed by the equally impressive triumph over British soldiers in Princeton on January 3.

The army caught the town completely off guard. In that era of slow communication, townspeople were not yet even aware of the victory at Princeton, much less mindful that it must host Washington and his army for the winter. The startling sight of about 3,000 soldiers — about fifteen times the population of the village — could only have overwhelmed the inhabitants.

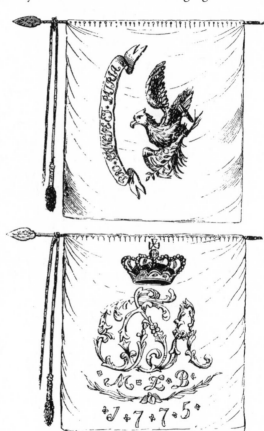

These men were a dirty, ragged, tough-looking lot after nearly two weeks of battling, digging trenches, traveling, and sleeping on the muddy ground. Many were in their teens, and many were barefoot and clothed in threadbare garments. Any observant resident must have asked himself: How can we feed them? How will we house them? How can we live with them? Armies then traditionally lived off the land they occupied; caring for them in Morristown would call for unprecedented sharing.

On the first night in town, soldiers wrapped themselves in their blankets and slept on the ground wherever they found space. Campfires flared on the green and in nearby open fields.

The men quickly became acquainted with prosperous, comfortable Morristown. Its fifty or so houses and its tidy stores centered on the green or lined the five streets that led

These are the two sides of a four-foot square Hessian banner, made of heavy white muslin. All embroidery is in white or gold thread. The side with the eagle bears the message Pro principe et patria *(For prince and country). The 1775 date suggests the flag was decorated late that year as the Hessians prepared to sail for America. A gold British crown surmounts the embellishments.*

Morristown's most vital building facing the green during the Revolution was the Presbyterian Church. Its 124-foot tall steeple housed a bell which was made in England; when rung it could be heard for miles.

outward to surrounding villages. Shopkeepers displayed a miscellany that ranged from shoes to combs, silver and brassware, muslin and silk, wallpaper, and ribbons; hats, needles, ink, gunpowder, playing cards, and coffee. Spices and salt were valuable items for sale. Nearby in the town were many kinds of craftsmen; in the outlying areas, millers and farmers earned good livings by supplying the wants of the town. All of the merchants, craftsmen and millers accepted country produce in payment.

Stage wagons rolled up to the green once or twice a week to bring newcomers to town and to carry businessmen westward to the iron furnaces or forges or eastward to Springfield and Newark. Service to New York ceased when the war began.

The Morris County courthouse and jail occupied the northeast corner of the green. A small Baptist Church and the imposing Presbyterian Church faced the eastern edge.

A stream that rose to the west tumbled rapidly across what is now Speedwell Avenue on the northern edge of town and plunged into "The Hollow," creating power to run an iron forge owned by the Ford family. The forge area, although now greatly changed by twentieth-century urbanization, is still known as "The Hollow." The founders initially called their settlement West Hanover, a nod to Hanover Furnace, the bustling iron-manufacturing town four miles to the east. Settlers soon moved up to the plateau from The Hollow, laid out the green, and began to expand their prosperity.

The settlement officially was renamed Morristown in 1740, a year after the founding of Morris County. The town and county were both named for Governor Lewis Morris, a native New Jerseyan who in 1738 was appointed Royal governor of the colony. It was the first time New Jersey had a governor of its own rather than one who ruled both New Jersey and New York.

In Morristown's year of christening, the Presbyterians started to build their substantial church. It was finished in 1742, the year twenty-five-year-old Reverend Timothy Johnes, newly ordained by Yale, was called as pastor. He became a powerful force in his fifty-two-year ministry in Morristown.

Soon after the arrival of Johnes, townspeople stood in awe of the 124-foot-tall steeple

The First Baptist Church, also on the green, was moved into its new building across the street from the courthouse in 1894.

the Presbyterians raised atop their church. It could be glimpsed for miles around, as a symbol that Morristown was far more than a widened place on the King's Highway. Knowledgeable visitors marveled that the steeple was twenty-five feet taller than the vaunted ninety-five-foot-high Trinity Episcopal Church spire in Newark.

Housing the 3,000 soldiers became both the immediate priority and a tremendous challenge for the small, compact community. It was somewhat alleviated when contingents of soldiers were detached to patrol duties atop the mountains or on the plains to the east. Pressure also was eased when enlistments expired or when soldiers left town to live in nearby villages, to guard outposts, to take approved leave, or to desert.

Those who remained had to be placed in private homes in Morristown and in a wide circle outward. Local civilian commissioners went house to house within a wide radius and simply announced to the householders how many men must be accommodated for as long as the army stayed. Homeowners were not permitted to argue the allotments.

The task was completed in a relatively short time, despite the fact that many residents already were voluntarily housing civilian refugees. Many of them had fled westward from Newark, Elizabethtown, and other towns when British troops pursued the American Army across eastern New Jersey in late November and early December of 1776, in the dismal flight toward New Brunswick, Princeton, and beyond the Delaware River to the Pennsylvania riverbank.

Lieutenant Charles Willson Peale, who would become a noted American painter and the patriarch of a distinguished family of artists, had been with the troops at Trenton and Princeton. In Morristown he found a household willing to take him in but had no available extra bed. Peale wrote that he "slept on the planks rather coldly." He felt lucky, noting that a person had to walk "a few miles" to find a house without soldiers.

Troops were spread in a long, thin line from Princeton to the Hudson River Highlands. Captain Elias Bloomfield saw a strategic value in the dispersal of the soldiers:

> *Our army was exceedingly reduced so that 3,000 effective men were the full of the whole. To prevent this being known, Genl. Washington distributed them by 2 & 3 in a house, all along the main roads around Morristown for miles, so the general expectation among the country people was that we were 40,000 strong.*

Captain Bloomfield either did not know or did not tell the full truth about army quartering. Some extreme crowding was inevitable and far surpassed the "2 & 3 in a house" described by Bloomfield. Rev. Jacob Green of Hanover, an outspoken advocate for independence, invited fourteen officers and men to share his home with himself, his wife, and their eight children. Although not ordered to do so, some hosts fed the visitors. Mrs. Anna Kitchell, who housed sixteen soldiers, also fed as many as forty men every day. In homes designated as soldier billets, hay was piled thickly on the floor and soldiers bunked there, "numbering sometimes six, sometimes twelve, and sometimes even twenty," as one soldier described the housing. Each man covered himself with a single blanket and the fireplace cast enough basic heat to keep the soldiers reasonably warm.

Most officers found less crowded accommodations and were expected to pay their way. Washington and his aides established his first Morristown headquarters in Jacob Arnold's substantial tavern that faced the town green on the corner near the road to Mendham. Washington knew at least casually of Arnold, captain of a local mounted militia unit.

Arnold's sumptuous three-story establishment was the center of the community's political and social activity, in the tradition of colonial inns. Gracious circular interior stairs led upward from a broad first floor hall to well-furnished rooms on the second and third floors, enough to accommodate not only most of Washington's staff but also visitors who needed to do business with the commander. The dining room, enhanced by large mirrors hung on the walls, could seat twelve persons at a big mahogany table.

Other generals took whatever other housing was available. General Nathanael Greene, Washington's close associate, lived in the home of Nicholas Hoffman. Greene doubted Hoffman's loyalty, but there was no question about his hospitality. Jacob Ford's mansion, the finest building in town, was allotted to Captain Thomas Rodney and the thirty-five officers of his short-term Delaware troop, a curious assignment in the light of the numbers of men involved, the fact they all were due to be discharged in a few days, and worse, the fact that Colonel Ford lay dying in the home.

Washington was about to lose his most important link in Morristown. On December 30, four days after the victory at Trenton, Ford had received written orders from Washington to advance his militia company six miles eastward to Chatham. Ford ordered his men to meet him on January 4, armed and ready to march. He knew nothing of the triumph at Princeton, much less that on January 4 the main army was headed for Morristown.

Ford collapsed as he was reviewing the gathering troops. Two soldiers carried him to his home, where he was put in bed with a raging fever probably caused by pneumonia. He died on January 10. He was forty-eight years old.

Washington ordered a military funeral, attended by scores of Continental officers, soldiers, militiamen and townspeople. There is no record, however, that Washington took any personal part in the funeral or the burial in the Presbyterian cemetery. Rodney's men stayed on in the stricken house for three more days before their enlistments ended and they returned to Delaware. About a week later, on January 19, Jacob Ford, Sr., the colonel's father, followed his son in death.

Major Wilkinson later wrote of the high optimism that the army entertained about Morristown:

Jacob Ford Jr. erected this small gunpowder manufactory on the Whippany River to meet a growing need of the army.

This position, little understood at the time, was afterward discovered to be a most safe one for the winter quarters for an army of observation, and such was General Washington's; the approach to it from the sea-board is rendered difficult and dangerous by a chain of sharp hills, which extend from Pluckemin by Bound Brook and Springfield to the vicinity of the Passaic River [at what is now Paterson].

It was a shrewd and accurate description of the Watchung Mountains. With lookouts patrolling the ridge tops and a few sharpshooters manning the single gap in the ridges, the position seemed to be as nearly impregnable as any location in the nation. It also emphasized a very important fact: this army was to be an army of observation, not a force geared to strike New York at any moment.

Wilkinson also waxed optimistic (too much so, as it turned out) about a second vital element in the army's encampment — food: "It [Morristown] is situated in the heart of a country abounding with forage and provisions."

His complacency would soon be shattered.

America's Iron Backbone

Morristown had a tremendous asset in the hills to the west and north when the Revolution began: iron ore, from which could be fashioned much of the army's needs on the battlefield and in camp.

In about 1700, Indians told early settlers of "suckysunny," their name for the "black stone" found on the surface near what is now Succasunna. Prospectors poured into the area, hoping for a stake in the Highlands (a name later bestowed by geologists, not by a Scot yearning for the bonnie braes of home).

When Washington brought his troops to Morristown in 1777, he surely knew that dozens of furnaces (where the ore was melted and cooled into pig or cast iron) and forges (where the pigs were reheated and hammered into wrought iron, iron which then could be wrought or shaped) were operating around the clock.

The Highlands had everything needed by early iron makers — iron ore, of course; rapidly flowing streams to provide power; limestone to hasten melting and to draw out impurities; and thick forests for fuel. Estimates indicate that a single forge fire consumed one thousand acres of woodland annually.

The Jacob Fords, Sr. and Jr., of Morristown were major powers in the industry. Together they owned or controlled more than a dozen iron works in Morris County. Their major holding was the Mount Hope furnace, opened in 1772, the year the Fords leased the property to noted ironmaster John Jacob Faesch.

An early smithy — where iron bars were heated red hot and beaten into horseshoes, wagon wheel rims, hardware, kitchen utensils, and a wide variety of other iron products — was, in reality, a small foundry.

Chapter Two

The GREAT SCOURGE *of* 1777

T he sudden demise of the Fords shocked Morristown, but the village had to put that grief aside immediately: it stood on the edge of a siege of deadly smallpox — as great a killer as the world has ever known. Before January's end, fourteen more members of the Presbyterian Church, ranging in age from twenty-five to eighty-one, followed the Fords to their graves. Most of them died of smallpox.

Other diseases, such as typhoid, consumption, pneumonia, and most devastatingly, dysentery, also swept through Morristown and outward into all of the surrounding area. These familiar diseases, however serious and potentially disastrous, took second place to the fear of what a raging smallpox epidemic could bring.

Washington personally knew the physical debilitation that the scourge could generate. In 1751, while visiting the British colony on Barbados with his brother, he was stricken with smallpox. After a severe three-week illness, he gradually recovered, with only a few pox marks on his nose as an outward manifestation of the disease. He was, of course immune to smallpox in 1777, but during the winter he became so seriously ill with quinsy (tonsillitis) that it was feared he might not survive.

According to Elizabeth A. Fenn's highly readable book, *Pox Americana* (published in 2001), more than 100,000 people died of smallpox in North America as the disease ravaged the New World between 1775 and 1782. Hundreds of thousands of others were scarred and maimed. The only consolation, however bitter, was that anyone who recovered was immune to smallpox for life — and that led to America's first crude inoculations.

This view of Revolutionary War Morristown showed the Presbyterian Church steeple dominating the town and the few shops and houses that surrounded it.

The Continental Army came in direct contact with smallpox in Boston in the autumn of 1775, but no army-wide action was undertaken. On the other hand, Sir William Howe, commander of British troops in America, ordered his troops polled; those who had not suffered from smallpox underwent immediate inoculation. This policy continued throughout the war, accounting for the fact that the English and German soldiers did not face severe epidemics. However, the disease was rampant among non-inoculated civilians in New York City.

Infected soldiers were among the regiments that marched into Morristown on January 6. A day later, Washington wrote of smallpox: "We should have more to dread from it than from the Sword of the Enemy." Smallpox stalked Morristown and the entire region for miles around. Soon after the first cases appeared, Washington wrote William Shippen, head of the army medical corps, declaring that if the disease were left unchecked it might ravage the entire military force in all the states. In Morristown he ordered Dr. Nathaniel Bond to begin inoculating the troops, the first mass inoculation of Americans.

The enormity of the task forced Washington to have second thoughts within three weeks after the inoculations began. On January 28, he ordered Dr. Shippen to end the process in Philadelphia. He feared that smallpox might be transmitted via the clothing that the soldiers wore; new clothing would be difficult to find. Inoculation, however commendable, had become "impossible," Washington wrote.

The Morris County courthouse and jail were prominent buildings on the public land. The village green is still in place; the courthouse moved into a new building on Washington Street in 1824.

A week later the commander ordered resumption of the inoculations: "The smallpox has made such head in every quarter that I find it impossible to keep it from spreading thro' the whole army the natural way." All men in service not yet victims of smallpox would be inoculated, as would all recruits before they were sent to organized regiments.

Inoculation was neither a preventative nor a cure: it induced the disease and minimized the effects of smallpox. The placing of a small amount of pox fluid in a slight scratch in a well person's skin was meant to give the patient a lesser case. Soon after being inoculated, a patient could expect a rising fever and possibly a few pox, but recovery was quite rapid for nearly all. Some estimates indicate that while fifteen percent of untreated patients died, only two percent of every 500 inoculated soldiers were lost as a result of inoculation.

By February, nearly all Continental troops not yet infected were in the process of inoculation. The work spread outward from Morristown, to Philadelphia, to the Carolinas, up the Hudson River, to Pennsylvania and Connecticut, and wherever else large contingents of American solders were billeted.

Washington chose to live in and make his headquarters at The Arnold Tavern, facing the green, on the corner where the road to Mendham went west. He had his office on the second floor in a room that gave him a view of the common.

More than a thousand inoculated soldiers were recovering in Morristown area homes or makeshift hospitals and others were being called in from the outposts for inoculation. Washington then ordered militia commanders in New Jersey, Pennsylvania, New York, and Connecticut to expose their troops to the disease. Haste was both the dilemma and the necessary order of the day; inoculations could not be long delayed, but neither could all soldiers be treated at the same time, lest there be no fighting force left.

Since each inoculation created another ill man, space for convalescence and treatment became a major concern. Morristown's Presbyterian parson, Timothy Johnes, first filled his sanctuary with smallpox patients then became a one-man committee seeking space in other churches and large buildings. He located several private homeowners and many pastors in surrounding towns eager to help. He and other ministers, as well as local doctors, assisted in the inoculations.

Citizens did not fare as well as the soldiers, but not because the army denied them the chance to escape serious illness. Ministers urged their members to participate but fear and ignorance kept many out of the inoculation lines. The army could not force civilians to accept the experiment. Thus, large numbers of citizens died of smallpox. In the Morristown Presbyterian Church alone, sixty-eight parishioners died in that winter of 1777. Five members of the church's Hathaway family died of smallpox in a single day. No other family in the area suffered so appalling a loss, but before the epidemic faded away, nearly every family in Morristown had at least one death and most of those who lived were scarred for life.

Private Joseph Plumb Martin, the common soldier's symbol of survival, received his inoculation with about 400 other Connecticut soldiers in the summer of 1777. The men were housed in an old barracks in the Highlands of New York and attended by previously immunized troops. Martin summarized the experience: "We lost none. I had the smallpox favorably, as did the rest."

More than a thousand soldiers were in the makeshift hospitals at the peak of the inoculations. Washington's greatest fear was that General William Howe might launch an enemy attack with so many of his soldiers incapacitated. He wrote: "Should we inoculate generally, the Enemy, knowing it, will certainly take advantage of the situation."

Ashbel Greene, a sixteen-year-old Bottle Hill (Madison) schoolteacher and militiaman, an outspoken patriot and fervent advocate of independence, left a different feeling in a diary notation. He felt, with perhaps an unwarranted teen-age optimism, that side effects were so slight "there was not, probably, a day in which the army could not have been marched against the enemy."

Despite the smallpox epidemic, American militiamen were ferociously battling the enemy in was has been called "The Forage War." British Colonel Charles Stuart on March 29, 1777, wrote that a "petit guerre" had been thrust on his army by the lack of forage for his horses. Enemy soldiers apparently were well fed in Perth Amboy and New Brunswick, but fodder for their mounts was scarce. Without horse power, the British were stymied. Their cavalry could not be mounted, cannons could not be towed into strategic positions, and supplies could not be hauled to their troops. Orders from New York told the British army it must sweep through Middlesex County hay barns and fields to seize forage.

Militia attacks against the desperate Royal forces began even as the main American army was moving north from Princeton to Morristown. On January 4, when the army advanced toward Pluckemin, twenty mounted militia cut off British supply wagons near Maidenhead (now Lawrenceville). The enemy fled, leaving behind "numerous" wagons loaded with woolen clothing, far more precious than gold to freezing Continental soldiers.

Two days later, about sixty German Waldeck infantrymen, escorted by British dragoons, set out from Elizabethtown to punish the American militia. The dragoons rode

Part of the earthenwork reproduction of Fort Nonsense, built in the summer of 1777 at Washington's direction. Built in the 1930s when the National Park Service decided the hilltop just west of Morristown needed a graphic depiction of the size and nature of the fort, it was stern reality during the war. The implication that it was a make-work program was suggested during the 19th century.

back into town within a few hours; all of the Germans had been killed or captured. General Howe ordered British and German troops to evacuate Elizabeth to seek safety in Perth Amboy. The departure was so hasty that the pursuing American militia took 100 prisoners and "the baggage of two regiments besides a quantity of provisions."

Call it Fort Missing

To call the 1777 redoubt built on the heights overlooking Morristown Fort Nonsense is to pay tribute to mythology. The fort had a very serious purpose, yet the nonsensical name endures as part of Morristown National Historical Park's lore.

It might better be called Fort Missing — although there is a clear paper trail to show the fort was built and manned.

In the spring of 1777, Washington ordered a fort built on Kinney's Hill, 230 feet above Morristown. When the Continental army moved to Middlebrook in May, Washington ordered Lieutenant Colonel Jeremiah Olney to "strengthen the works already begun upon the hill near this place, and erect such others as are necessary for the better defending of it, that it may become a safe retreat in case of necessity."

No on-the-scene letter, diary or remembrance mentions that there was nonsense or "make work" of any kind on Kinney's Hill. There were, in fact, two redoubts (fortifications) on the hill, the upper and the lower. The name Fort Nonsense was first used by a fanciful writer in 1833 and it has never gone away.

Strengthening "the works already begun" on the hill had to be a priority. Washington felt the earthworks must be a safe retreat in case the British ever got as far as Morristown. He ordered that at least a "trusty sergeant and a select body of men" be kept in the fort after the army left. If the British or Loyalists had any hope of regaining Morristown, he said, "their first attempt will be to seize the height and turn our works against us."

The British never entered Morristown nor did the Loyalists gain sufficient strength, but Washington believed earnestly that a hilltop fort by any name would be Morristown's best defense.

According to a report prepared for the Washington Association, an archaeological dig established the presence of the fort three years after the National Park Service acquired the site and an earthwork was constructed. It became a major attraction in the park. But National Park Service regional administrators insisted in the 1960s there was no "sound historical basis for the present Fort Nonsense area."

Melvin Weig, a National Park Service employee and a highly respected historian of the Morristown encampments, called this "the most preposterous piece of 'historical writing' I've ever seen, completely ignoring the evidence and the logical conclusions therefrom."

The administrators had their way. In 1965, a bulldozer employed by the park service leveled the rebuilt fort on the grounds that it had been "purely hypothetical."

It is as if the fort were, indeed, pure nonsense.

Militia attacks picked up pace between January 5 and January 20 — at Spanktown (now Rahway), Chatham, Connecticut Farms (now Union), and Bonhamtown, now edging ever closer to the large British stronghold in New Brunswick.

Washington responded quickly. He ordered most of his Continental troops to reinforce the militia, an unusual reversal of his army's role. In ordering his officers to take the initiative against the invaders, he declared, "the enemy are afraid of us."

Particularly brilliant was General William Maxwell. Washington sent him into the Forage War with orders to "annoy and harass the enemy" wherever possible, but without risking a general engagement. Maxwell's soldiers affectionately called him "Scotch Willie" because of his thick Ulster accent. They admired his skills, his tactics on the field, and his poise during a battle.

The fully-manned British attacks in late January and throughout February — at Metuchen, Piscataway, Bonhamtown, Spanktown, Ash Swamp, and many other places — netted them only a loss of increasingly large amounts of forage ground and large numbers of killed and wounded. The most crushing blow might have come on January 24, when General Philemon Dickinson pressed his 400 New Jersey militia and fifty Pennsylvania Riflemen to attack about 550 strongly positioned British soldiers at Somerset Court House. The Americans broke the ice on the frozen Millstone River, crossed to the opposite bank, and routed the enemy. The British lost about twenty-five killed and wounded to an American loss of four or five men. The Americans captured forty-three baggage wagons, 104 horses, 115 head of cattle, and about sixty or seventy sheep.

In about thirty-five battles and skirmishes between January 4 and March 21, 1777, one estimate (probably very low) said that the British and Hessians lost more than 900 men killed, wounded, captured, or missing in action. American losses were not even half that. Estimates by Washington and Nathanael Greene put enemy losses at "between two and three thousand men" in the foraging skirmishes.

Howe had no intention of launching a New Jersey campaign that winter, partially because of his usual lassitude but mostly because he had been tricked into believing Washington's army was larger than it actually was. The Forage War should have erased even the faintest doubts about the ability and courage of the American militia.

Howe's soldiers and officers in New York faced unprecedented housing woes, created by a disastrous fire that swept through the city in mid-September 1776, about a week after the English came to occupy the city. New Yorkers had fully expected to see the city torched by fleeing Continentals, many of whom believed the city should be sacked.

General Nathanael Greene had argued openly in favor of destruction of New York:

If the enemy gets possession of the city, we can never recover the possession without a su-

An artist's impression of the dreadful fire that swept through New York City on September 21, 1776, shortly after the British took control of the city. Flames destroyed 493 buildings and damaged hundreds of others, engulfing areas ranging from "lowly wooden houses of the poor to the mansions of the rich." Problems caused by the fire lasted throughout the British occupation.

perior naval force to theirs; it [destruction] *will deprive the enemy of barracking their whole army together* [and] *it will deprive them of a general market.*

Since "two thirds of the city of New York and the suburbs belongs to the Tories" Greene wrote, "We have no very great reason to run any great risk for its defense."

Washington decided to place responsibility for the city in the lap of Congress: "If we should be obliged to abandon the town, should it stand as winter-quarters for the enemy?" Congress ruled the city must be spared, on the grounds that the Americans would in time "recover the same."

Soon after midnight on September 21, however, a fire broke out in a small wooden house on the wharf on the Hudson River. It spread rapidly, engulfing block after block of houses that ranged "from lowly wooden houses of the poor to the mansions of the rich." Venerated Trinity Church, a symbol of New York wealth and power, stood in the path of the fire. Flames quickly rose high above the roof to engulf the 140-foot-tall steeple. A mile-long swath of fire cut through the city, completely destroying 493 buildings and severely damaging hundreds of other structures.

The fire was a major disaster for the British and the Tories from New Jersey and Connecticut who less than ten days previously had joyfully flocked to the city to welcome Howe's conquering army. One source said: "Our distress was great before but this calamity has increased them ten-fold. Thousands are hereby reduced to beggary."

Problems caused by the fire would last throughout the entire British occupation of the city. In 1777, the British counted their immediate losses in military supplies and food stored in destroyed warehouses, the loss of proper quarters for the soldiers, and great difficulty in accommodating the increasing numbers of Tories fleeing to the city.

There is confusion about whether any individuals or groups were ever definitely identified as the arsonists, but many sources understandably laid the blame on the Patriots. During the fire several men deemed suspicious were hanged on the spot or thrown into the flames.

An American suspect allegedly confessed to the deed much later. According to William S. Stryker, who published his *Extracts from American Newspapers* in 1901, a New York newspaper identified the arsonist as Abraham Patten of Baltimore, an alleged American spy. The account, dated June 9, 1777, nearly nine months after the fire, described Patten's arrest in New Brunswick for trying to bribe a British grenadier to smuggle out of the city four incriminating letters addressed to Washington. The grenadier took the money and promptly delivered the letters to British headquarters.

Patten's letters, it was reported, revealed that he "proposed on a certain day to set fire to New Brunswick in four places, blow up the magazine, and set off a rocket as a signal for the Americans to attack the city." That set Patten on a fast track to the gallows. He was arrested, expeditiously tried, found guilty, and sentenced to die by hanging. On the scaffold before he was hanged, Patten acknowledged all the New Brunswick crimes, then startled the audience by declaring he was a principal in setting fire to New York, but would not name any of his accomplices.

Newspapers of the time were biased and often served as conduits for propaganda. However, as a strong confirmation of Patten's guilt, the journals of the Continental Congress include a citation that Congress voted money for a pension to be paid to his widow for Patten's "services rendered to the government."

Washington was in no position to gloat about the fire or to argue about Patten or anyone else, but when he heard of the disaster and the suspicions about American culpability, he had written: "Providence, or some good honest fellow, has done more for us than we were disposed to do for ourselves."

During the winter, the British garrisoned more than 10,000 soldiers in New Jersey to oppose the incessant guerrilla attacks by the Americans. Enemy strength was boosted in Perth Amboy and New Brunswick. The force on Staten Island, separated from New Jersey

This sketch drawn after the war shows New Amsterdam (New York) as it appeared from near Paulus Hook (Jersey City). The windmill shows the early Dutch settlement.

only by the narrow Arthur Kill, was bolstered.

Winter attrition of troops usually is considered the particular hallmark of Valley Forge in 1777-78 and Morristown two years later. But on January 19, 1777, one day shy of two weeks after the army had marched into Morristown, Washington declared that the nation had reached a point of "scarce having any army at all."

The army continued to melt away. Many units refused to reenlist after their terms of service expired. Worse, soldiers simply walked away from camp and headed for home, some believing that without any military action they were not needed. Desertion became such a problem that Washington asked the New Jersey legislature to enact a law forbidding the harboring of deserters, lest "our new army will scarcely be raised before it will dwindle and waste away."

Soldiers who remained were "marching over frosted snow, many without a shoe, stocking or blanket." On February 22, Washington complained bitterly to Matthew Irwin, a Deputy Commissary of Issues, that his troops could draw no provisions. That said, he lost his temper in scolding Irwin, a rare happening for the general:

What Sir is the meaning of this? And why were you so desirous of excluding others from this business when you are unable to accomplish it yourself?

Howe's well-defined inability to make a decision became, paradoxically, a matter of strength for him. Americans had to ask constantly, will he strike north along the Hudson River, perhaps to unite with British forces in Canada? Or would he opt to move his headquarters to Philadelphia? Concerning the latter, Washington mused:

> *With what propriety can he miss so favorable an opportunity of striking a capital stroke against a city from whence we derive so many advantages, the carrying of which would give such éclat to his arms and strike such a damp to ours?*

As the American Army waited in Morristown, an incident happened that might have been relegated to an obscure footnote had it not foretold major events to come. On February 19, 1777, five officers were advanced to the rank of major general. One was not. He was Benedict Arnold. Justifiably furious, he submitted his resignation. Washington convinced him to retract it. Arnold was promoted but the initial exclusion remained fixed in his mind.

Spring brought dogwoods into full flower on the mountains and touched the Jockey Hollow forest with delicate green. Martha Dangerfield Bland of Virginia came to Morristown that spring to visit her husband Theodorick, a colonel in the Virginia Light Dragoons. She described Morristown in a letter to her sister-in-law, Frances Bland Randolph, on May 12:

> *I find Morris a very clever little village, situated in a most beautiful valley at the foot of 5 mountains, It has three houses [churches] with steeples which give it a consequential look — and is something larger than Blandford (Virginia).*

She rode through surrounding villages, "all of them having meeting houses and court houses decorated with steeples which gives them a pretty airy look & the farms between the mountains are the most rural sweet spots in nature."

Mrs. Bland found a few people in Morristown she considered to be highly agreeable human beings, but dismissed most as "the errentist rusticks you ever beheld."

She could not disguise a strain of social cattiness when she discussed Morristown women:

> *There are some extremely pretty girls but they appear to have souls formed for the distaff rather than the tender passions and realy (sic) I never met with such pleasant looking creatures & the most inhospitable mortals breathing; you can get nothing from them but "dreadful good water" as they term everything that is good. Desperate and dreadfull (sic) are their favorite words; you'd laugh to hear them talk.*

Mrs. Bland became very friendly with General and Martha Washington and told her sister-in-law that she often rode horseback with them through the county, "at which time General Washington throws off the Hero and takes on the chatty agreeable companion — and he can be downright impudent sometimes, such impudence, Fanny, as you and I like."

Spring also brought streams of volunteers back to the American cause. By May 20, there was reason to believe stability had come to the army; enlistments were for three years or the duration of the war.

In the belief that Howe surely would strike into New Jersey, Washington moved increasing numbers of soldiers to the southern slopes of the Watchung Mountains. On May 28, he moved his headquarters and his main army to Middlebrook, about fifteen miles south of Morristown. If Howe were ever to awaken from his torpor, the time had come for a significant move.

Finally, at 11 p.m. on June 12, Royal forces — 17,000 well-trained, well-equipped men — began to march westward out of New Brunswick, along the broad Raritan River. Howe hoped to surprise General John Sullivan's brigade at Princeton in the early morning. He would not be permitted to savor that. Quickly alerted Continental forces were immediately moved into defensive positions.

The supposed march toward Princeton or Philadelphia had been a ruse from the outset. Howe had written Lord George Germain in London that his "only object was to bring the American Army to a general action." The British had learned nothing: Washington, the man Howe sought to provoke into a head-to-head combat, was the man always most anxious to avoid any such dangerous confrontation.

Adding to the unlikelihood of an attack by the American Army was the strange fact that Howe took up his position with the Raritan River between his army and his quarry. Charles Stedman, an aide on Howe's staff, later wondered why Howe took "positions in which he could neither assail the enemy or the enemy him, if disposed to do so."

The British sat quietly on the flat land beneath the Watchungs and across the Raritan River. American sharpshooters picked off an occasional British straggler. Continental soldiers viewing the idle English campground had reason to wonder if it were some kind of a huge pageant or comic opera staged for their amusement. Howe abandoned his position after four days and led his embarrassed and confused Redcoats back toward New Brunswick. Howe's army left in its wake a trail of brutal pillaging and senseless burning of homes. The result was to transform many cautious neutral residents of the Raritan valley into virulent foes.

Washington immediately dispatched General Maxwell's New Jersey brigade on a forced march toward a position north of New Brunswick to hamper Howe if he decided to attack the American left. Simultaneously, General Greene led three brigades along the north bank of the Raritan River to monitor the British rear and to attack if the chance arose.

The waiting and watching ended on June 19, when the British left New Brunswick and began to march toward Perth Amboy. Washington moved his main army to Quibble-town (New Market). Howe countered by moving his forces sharply to the left and north and headed for Scotch Plains and Westfield, hoping to outflank Washington.

Lord Cornwallis led a major detachment out of Woodbridge on June 26, seeking to encircle Washington's position. Brigadier General William Alexander had moved his division toward Woodbridge and met Cornwallis in an unplanned encounter. Outnumbered two to one, Alexander's forces suffered grievously, losing more than 200 men killed, wounded, or captured. The British losses were no more than seventy, but the British triumph was in vain. Stirling's stand had given Washington time to return to the safety of the Middlebrook heights.

Howe had decided to relinquish New Jersey. He moved his army to Perth Amboy, then across the Arthur Kill to Staten Island, His mystifying, bungled expedition toward Middlebrook perplexed even his closest advisors.

Charles Stedman, a member of Howe's staff, praised Washington for "cool, collected and prudent conduct" — even as he found Howe's charade confounding. Howe foolishly blamed his caution on being "outnumbered." Stedman rebutted that, listing British forces at 30,000, compared with Stedman's estimate of 8,000 "rebel" soldiers.

General Henry Knox, who witnessed the debacle from his artillery position at Middlebrook, said the British conduct was "perplexing," He added:

> It was unaccountable that people who the day before gave out in very gasconading terms that they would be in Philadelphia in six days should stop short when they had gone only nine miles.

Howe continued to dawdle on Staten Island. Finally, on July 5, he loaded thirty-six battalions of British and Hessian troops, including a regiment of light horse, on transports in a huge fleet numbering 228 vessels. The 15,000 officers and men and the horses languished in the holds under the hot summer sun until July 23 when sails were hoisted and the fleet moved slowly toward Sandy Hook Bay.

Howe's second in command, the moody, egotistical Sir Henry Clinton, was left to rule New York until Howe returned. Clinton had strongly opposed the Philadelphia venture, believing it would have been far better to attack up the Hudson River for a union with forces in Canada.

Howe tried another ruse, leaking a letter supposedly meant for John Burgoyne, the

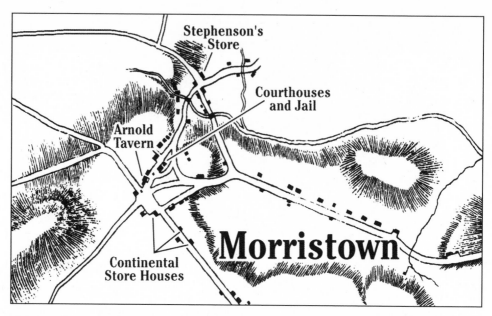

A section of a map used to train teachers shows Morristown and its green, facing The Arnold Tavern. The courthouse was on the green; storehouses were to the south of the town center.

overlooked British general in Canada, who was eager to move southward toward New York. Howe said he would cooperate in any venture Burgoyne proposed. Washington did not take the bait.

On July 23, the British fleet set sail and finally rounded the point of Sandy Hook and headed full sail toward the south. Howe finally had made up his mind: he would seek to control the Delaware River and overwhelm the Americans in Philadelphia.

Once he knew definitely where Howe was headed, Washington broke camp and headed his troops rapidly over land to Philadelphia. The war was about to resume, with a vengeance.

This bronze panel shows Washington in a religious rite with Morristown's Pastor Johnes.

The Original G.I. Joe

America's typical enlisted man in World War II came to be known as "G.I. Joe," thanks to the drawings and comments by cartoonists Bill Mauldin and Herb Block. G.I. ("Government Issue") Joe went with the flow, grumbling, complaining, resisting, but always ready when a battle cry sounded.

That description almost exactly fits Joseph Plumb Martin of Connecticut, whose post-war recounting of the Revolution, from a foot soldier's viewpoint, provides the most vivid account of the war by a man of the line. Martin published his account in 1830, when he was sixty-nine years old. It appeared as *A Narrative of Some of the Adventures, Dangers and Suffering of a Revolutionary Soldier Interspersed with Anecdotes of Incidents that Occurred Within His Own Observation*. Although Martin's descriptions and accounts were written about fifty years after the war, the private's words are remarkably accurate when tested against more official (and much less down-to-earth) writings.

Martin enlisted on July 6, 1776, when he was fifteen years old, He was present at the American defeats at Brooklyn and Manhattan, then went home for six months before reenlisting. Thereafter, he saw service in the battles outside Philadelphia in 1777, at Monmouth, and in other battles including Yorktown. He endured the winter at Valley Forge and described his hut building and misery at Morristown.

His account of the mutiny at Jockey Hollow on May 25, 1780, has influenced every modern recounting of that critical event. Without him, it might have become a mere footnote — if that.

Perhaps because of the weighty original title, the book sold poorly and for 130 years Joseph Plumb Martin was a non-entity. In 1960, Dr. Francis Ronalds, director of the Morristown National Historical Park, found the rare little book in the park's library.

Soon after, when historian George F. Scheer was researching another subject in the park library, Ronalds suggested that he read Martin's book. Scheer read it, edited Martin's prose sparingly, and it was published in December 1961 as *Private Yankee Doodle*. It became an overnight hit, aided by an article in *American Heritage Magazine*, with illustrations by Bill Mauldin, who pictured Martin as the prototype of World War II's G.I. Joe. Martin's straightforward, witty little book is likely to be forever a best seller in national historical parks.

Modern Revolutionary War historians began incorporating long excerpts from *Private Yankee Doodle* in their books after Scheer's edition of Martin's work appeared. Martin became the unofficial spokesman for all the "Joes" in Continental

Private
YANKEE
DOODLE

BEING A NARRATIVE
of some of the Adventures,
Dangers *and* Sufferings *of a*
REVOLUTIONARY SOLDIER

JOSEPH PLUMB MARTIN

EDITED BY
George F. Scheer

American uniforms. Few books, if any, have had greater influence on shaping the interpretation of the role of common soldiers in the American Revolution.

Chapter Three

The LONG ROAD BACK

General William Howe's 228 transports and escort vessels arrived on July 30 at Delaware Bay, where the slow-moving Delaware River waters mingle with the Atlantic ocean's swelling waves. The temptation to enter the twelve-mile-wide bay must have been nearly overwhelming, but the bay's well-known shoals prompted extreme caution.

The shallow sandbars, constantly shifting positions during even mild storms, had been a known hazard for more than 150 years. Henry Hudson, the British captain piloting the Dutch ship *Half Moon*, sought to enter the bay on August 28, 1609, hoping to find a new route to the Far East. Hudson's mate recorded that the little ship encountered shoals and "once we strooke" before Hudson pulled away and left the bay. If one small ship could go aground, the thought of 228 larger vessels trying to avoid the shallow sand bars was not reassuring.

Equally troubling, Howe certainly knew of the deadly American *chevaux-de-frise* spread across the river a few miles south of Philadelphia. (*Chevaux-de-frise* were iron-spiked wooden beams embedded in enormous crates sunk in the river.) The spikes could impale a ship or splinter its wooden hull.

If ships veered toward either shore to escape the *chevaux-de-frise*, the guns at four river front Continental forts below Philadelphia — two in New Jersey and two in Pennsylvania — could shatter the lightly armed British ships. (The imposing barriers ultimately were not overcome until October 1777 by British land troops attacking from Philadelphia).

Howe apparently did not even consider putting his troops ashore near Lewes, Delaware, and marching them northward to Philadelphia through the rich vegetable fields and orchards of Delaware on the west side of the river. Within three or four days the British might have been in Philadelphia, refreshed by the fresh foods pilfered in Delaware and stimulated by being freed from the oppressive lower decks of the ships,

Instead, eight days passed at anchor in the blistering summer sun before Howe made his decision not to risk the bay, the river, or an oceanfront landing in Delaware. On July 31, the ships sailed for the headwaters of the Chesapeake River, only a few miles from Delaware Bay by land but a long trip by ship. Buffeted by adverse winds and hampered by poor navigation, the fleet sailed about 300 extra miles before anchoring in the Elk River on August 24.

Howe had been about sixty miles north of Philadelphia in June when he pulled up stakes at Middlebrook and returned to New Brunswick. Now, after nine weeks of horror aboard the ships, he was still sixty miles from Philadelphia — south of

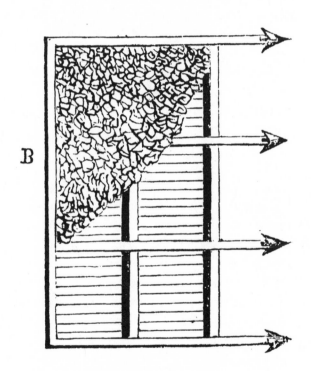

Drawing A shows a profile of a cheval de frise, *used effectively in 1777 by Americans to block the Delaware River south of Philadelphia. The stout poles, mounted at a forty-five-degree angle, were thirty-feet long, with sharp iron points. Drawing B shows an overhead view of the cheval, which is partially filled with stone to anchor it on the river bottom.*

the city. His men had been virtually imprisoned in the holds for more than seven weeks. Debilitated and emaciated, the men staggered ashore. The 300 horses that had not perished on the trip were let loose to graze; half of them died from colic caused by overeating.

Washington in early June was almost as cautious as his British counterpart, worrying that Howe's ships might sail up the Hudson River. When it was clearly established that the British had sailed for Philadelphia, he put his army in rapid motion. It took three days to march from a position near West Point to Morristown. Two days later, the army was at Coryell's Ferry (Lambertville), ready to cross the Delaware River for the short march to Philadelphia.

The fast-moving American army entered Philadelphia at about 7 a.m. on July 31, striding briskly in light rain from the old York Road into Broad Street. Despite the city's known large Tory population, Philadelphia greeted the Americans warmly.

The Continental soldiers had used the day before to prepare for a grand entrance. Clothes were washed, weapons burnished, and to offset their shabby uniforms, each man wore in his hat a "green sprig, an emblem of hope." John Adams, a member of Congress from Massachusetts, watched the impressive procession and wrote home to his beloved wife Abigail:

> Four grand divisions of the army and the artillery… marched twelve deep and yet took up above two hours in passing by. General Washington and the other general officers with their aides were on horseback.

Adams saw the army as "extremely well-armed, pretty well clothed, and tolerably well disciplined," although the soldiers actually wore threadbare uniforms and often marched out of step. The sight made Adams feel "as secure as if I were in Braintree, but not so happy." Many Philadelphians felt relieved by the sight of the army, however weak its marching skills.

The troops paraded through Philadelphia and headed for Wilmington, Delaware, where word had come that the British ships finally were unloading men and equipment six miles below Head of Elk, Maryland. Washington, General Nathanael Greene, and a very new acquaintance, the Marquis de Lafayette, made a quick dash on horseback through the region between the opposing armies, coming within two miles of Howe's temporary headquarters

Lafayette's presence on such an important mission surely raised some eyebrows in the officer corps. Washington had met Lafayette for the first time only the day before in Philadelphia. Congress had made the nineteen-year-old Frenchman a major general in the American army on July 31, without pay and without the privilege of leading troops. This despite the fact that Lafayette had held only a captain's commission in the French army reserve and could speak only a few words in English.

Washington liked the intelligent, willing, and eager teenager on sight, despite the general's usual antipathy (shared by his officer corps) toward the many pompous, self-serving foreigners who flooded into America seeking high rank and privileges. After Lafayette was wounded at the Battle of Brandywine, Washington told the surgeon, "Treat him as my son, for I love him as if he were." Young Lafayette would become a valuable ally and a good soldier.

If Colonel Alexander Hamilton — the same age as Lafayette and considered to be Washington's top aide — had any inclination toward jealousy, he never manifested it. But he had ample reason to wonder at his own relationship with the commander. After proving his valor and skills as an artillery officer on Long Island and at Trenton and Princeton, he had been promoted only to the rank of lieutenant colonel.

Washington decided a proper place to slow, if not stop, Howe's entrance into Philadelphia was at one of the shallow fording places on Brandywine Creek, southwest of the city. There, on August 10, the armies clashed. It would be the kind of head-to-head engagement that Howe had long claimed was his desire.

Greene commanded the forces at Chadd's Ford, facing Hessian General Wilhelm von Knyphausen's troops in what became a diversion while Howe moved a good part of his army in a flanking movement. Other American units were assigned to guard shallow fords up and down the creek.

The early fighting established an edge for the Continentals, but British soldiers crossed at an upper ford and drove the Americans away from the stream. By day's end the Continental defenders were in full retreat, allowing themselves the somewhat thin satisfaction that at least the battle had not become a disorderly rout.

American officers in the confusion of battle initially thought that Howe's losses exceeded theirs but in the aftermath this proved to be grievously wrong. The British losses of eighty-nine killed and 488 wounded were well below the Continental loss of between 1,200 and 1,300 men. Far from being a standoff, it was a major defeat.

The Battle of Brandywine Creek was not Washington's most commendable exploit. Critics later faulted his failure to study the terrain before the battle, his confusion in using his cavalry, and his inability to analyze properly whatever intelligence about enemy movements he had received. It was a failed report card. Worst of all, the road to Philadelphia appeared to be wide open for Howe.

Panic reigned in the city. Members of Congress fled westward, first to Lancaster, then to York. American military units packed or crated as many munitions and supplies as possible and hauled them to Reading in ox-drawn wagons. Citizens favorable to the revolution fled, leaving cheering Tories to welcome advance British forces to the city on September 20. Howe encamped his main army in Germantown.

About 2,600 additional American troops arrived to join the Americans in Pennsylvania on September 28, marching in from upper New York State, New Jersey, and Maryland. They bolstered the morale of Washington's troops and boosted the force to 11,000 strong. For one of the rare times during the war, the Americans had an advantage in numbers; Howe's force at Germantown did not exceed 8,000.

When word reached Washington that about 3,000 British troops had been dispatched southward along the Delaware in an attempt to dislodge Americans from forts that were greatly hindering British shipments to Philadelphia, he and his council of officers agreed to launch a surprise attack on the English garrison in Germantown.

Heavy fog shrouded the Schuylkill River valley at 11 p.m. on October 4, when the Continentals began a slow, silent advance. Troops were halted three hours later, two miles from the enemy lines. By 5 a.m., when advance units were ordered forward to bayonet — not shoot — sentries or anyone else they encountered, the fog was thicker than ever. Each advancing American was told to "have a piece of white paper in his hat" to tell friend from foe.

The artfully planned, logistically difficult, pre-dawn attack called for four simultaneous thrusts over a seven-mile-wide area. In the darkness and fog, the Americans had difficulty maintaining communication. The assault could have been a complete surprise except that gunshots began echoing from sentinel posts. A British officer reported his amazement at the sight of Americans creeping silently toward his position. He wrote:

> *We charged them twice, till the battalion was so reduced by killed or wounded that the bugle was sounded. Indeed had we not retreated at the very time we did we all should have been killed or taken, as two columns of the enemy had nearly got around our flank. This was the first time we had retreated from the Americans and it was with great difficulty we could get our men to obey our orders.*

After about three hours of fighting, a great American victory was almost at hand, a victory that might well have forced the British to alter their plans for taking Philadelphia. The stone Chew house on the battlefield, manned by British sharpshooters, served as a critical fort and delayed some American troops. Other units ran out of ammunition.

Suddenly, something cataclysmic happened that no officer in the field, British or American, could ever explain fully. Perhaps the thick fog bewildered two American units that approached each other, mistaking the other for the enemy. Perhaps someone, on either side, carelessly yelled the word retreat. Perhaps the chance for a smashing victory was too much for the Continentals to comprehend. General George Weedon, commanding a Virginia contingent, recalled the bewildering reversal:

In the battle for Germantown, the large, sturdily built stone mansion on the battlefield was a formidable obstacle. It was owned by Benjamin Chew, regarded as "having Tory sentiments." The house, fortified by British marksmen, held up the American drive for more than an hour, disrupting Continental plans.

Our men behaved with the greatest intrepidy for about three hours, driving them [the British] from their camps, fieldpieces, stone walls, houses, &c. Trophies lay at our feet, but so certain were we of making a general defeat of it that we passed by in the pursuit and by that means lost the chief part of them again, when the unlikely idea struck our men to fall back. The utmost exertions to rally them again was in vain, and a few minutes evinced the absolute necessity of drawing them off in the best manner we could.

Washington marched his abject, bewildered army back twenty-four miles to Penny-packer's Mill. Every man had marched, walked, or run at least fourteen miles the night before. The exhausted men dropped to the ground in almost instant sleep. Washington counted up the cost of Germantown, over and above the incredible battlefield letdown and the psychological damage it might have done to his men.

The total American loss, including prisoners taken, was about 1,100 men. Howe had lost about half that number. Yet there were major positives: The Continentals had performed superbly for three hours. There was no question that this was a tougher, more skilled American Army than it had been a year ago. Washington believed that Germantown was "rather more unfortunate than injurious."

Baron von Steuben instructs soldiers at Valley Forge. He is often credited with turning the Continental Army into a well-drilled fighting force.

Stunning news, wonderful from an American viewpoint, was drifting down from Saratoga. There, British General John Burgoyne had surrendered his army on October 14, a victory that lifted American troop morale. Still, soldiers and officers could not help but wonder that if the battle at Germantown had become the success that seemed imminent, it might have brought the British close to the peace table.

There was one more episode to play before the foes could repair to their winter camps. On December 4, Howe marched 14,000 men out of Philadelphia, with colors flying, bagpipes keening, and drums throbbing. He headed his massive army to Chestnut Hill, about four miles from the American outpost. Two days later, after a brief skirmish which caused losses of only about fifty combatants on each side, Howe surprisingly withdrew and returned to Philadelphia.

The British general's bewildering move invited questions. He offered his usual simplistic reason for the withdrawal: the Americans outnumbered him. It was a great distortion; the British actually held a two-to-one edge on the battlefield.

Howe's hold on Philadelphia was complete when, within a few weeks, his troops overwhelmed the four American Delaware River forts that had blocked British shipping for months. Supplies, arms, and new troops poured up the river into Philadelphia. It was a tempting time for celebration. Howe and his officers joined in wholeheartedly.

A young female Tory, Rebecca Franks, summed up the Philadelphia mood in a letter to an exiled rebel friend: "You can have no idea of the life of continued amusement I live in. I can scarce have a moment to myself…and most elegantly am I dressed for a ball this evening at the Smith's, where we have one every Thursday."

The city's numerous Tory families, including the haughty Shippens (one of whom would soon become a noted figure in American history) hailed the British as conquering heroes. Howe was joined by his Massachusetts mistress, Mrs. Elizabeth Loring, wife of retired British Army sergeant Joshua Loring. The former non-com did not make the trip; as Commissary of Prisoners he stayed in New York enjoying the many perquisites received by lending his wife to the general.

The American army went into winter quarters on December 19 at Valley Forge, about twenty-one miles north and west of Philadelphia, sufficiently close to the city to keep tabs on the British. Only 8,200 men were fit for duty; 2,898 were unfit, because, in Washington's words, they were "barefoot and otherwise naked."

Washington lived in a tent (as did his men) until the army was "hutted". Then he moved into the Isaac Potts house. Martha Washington arrived in mid-February, added a makeshift dining room to the house, and feted George on his forty-sixth birthday. She hired an army band for the occasion and scrupulously paid its musicians a total of fifteen shillings.

Anyone who has had even a light brush with American history knows that the American army wintered, suffered, and seemed close to total collapse at Valley Forge. The soldiers barely survived on a farmland plateau above the forge, in a sparsely settled section of Pennsylvania.

Three months before the encampment began in mid-December, the Americans had suffered a loss that should have been a dire foreboding. Advanced units under Knyphausen and Cornwallis raided a rebel depot at Valley Forge. They took away 3,500 barrels of flour, twenty-three barrels of horseshoes, several thousand tomahawks and quantities of kettles and other desperately needed supplies that would have eased the approaching winter for the Americans.

The winter weather was not severe, but the poorly fed men, barefoot in the snows of Valley Forge, knew the ever-present specter of death. Soldiers faced the bitterness of hunger in the midst of plenty. The eagerness of local farmers to profit, whether by selling to American speculators or to the British in Philadelphia, heightened the suffering. General Nathanael Greene, heading a patrol on foraging duty, said, "Harden your hearts; we are in the midst of a damn nest of Tories."

Neither cold nor snow were the main enemies of an army that, at one time at Valley Forge, had 4,000 men so destitute of clothing that they could not leave their huts. Food often was meager. But the signature of Valley Forge was death — appalling, incessant, terrifying death. An estimated 2,500 soldiers of the total complement of troops died that winter, a one-in-four ratio that vied with the worst of plagues. They died, in the main, from disease and neglect.

Historian Willard M. Wallace has written that the "suffering was due to American mismanagement, graft, speculation, and indifference more than to the enemy or the weather." Pennsylvania's rich harvest was sold to the British in Philadelphia. Loads of New Jersey pork rotted on wagons because of a lack of transportation. Much of the difficulty was blamed on Thomas Mifflin's inept performance as quartermaster general. He was replaced eventually by the highly efficient General Nathanael Greene.

Valley Forge's bright side was the intensive military training a received by Continental soldiers. By spring, General Friedrich von Steuben had soldiers seemingly enjoying, or at least respecting, the rugged marching drills and battlefield tactics he imparted. He was rough speaking and often impatient, but American soldiers earned a sense of belonging to a well-disciplined, well-trained army.

Valley Forge tested Washington's demeanor in the face of harsh criticism and the scheming actions of members of his officer corps as they fought for promotions and harped to Congress (or anyone who would listen) on Washington's weaknesses as they saw them. When the Pennsylvania assembly rebuked him for not trying to recapture Philadelphia, Washington answered in what were his sharpest jabs at the highly critical (and quite comfortable) civilians. He wrote:

> I can assure these gentlemen that it is a much easier and less distressing thing to draw remonstrance in a comfortable room than to occupy a cold bleak hill, and sleep under frost and snow, without clothes or blankets. However, although they seem to have little feeling for the naked and distressed soldiers, I feel superabundantly for them, and from my soul I pity their miseries, which is neither in my power to relieve or prevent.

Stimulating news came in the worst of the winter. On February 6, 1778, France finally signed the long-awaited treaty that formally recognized the United States. France vowed to help the new nation achieve independence. And, if England ever waged war on France, the United States would in turn come to its ally's aid. The portentous treaty was made public on May 5.

On April 14, word came that the British ministry had eagerly accepted Howe's request that he be replaced and called home. The querulous, self-doubting Henry Clinton,

George Washington visiting soldier's huts at Valley Forge. This bleak artist's view reflects the erroneous belief that the Valley Forge weather was the most dreadful of the war.

Howe's second in command in New York City, succeeded him.

Clinton's hands were tied almost from the start. His instructions, straight from the home office, were to return the army from Philadelphia to New York, and simultaneously weaken its position by immediately dispatching nearly 10,000 men to points in or near the Caribbean — 5,000 to help attack St, Lucia, an important French port in the West Indies; 3,000 to Florida, and hundreds of soldiers to Bermuda and the Bahamas. French and British forces were vigorously fighting for control of the islands.

The full evacuation of Philadelphia took several weeks, with many wealthy Tories being placed aboard ships, along with their abundant baggage, ranging from valuable works of art to dining room furniture. Clinton did not dare send his troops to New York on ships for fear of a French naval attack. He worried as well that unpredictable winds and seas might so long delay his arrival in New York that his force would be easy prey for the Americans.

On June 18, the British evacuation became complete, so skillfully planned and carried out that by noon the New Jersey side of the Delaware River was crammed by the British army, its camp followers, Tories who preferred to be with the army, and various Philadelphia officials who did not dare stay in the city.

The military units moved off; when the last baggage wagon left the riverside, the line

In 1854, Emanuel Leutze painted Washington at Monmouth, *brilliantly depicting Washington rallying his troops after sending General Charles Lee to the rear. Leutze's most inspiring Revolutionary War depiction,* Washington Crossing the Delaware, *was painted three years earlier.*

of march (including camp followers and other civilians) was twelve miles long. General William Maxwell and his New Jersey brigade soon engaged Clinton's advance guard at Haddonfield, a few miles east of the river.

Washington was ready to move on the same morning that the British evacuated Philadelphia. Advance militia units were in place on the route Clinton must take to impede the British advance. They felled trees across major roads, poisoned wells, burned bridges, and constantly shot at the flanks of the ponderous army's line of march.

The main American army of about 12,000 men crossed the river to Coryell's Ferry [now Lambertville] and moved eastward into the Sourland Mountains northeast of Trenton. A council of generals, convened the night of June 18 in Hopewell, debated the wisdom of attacking Clinton's army on open, level ground. Disgusted by the timidity, Colonel Alexander Hamilton said the session "would have done honor to the most honorable society of housewives."

Washington overcame all the objections: he would engage Clinton whenever and wherever possible. The Marquis de Lafayette, barely twenty years old, was picked to lead the advance forces into battle after the inscrutable Major General Charles Lee, often an outspoken critic of Washington, refused the command. Lee then changed his mind after the choice of Lafayette; he demanded leadership when the Battle of Monmouth began on June 28. Because Lee outranked Lafayette, the command was his.

It was by any standard a curious choice. Charles Lee, born in England in 1732, served as a career officer in the British army and fought in America for England during the French and Indian War. He returned to America in 1775, espoused the revolution and won wide popularity despite his wretched manners and slovenly appearance.

Lee had dallied, peculiarly when Washington ordered him to bring 3,000 soldiers to the camp on the Delaware River in December 1776. The British captured him in Basking Ridge, even as he was writing a scurrilous letter about Washington. When exchanged, he rejoined the American army, and as the Battle of Monmouth impended, he declared that an open battle with the British would be "insanity."

Yet Lee led the attack on June 28, a day that dawned blisteringly hot. Washington had ordered Lee to open fire at dawn, "acquainting him at the same time I was marching to support him." Lee did not obey, doing little more than jab at the aggressive enemy before moving his troops in retreat. Within an hour the American position verged on chaotic. When Washington heard of the withdrawal, he dismissed it as a rumor even as he spurred his horse to the scene.

Washington met the retreating Lee and the two argued vehemently. Lee allegedly declared that his troops were "not able to meet British Grenadiers." Washington retorted

Washington's encounter with Lee on the Monmouth battlefield is one of the classic stories of the war — and a favorite of nineteenth-century illustrators.

furiously, "Sir, they are able, and by God they shall do it!" He gave orders to countermarch toward the front. Lee was sent to the rear.

Taking command, Washington spurred the troops forward. Lafayette was amazed at the way he rode " all along the lines amid the shouts of the soldiers cheering them by his voice and his example and restoring to our standard the fortunes of the fight. I thought I have never beheld such a superb man."

Temperatures soared above a hundred degrees, felling men with the same deadliness as the cannon and musket balls. The front swerved back and forth; neither side could claim a decisive advantage. Clinton quit the battlefield at twilight, marching over the steep Atlantic Highlands to Sandy Hook Bay, where the British forces boarded boats and escaped to New York.

Although Clinton cut off the battle, the Americans were too exhausted and too disorganized to follow. They nursed the wounded and buried the dead before falling into deep sleep on the open field. Washington spent the night wrapped in his cloak, sleeping on the ground with his men. Both armies suffered severely. British losses were more than 500 killed or wounded, against more than 400 American casualties. One source also lists thirty-seven American and fifty-one British deaths from sunstroke.

The summer of 1778 dwindled away, with neither side making any kind of decisive move. Late autumn brought Washington's army back to the security of the New Jersey hills. This time the commander chose Middlebrook near the southern slopes of the Watchung Mountains. The location was considerably more exposed than Morristown's position well behind the ridges, but the mountains provided a sanctuary in the unlikely case that the enemy ventured as far as Middlebrook.

The days grew shorter and in early November the first sharply cold winds gusted down from the Hudson River valley. Within a month, snow sifted softly across the wooded slopes. The Continentals would have to face another winter in the mountains.

General Lee, depicted in this caricature, proved to be a detriment in the Battle of Monmouth because of his indecisive, almost calamitous behavior on the battlefield. Lee demanded a court martial; his wish was granted. The trial found him guilty of leaving the battlefield, and suspended him for a year without pay. Lee died in 1782, and even in death he showed his lasting contempt for all society. In his will Lee asked that he not be buried "in any church or church yard within a mile of any Presbyterian or Anabaptist meeting house, for since I have resided in this country I have kept so much bad company while living, that I do not chose to continue it when dead."

A Day of Thirst

The setting sun went down a fiery red, a fitting end to June 28, 1778, the day in which the fierce Battle of Monmouth was fought in blazing temperatures. That much was truth, but in the gathering dusk after the battle, a legend was growing: Molly Pitcher had begun a vigorous, if much disputed, walk through history.

There likely was a "Molly" at Monmouth that Sunday, said to be Mary Ludwig Hayes of Carlisle, Pennsylvania, wife of William Hayes, a gunner in a Pennsylvania artillery regiment. Mary was always called Molly. Mary (Molly) had followed her husband to the showdown at Monmouth.

As the sun rose progressively higher, the day became almost intolerably hot. Men began to fall from heat and exhaustion. Molly's legend says Molly began carrying water across the battlefield, dipping her pitcher into a nearby spring again and again. As she ran across the field with the water, it is said soldiers called, "Molly, bring the pitcher," or just "Molly! Pitcher!"

Other, more likely, reports tell of soldiers fainting on the field because of thirst, many of them dying or near death. Other tales tell of soldiers dipping their hats in the spring to get water to drink or to pour on overheated brows.

Molly has remained a considerable enigma. One version says that when her

The story of Molly Pitcher carrying water to the troops has become a favorite legend. More likely, soldiers dipped water from a spring to drink or to throw over themselves during heat that soared above 100 degrees.

husband was killed, she replaced him at his cannon. That was not true: William Hayes lived to earn a pension for his army service. Other accounts say she helped him at the cannon. Anything goes in a legend.

Her birthplace, parentage, and nationality are as much fiction as fact. Artists have depicted her as everything from a hoyden to a saint. Descriptions of her also vary, although every account comments on her strength: "with ease she could carry a three-bushel bag on her shoulders," or "she was healthy, active and strong; fleshy and short in stature."

Several soldiers at Monmouth remembered a woman at a cannon. Joseph Plumb Martin recalled that "a cannon shot from the enemy passed directly through her legs without doing any other damage than carrying away the lower part of her petticoat." Martin did not name her; he merely confirmed that at least one woman was active in the battle.

Molly deserves to be remembered, whether as a soldier in action at a cannon or as a legendary humanitarian serving those stricken on a field of war. Someone (or many "someones") carried water to the parched soldiers and it does little harm to think of one named Molly, with a pitcher.

Chapter Four

PLEASANT DAYS *at* MIDDLEBROOK

After the sufferings and miseries of Valley Forge, the winter at Middlebrook in 1778-79 gets minimal attention in most Revolutionary War accounts. It is as if a New Jersey winter on the southern slope of the Watchung Mountains were a holiday of rest and relaxation compared with other winter encampments.

In fact, winter came early that year, sending snow swirling across the middle colonies in December, with an especially heavy snowstorm on Christmas Day. It came from the west, sweeping across Pennsylvania and New Jersey and was called "violent" in New Jersey. It was not, however, an augury of things to come; that was the only major storm of the winter.

But that first, and only, consequential snow of the Middlebrook encampment was described by General Anthony Wayne as "a very severe storm from Christmas to New Years." It plunged temperatures to near zero. Wayne had particular reason for concern. His Pennsylvanians had arrived late at Middlebrook, after being detained "by the maneuvers of the enemy up the [Hudson] river."

On December 23, with their huts scarcely begun, Wayne's soldiers were "exposed to wind and weather in their old tents." Many were "quite destitute of blankets" and without hats. Wayne wrote Joseph Reed, a member of Congress and a powerful Pennsylvania leader, that the plight of his officers was "more intolerable than the soldiers." He warned that many of them sought to go home, leaving their men "unofficered." If permitted to depart, Wayne predicted they were likely "never to return to this army again."

The View from Washington Rock

A bold, rocky prominence on the southern slope of the Watchung Mountains, overlooking the Raritan River and valley in central New Jersey, gave the American army a lookout across a broad and fertile area of New Jersey.

This earliest known depiction of the famed Washington Rock appeared in *Historical Collections of the State of New Jersey*, written by the noted wandering artist-historians, John W. Barber and Henry Howe, and published in 1844.

The collaborators said Washington Rock offered views extending to "the spires of New York" and the Atlantic Highlands overlooking Sandy Hook. They estimated the rocky protuberance was about twenty-five feet high and from thirty to forty feet in circumference. It is still a popular lookout, as part of the small Washington Rock State Park in North Plainfield.

Weather was neither a motivating factor nor a deterrent when Washington decided late in November 1778 that his main army would return to the strategically secure Watchung Mountains. General Henry Clinton again kept the Americans on tenterhooks by creating fear that he might speed troops up the Hudson River valley to attack West Point and possibly split the infant nation in two. The enigmatic Clinton did not move, but Washington felt he must keep him under close observation.

Washington divided his army into three sections for the winter. The North Carolina Brigade was stationed on the west side of the Hudson River north of New York City

The home of John Wallace in Somerville, where Washington spent the winter of 1778-79. The house still stands and can be visited.

to counter any British thrust toward West Point. The New Jersey brigade was quartered at Elizabethtown, to give early warning and to provide a delaying action if the British marched west toward Morristown. The third, and largest, unit — about 8,800 men from Virginia, Maryland, Delaware, and Pennsylvania regiments — began heading to Middlebrook (now Bound Brook) in late November. Washington established his headquarters in the newly built residence of John Wallace in Somerville.

With the army spread so widely, quartermaster officers reasoned that the quest for food would be easier than it had been at Morristown in 1777 or at Valley Forge a year later. It would not be so: central New Jersey farmers were as unwilling to feed the hungry soldiers, as were the Dutch farmers near Valley Forge.

Hut building that winter went rapidly, thanks to the generally good weather and the experience gained at Valley Forge. Soldiers built their huts from trees they felled, but they were rested after five months of idleness and the little snow that lingered on the ground at Middlebrook offered no problem.

Washington ordered that huts not be sunk into the ground as they had been at Valley

Forge and that "boards, slabs or large shingles" were to be used for roofing. Inside, bunks for twelve men were arranged in tiers on three sides of the single room; a large fireplace took up the fourth side. Each soldier received straw for his bunk and one blanket

According to Dr. James Thacher, a twenty-four-year-old Massachusetts army doctor and historian, the huts were built in six to eight weeks. He added that "having continued to live under cover of canvas tents most of the winter, we have suffered extremely from cold and storms." He seemingly exaggerated the situation; he later characterized the winter as mild.

Thacher and his fellow officers did not let wintry days

Washington's fondness for dancing was demonstrated in January 1779 at the home of General Nathanael Greene and his vivacious young wife Kitty, during the Middlebrook encampment. Greene wrote "the commander-in-chief evinced his esteem for Mrs. Greene by dancing with her for three hours without sitting down."

interrupt their social life. "Our officers have not permitted the Christmas days to pass unnoticed," wrote Thacher. There was not a day "without invitations to dine, nor a night without amusement and dancing." He and fellow officers celebrated Christmas with a lavish dinner, followed by dancing until 3 a.m.

It was a barometer for a joyous winter — for the officers.

On New Year's Day, Thacher and some other officers (called "gallant Virginians" by the young doctor) feasted at the nearby country home of Colonel John Gibson, followed by the luxury of dining at an "amply furnished" table at a general's quarters. The celebrants then went to Colonel Peter Muhlenberg's home, where a "very elegant supper" was provided. On hand were "a number of ladies," mostly wives or special friends of officers, for a marathon dance session. A weary but happy Thacher reported, "not one of the company was permitted to retire until three o'clock in the morning."

Washington reached the encampment on December 11, 1778, declaring that he was ready "to indulge in more agreeable amusements." Such pleasures would have to wait. The

In an army short on horses, it was not unusual for artillerymen to drag their guns themselves. The guns ranged from four pounders to twenty pounders, as well as howitzers and mortars. Henry Knox set the tone when his men supplied their own artillery weapons by dragging 120,000 pounds of guns from Ticonderoga to Boston in the winter of 1775-76. The 300-mile journey took nearly three months but it gave America a well-equipped artillery corps.

---

general was summoned to Philadelphia on December 22 to confer with Congress.

The chief remained in the city for forty-five days, cooling his heels and observing the woeful inertia of the governing body. The showy comfort of the Americans in the City of Brotherly Love, verging on lavish indulgence, appalled him. Shortly after reaching the nation's war capital, he wrote to Benjamin Harrison:

> *If I were called upon to draw a picture of the times and of men from that I have seen, heard, and in part know, I should in one word say that idleness, dissipation, and extravagance seems to have laid fast hold to most of them. Speculation, peculation and an insatiable thirst for riches seem to have got the better of every other consideration and almost of every order of men.*
>
> *Party disputes and personal quarrels are the great business of the day whilst the mo-*

mentous concerns of an empire — a great and accumulating debt, ruined finances, depreciated money, and lack of credit — which in their consequences is the want of everything — are but secondary considerations and postponed from day to day, from week to week, as if our affairs bore the most promising aspect.

Our money is now sinking 50 percent a day in this city…and yet an assembly, a concert, a dinner or supper, will not only take men off from acting in this business, but even of thinking of it…. After drawing this picture, which from my soul I believe to be a true one, I need not repeat to you that I am alarmed and wish to see my countrymen aroused.

Mrs. Washington joined the general in Philadelphia as house guests of Henry Laurens of South Carolina, the president of the Continental Congress. The couple attended a few social affairs and the general sat for a portrait by Charles Willson Peale. Washington called this "the only relief" he had enjoyed since entering into service.

The Washingtons returned to Somerville on February 8, 1778. Mrs. Washington hoped the active social life Middlebrook officers purportedly had been enjoying might lift the general from the despair that had overwhelmed him in Philadelphia.

Enlisted men did not have the opportunity, the money, the social status, or the energy for such sprees. They were felling trees and building their own quarters, and spending other long days raising huts for the sleep-deprived officers. There was no evidence that Thacher and his fellow officers ever wielded an axe or hoisted tree logs to help themselves.

Foot soldiers who could afford it quickly found their own sub rosa winter pleasures. They bought illicit liquor in shacks built behind their huts. Some dallied with the prostitutes who lingered near the edge of camp, and many of them gambled in their huts. Army enforcers burned down the illicit bars, gaming was stopped (or pushed further underground) by a stern decree from Washington, but the ladies of the evening usually stayed one step ahead of the law.

No one enjoyed the return to the Watchung Mountains in 1778 more than twenty-eight-year-old Brigadier General Knox, the tall, corpulent commander of the artillery. His pleasant little wife Lucy journeyed to Pluckemin. She followed her husband each winter wherever he went, confirmed by the fact that eventually she bore him twelve children. Most higher-ranked officers also regularly brought their wives to camp during the winter seasons.

The Knoxes were party people who enjoyed the frequent officer frolics; before the winter ended they would host the most glittering affair of the season (and perhaps of the entire war) at the newly built Artillery Academy in Pluckemin. By day, Henry Knox devoted himself to completing the dream of his young life.

Knox had taken an almost non-existent artillery unit in 1775 and molded it into a competent fighting force. His artillery had distinguished itself at Trenton and Princeton, in the 1777 battles outside Philadelphia, and on the open field at Monmouth. By 1778, the artillery was achieving most of what Washington had hoped for when he appointed Knox to lead the brigade. But Knox wanted more — much, much more.

Artillerymen enjoyed a high status in the eyes of Knox. Tall and verging on 300 pounds, he was often described as "beefy," with a "pompous, self complacent walk" caused by his weight. He believed that fair, intelligent treatment of "his lads" produced discipline more effectively than the harsh, cruel punishment that Army regulations allowed.

That attitude enabled Knox to tackle his fantasy, an "artillery academy" that had been shaping in his mind for more than two years. If it could become a reality, winter months could be spent lecturing on, and demonstrating, the art and craft of using heavy cannons in battle. Soon, the academy began to rise on the hillside east of Pluckemin.

The site, about five miles north of the main encampment, was carefully acquired before Knox led about 1,000 on-the-job trained gunners and their sixty cannons into the area. The artillery's highly motivated troops swiftly completed upgraded quarters for both officers and men, as well as other huge, permanent buildings for the academy, and for storage, as well as other structures for planning, forging weapons, and teaching the art of handling the big guns.

Work proceeded on the academy at a furious pace in the last two weeks of January and the first two weeks in February 1779. An original completion date of February 5 had been set, as an occasion to celebrate the first anniversary of the French Alliance proclaimed at Valley Forge The buildings were not finished; but fortunately the original date had to be postponed because the Washingtons did not return from Philadelphia until February 8.

The commander in chief's unproductive stay in Philadelphia had left him in a dark mood. If he had known, more worries would have been added by affairs that threatened much of the camp. With the leader away, discipline had become lax, and men used any excuse to avoid work, excepting most of the artillery regiment, but even some of Knox's "lads" shirked their duties. Large numbers of officers were taking long furloughs (sometimes not authorized), men were deserting, and courts martial sat every week.

Guilty verdicts in the army trials brought dismissal from the service for officers, reduction in rank for the men, plus lashings and a few hangings. The day after Christmas, a delayed "gift from the government" brought 100 pairs of shoes to camp. It was said that many men spurned the new shoes because well-shod feet might eliminate a sure excuse for not working.

The reasons for despair were put aside, at least temporarily, in Pluckemin, where enlisted men and officers worked furiously to get the big new rooms in the Academy present-

General Henry Knox, a Boston bookseller before the war, founded the American artillery corps and led it throughout the war. Knox's artillerymen excelled at Princeton, at battles outside Philadelphia in 1777, and at Monmouth and Yorktown.

able for the great celebration that Henry and Mrs. Knox planned to host on February 18 to honor the first anniversary of the French alliance. The Academy was finished on the morning of the grand fete, a tremendous task accomplished by fewer than 200 men in slightly less than two months.

Enlisted men and a few low-ranked officers attended to every work detail of the celebration — decorations, lighting, gathering of tables and chairs, fireworks, and even preparation of the food and cleanup. Sufficient food and drink were on hand, presumably paid for at the high prices area suppliers were demanding. An enlisted men's band would play for dancing; they likely were paid a few shillings for the evening, as was the custom. Enlisted men did not attend as guests, although they were permitted to enjoy the fireworks.

The Knox-supervised party was the social event of the year and perhaps of the entire war. Guests from all over the state rolled into the park in carriages and wagons and stepped down at a 100-foot-long pavilion that enlisted men had constructed for the occasion. Thirteen huge paintings showed colorful facets of the revolution and the glories of war itself. Sixteen roaring cannons summoned guests to a multi-course dinner, followed by fireworks and an evening of dancing that lasted nearly until dawn.

General Knox, who knew a party when he attended or planned one, said of his gala event: "everybody allowed it to be the first of the kind ever exhibited in this state at least. We had about seventy ladies, all of the first tun [meaning beauty, not weight] in the state, and between three and four hundred gentlemen." Knox was proud beyond belief when Washington opened the party by dancing with his wife Lucy.

As soon as possible after the fete, the men cleaned the Academy, and classes on handling cannons and other heavy weapons began for officers. According to reports by a perplexed and saddened Knox, very few officers took advantage of the unprecedented opportunity

Meanwhile, the winter weather cooperated. Thacher wrote on April 13, 1779: "We have passed a winter remarkably mild and moderate; since the 10th of January we have scarce had a fall of snow, or a frost and no severe weather."

An unwilling participant in Middlebrook's fine spring weather was Major General Benedict Arnold, called to Middlebrook from Philadelphia to face a court martial on June 1. He was to be tried for minor misdeeds he allegedly committed while he was the commander assigned to govern Philadelphia after the British left in June 1778 to head toward what would become the Battle of Monmouth.

Washington surely had paid Arnold at least one courtesy visit while he was in Philadelphia the previous December and it is likely that no day passed that he did not see, or hear, evidence of Arnold's new-found wealth in the city. However, Arnold was admired by Washington and highly regarded by most American officers.

The first date set for the court martial was inconvenient for members of the court, since the army was preparing to leave Middlebrook. The board would not be able to meet again until December in Morristown. Arnold returned to Philadelphia to marry nineteen-year-old beautiful and wealthy Peggy Shippen on June 8, 1779. (Arnold was thirty-eight at the time.) Their life style immediately expanded. Resentment grew in the city and charges were made that Arnold had misused government wagons and had engaged in other misfeasance to line his pockets. This was the substance of his forthcoming court martial.

Middlebrook's pleasant weather and busy social calendar did not dispel the sense of dread that depressed Washington. Recruiting was going badly, the nation's currency was sinking rapidly in value, desertions were frequent, and the army had concluded another winter in desperate need of both food and clothing. Washington wrote on May 8: "Our army as it now stands is but little more than a skeleton of an army and I hear of no steps that are being taken to give it strength and substance."

The army broke camp on June 3 and headed by way of Morristown for West Point, which Washington feared might be in imminent danger of an attack by the British. The attack never came; British attention, by orders from London, had become focused on the South.

Most of the army, officers and men alike, welcomed the unhurried march to the cool summertime shade in the Hudson River valley. Yet Knox's Artillery surely left Pluckemin with mixed emotions. Their feat in constructing in two months the most imposing army structure built during the war was a matter for enduring pride. Some historians have called it the forerunner of the West Point Military Academy.

But the buildings were never again used as an academy. They became a hospital in the winter of 1779-80, then gradually disappeared, ravaged by looters and local farmers who used the logs and boards in their own buildings, or for easily cut firewood.

The days grew shorter and the first cold winds once again gusted down the Hudson River Valley in mid-October. Another winter was fast approaching. Would the Watchungs again provide the haven Washington needed for his out-manned and ill-equipped army?

Artillery Park

One of the very rare on-the-spot drawings made during the war was this precise pen-and-ink drawing of the Artillery Park "academy" built on the mountain east of Pluckemin during the winter of 1778-79. It was drawn by Captain John Lillie ("J. Lillie") of the Third Continental Artillery. His depiction features the big academy structures surrounded by affiliated buildings and the barracks of both officers and men. The buildings were finished on February 18, the day of the scintillating party staged to celebrate at Pluckemin the first anniversary of the French Alliance.

Henry Knox, the former Boston bookseller chosen by Washington to establish a utility corps for the army, had suggested to Congress in October 1776 that "an academy" be built where "the whole theory and practice of fortification and gunnery should be taught." Congress took no action but Knox established an academy in one of the large tents that traveled with his artillery.

Everything had to be special in Knox's view; there is evidence that even the one-story enlisted men's barracks were on stone foundations, with wooden floors. But the shining symbols of the facility were two of the largest public rooms in America at that time. One of the rooms, measuring twenty-by-forty-feet long, was called the Long Room. The largest room, measuring fifty-by-thirty feet, was housed in the academy building itself, whose elaborate cupola could be seen for miles around. The room had a high arched ceiling, plastered walls, and highly polished floors.

The *Pennsylvania Packet* published an eyewitness account of the structures in March 1779. It said in part that the buildings "unfold themselves in a very pretty manner as you approach. Field pieces, mortars, howitzers, and heavy cannon make the front part of a parallelogram; the others sides are composed of huts for the officers and men." The account said "there is also an academy where lectures are read on tactics and gunnery."

There can be little doubt that Knox intended the imposing structure to be the permanent home of the United States Artillery Corps. It has been written that the academy was the predecessor of the military installation at West Point, but no positive evidence of that has been produced.

The academy was used as a hospital during the winter of 1779-80 but failure to use the academy's well-built and most imposing structures during the rest of the war is mystifying. Some of the suffering men at Jockey Hollow with

Without this on-the-spot drawing by Captain John Lillie, an American officer, the Artillery Park at Pluckemin would be little more than mentions in a few letters. Instead, the expansive, well-built facility is fully understandable. It centered on the very large hall; surrounding buildings were workshops to the rear and housing for the men on either side of the complex.

minor injuries such as frozen feet might well have been temporarily housed at the academy rather than languishing in their sparse huts.

No above ground physical evidence of the buildings remains, and what should have been a major New Jersey historical site has been obscured by a huge housing development on the hillside.

Fortunately, an extensive archaeological project on the site, led by John L. Seidel in the late 1970s, verified the existence and magnitude of the installation. There had been considerable written documentation but the on-site archaeological digs provided the first tangible proof that the academy existed.

Chapter Five

STALEMATE *on the* HUDSON

A half hour before midnight on July 16, 1779, nearly 1,300 Continental soldiers maintained strict silence as they stood in muddy marshes a half mile west of the British-held fort at Stony Point on the Hudson River. Sixteen miles to the north lay the emplacements at West Point, considered by Washington to be the "key to the Continent."

Stony Point would not have been considered a major emplacement if either the British or the Americans had been waging a vigorous war, or had planned any major campaign during the summer of 1779. It was as if Washington at West Point and Clinton in New York City were playing a peculiar game, well aware that the most important player (the French navy), although not even on the board, tended to influence nearly every move of both gamesters.

Clinton had made what was for him a bold move on June 1, sending a strong force northward on ships to land at King's Ferry, about twelve miles south of West Point. King's Ferry was a fine prize in its own right: it was the closest ferry point to New York and the easiest and safest place to operate barges that moved Continental brigades and supplies east and west. It was also important in maintaining communications between New England and the Middle States. More immediately important to the British, the ferry also linked forts at Stony Point, on the west bank of the river, and Verplanck's Point (Fort Lafayette) on the east. The Americans built both but had neglected to garrison either adequately.

West Point was hastily strengthened after the fall of Stony Point, and Americans dug

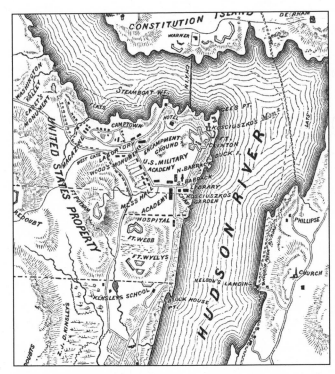

Benson Lossing's map of West Point showed the relative safety offered Washington's main army. However, it was useful only if General Clinton attacked northward on the Hudson River.

in to await what they felt surely would be a powerful assault toward West Point by Clinton. He had a chance to seize the initiative if he wished — or dared — to use it. Instead, the British commander left strong forces to strengthen and defend the captured forts and the ferry, then withdrew his ships to the city.

Washington quickly began planning to take back the forts. He asked Major General Anthony Wayne on June 28 to study the "practicability" of storming and retaking Stony Point. "If it is undertaken,' Washington told Wayne, "I should conceive it ought to be done by way of surprise in the night."

The assault on Stony Point began about noon on July 15, when Wayne's newly formed light infantry began the fifteen-mile march to the assembly point a mile or so west of the fort. Orders had been given that there would be as little sound as possible. One report of the advance said that all dogs on the route were killed, lest their barking alert the British. No weapons were to be loaded; one soldier was killed with a sword when he attempted to defy this at the assembly point.

Wayne's force had to cross a narrow causeway single file or wade through a half-mile of water in the deep marshes near the fort. Conquering the marshes, whether via the causeway or wading, merely brought any invader face to face with at least two, and at one point three abattises — fortifications of trees felled and placed with their branches facing the invader. These would have to be chopped away before any advance could be started. Beyond, on a steep rise, the fort walls might then be breached.

Wayne believed an attack could succeed, although the feat would require the darkness of night, extreme silence, and perfect timing. Leading the way would be two groups

Paulus Hook, now part of Jersey City, was built on a man-made island at the edge of a wide salt marsh. It was surrounded by the Hudson River and a wide ditch through which tidal waters flowed. To conquer the fort, American Major Henry Lee had to lead 400 men across the broad, trackless marsh in darkness, wade through the ditch at low tide and fight about 200 well-trained occupants.

---

of axe-wielding "Forlorn Hopes" (today such a force would be called a suicide mission). Their unenviable role was to hack paths with axes through the limbs of the abattisess. They would be working under heavy British fire.

The Forlorn Hopes moved through the marshes and began hacking at the abattises at about 11:30 p.m. on July 17. As expected, they worked under heavy fire; by morning, only three of their original number were still alive. Close behind, as pathways were hacked through the fallen trees, were Wayne's 1,200-man light infantry brigade, split into three prongs. The assault was a totally stealthy bayonet charge until the British started to fire. The Americans then unleashed their own muskets.

Wayne's plan was nearly flawless. Even though he was temporarily out of action after a bullet grazed his head, Wayne returned to the fight. The fort was quickly overrun at a cost to the Americans of fifteen killed and eighty-three wounded. The British suffered twenty killed, seventy-four wounded, fifty-eight missing, and 472 captured, a total of 624 casualties.

The Americans tried briefly and ineffectively to use Stony Point's guns against a nearby British sloop, the *Vulture*, and Fort Lafayette across the river to the east. British troops heading up the river stopped that effort. Wayne withdrew his men after they had removed or destroyed all the fort's weapons and ammunition. The British reoccupied the fort within a day, rebuilt it in a stronger fashion, and manned it with a more alert garrison.

Operation at Stony Point, for all its masterful show of skill, had little strategic worth and no lasting value, but the daring exploit built morale throughout the army and ignited flames of hope and pride in the American people. The British Annual Register admiringly called the assault on the fort a feat that "would have done honor to the most veteran soldiers."

One month later, on August 18, Virginia's cavalry under Major Henry Lee ("Light-Horse Harry") marched 400 men more than sixteen miles over rough New Jersey terrain to within two miles of the British fort at Paulus Hook (now Jersey City). The troops neared their objective at about 3 a.m. and began moving slowly and quietly toward the fort through a soggy marshland and tidal waters.

The action was an almost exact copy of Wayne's Stony Point success. Soldiers were warned that anyone firing a gun before action was joined would be killed on the spot. After a short, sharp skirmish, the Americans took control of the fort and damaged it as much as possible. But enemy support was again on the way from New York. Lee retreated across the wetlands, losing only about seven men. The British lost fifty-nine or sixty men to Continental bayonets and Lee took along 158 prisoners as his forces withdrew.

The attack on Paulus Hook was not a tremendous victory either, but in light of the non-active summer, it also assumed major proportions. Lee and Wayne were both awarded gold medals by Congress for back-to-back victories cut from the same cloth.

The rest of August, as well as September and October, slipped away as Clinton and Washington resumed their desultory game of live chess. By November 1, ice appeared in the coves of the Hudson River and temperatures dipped into the low 30s. North winds whistled through the leafless trees. Something had to be done — and quickly — about locating a site for the winter encampment.

Quartermaster General Nathanael Greene, whose duties included finding the proper site, warned his deputy, Colonel James Abeel, on November 4, 1779, that "the weather grows cold and puts us in mind of winter quarters." Abeel was ordered to examine "all the country within eight or ten miles" of Morristown. Greene assured the colonel he based his instructions on "the conversations I have had with the General [Washington] and other reasons." But he also told Abeel "not to let any person know of the matter, unless it is Lord Stirling, whom you may advise with and consult upon the occasion, as his knowledge and opinions will be of great weight in the matter,"

Abeel left immediately for Morristown. He was to start "away down below Baskenridge [Basking Ridge] and search on towards Chatham, and from Chatham to Boonetown." He was to look for and record the "water, wood, and make of ground." He was to map, however roughly, the roads leading to Morristown. This was no abstract hunting trip.

Conflicting letters began emanating from Washington's West Point headquarters, confounding Greene. Would the commander choose Scotch Plains, or perhaps Boonetown (Boonton), or Acquackanock (Passaic), or even somewhere else? The commander never mentioned Morristown in the early correspondence.

Washington clung to a waning hope of a major attack on the British in New York, if he could be sure of massive help from a French fleet commanded by Vice Admiral Count

Lossing's 1850 map of the narrows in the Hudson River between the forts at Stony Point and Verplanck's Point. King's Ferry, north of Stony Point, was the favored north-south river connection.

d'Estaing biding time in the West Indies. Finally, in the first week of October, word reached both Clinton and Washington that the French fleet was headed north. Clinton cancelled orders for Cornwallis to leave New York with 4,000 men to strengthen the defense of Jamaica. Washington hoped that the sails of the strong French fleet might soon be seen heading past Sandy Hook on the way to attack New York.

The fleet finally materialized off Georgia in September; d'Estaing had decided to cast his lot with American troops pressing against the British stronghold in Savannah, initially with considerable success. But in mid-November dreadful word (from an American viewpoint) came that the French and American siege on Savannah had been crushed. The siege was abandoned and d'Estaing hastily set sail for the West Indies. Clinton jubilantly hailed the news as "the greatest event that has happened in the whole war."

Even before he learned of the Savannah debacle, Washington admitted on November 13 that there was "uncertainty of an operation in conjunction with the French fleet" because of "the advanced state of the season." He said he "expected hourly to be relieved from this embarrassment [of waiting vainly for the French] and I shall then take instantaneous measures for making a disposition for winter quarters." The "relief" came with the departure of the French fleet from Savannah, headed for the West Indies. Several regiments were ordered to move toward Morristown — even though no site had yet been officially approved.

Two months had slipped away since Washington first talked of a winter camp and three weeks had elapsed since Greene's early November warning that winter was imminent. Two early snowstorms already had drifted across New Jersey; winter was sending a strong message. Washington's uncharacteristic indecisiveness was delaying the building of huts, the movement of supplies, and the numerous other details of a winter encampment.

Not surprisingly, Nathanael Greene wrote Washington on November 20, politely pressing for guidance: "I wish to know which would be your Excellency's choice — to hut below the mountains, nearly all together, or in a divided state in this [Morris] County?" The commander replied merely that he was "sorry to find that your perplexity as to a winter camp for the Army has rather increased." He offered no concrete solution; Greene had reason to wonder whether the general was reading his mail.

The quartermaster general seldom expressed frustration or annoyance to his chief, but with Washington still temporizing at West Point, Greene wrote Colonel John Cox: " I am almost worn out with fatigue in riding around the country in search of a position to hut the army in…. I have rode hot and cold, wet and dry, night and day…"

Greene's impatience intensified on November 26. He informed Washington that he had set out "in the snow storm" and had driven his horse through "Morristown, Mendon [Mendham] and Vealtown [Bernardsville]." He concluded, "a very good position may be had at Jockey Hollow, right back of Mr. Kimble's." "Kimble" — Peter Kemble — was a known Tory who had won liberty to remain in his house by promising not to be aggressive in proclaiming his beliefs.

Upon his return to Morristown, Greene met Colonel Alexander Hamilton and expounded on his day's arduous ride through the storm. He laid out his high opinion of Jockey Hollow, and in apparent belief that Hamilton's support would influence Washington, Greene wrote to the chief: "the Col. thinks we ought to make choice of the interior position [Jockey Hollow] especially as our force will be diminished bye and bye." Greene concluded his report to Washington on a not-subtle note: "The army is all halted between this and Rockaway Bridge waiting further directions."

Washington made the Morristown site official with only two days left in November. Orders to move went outward to the troops scattered north of Morristown, and on November 29 the commander left West Point and headed south. He paused in Pompton on November 30, from where he dispatched an express rider to Greene, ordering him to "proceed with laying out the ground" in Jockey Hollow for assignment to incoming regiments. Washington also asked if he was still slated to live "at Mrs Ford's" and, as a prudent man should, asked that a "late dinner" be available when he arrived.

Snow fell on December 1, the fifth storm of the year. Brisk winds beat cold flakes into the faces of the general and his retinue of aides, guards and servants as they trot-

The home of Peter Kemble, an avowed Loyalist, at the corner of what is now Mt. Kemble Avenue (Route 202) and Jockey Hollow Road. Kemble was permitted to stay in the house if he muted his sentiments; later the building was occupied by Continental officers. In 1840, the house was moved to a location about a quarter-mile north..

ted their horses over the snow-packed road between Hanover Furnace [Whippany] and Morristown. The falling flakes deepened the snow banks left by four November storms.

Washington likely had met Mrs. Ford during the winter of 1777, and he had known her husband, the late Colonel Jacob Ford, Jr. There is no record that he had ever been in the family mansion, even to attend Colonel Ford's funeral in January 1777. He could not expect to be greeted as a warm friend, but he hoped for a hospitable acceptance by Mrs. Ford, and that she and her four children would share the mansion for the next six months or more.

Jacob Ford, Jr. had planned well when he began building the house in 1772. It was the largest and most handsome place in town, set on a small rise and surrounded by two hundred acres of orchards and fields that sloped away northward toward the Whippany

River. He could well afford a magnificent home; his iron mines to the north paid fine profits. In the early days of the war he had also built a small gunpowder mill on the river at the rear of his property.

The house had eight very large rooms, four on each floor, centered on spacious halls that reached from the front to the rear of the house. Each hall equaled the space of two large rooms; the spaciousness was meant to impress visitors. The large front door, set in a frame that included small windows to let in light, offered a pleasant welcome.

There is no record of a meeting between Mrs. Ford and the general at that welcoming door, but her heritage and breeding as the daughter of the town's powerful minister, Rev. Timothy Johnes, assured that she would be at least polite. However, there exists clear, if indirect, evidence that she did not relish the thought of "sharing" her house, even with the American Army's commander in chief. She and her four children, ranging in age from eight to fifteen, would occupy only two first-floor rooms while Washington and his staff would have the run of the rest of the house — the very wide halls on both floors, the other two large rooms on the west side of the first floor, and all of the rooms on the second floor.

A letter from New Jersey Governor William Livingston, written on December 10 to Reverend Johnes, makes it abundantly clear that Mrs. Ford rushed to complain to her father, a firm revolutionist, when she learned she must share her house. Mr. Johnes immediately forwarded his daughter's woes to Livingston.

Without listing Mrs. Ford's objections or any mention of her discussion with her father, Livingston answered the minister. The governor first discussed other cases (but no names) of officers who had been placed in citizen's homes after ample warning and pleasant negotiations. The governor told the minister that he wished "General Washington could have been as well accommodated without taking up his Quarters at Mrs. Ford's." Livingston concluded:

> But his amiable disposition & the pleasure he takes in making everybody about him happy will, I am persuaded, induce him to make it as easy for her not to resent that her house has entertained such a general, nor the Neighborhood regret that a disproportionate quantity of their wood was sacrificed in such a cause.

It is very doubtful that Mr. Johnes ever revealed Livingston's letter to Washington and even more improbable that the mistress of the house ever softened her view of the occupation. Most likely, the Ford children were awed at having the nation's most important man as their guest, along with a cadre of notable young officer aides who dashed through the mansion each day.

As for the wood that "the Neighborhood" regretted losing, it probably went to build log cabins ("huts" in the lexicon of the army) for Washington's personal guard, which in various accounts numbered somewhere between 250 to 400 men. The lower figure just about equaled the entire population of Morristown. Washington's guard was stationed across the road that ran past the Ford's front door.

The anger and futility seemingly expressed to her father by Mrs. Ford reflected the attitude of many Morristown property holders. The regard for an occupying army had changed radically since January 1777 when the ragged, dirty, hungry heroes of Trenton ad Princeton first marched into town. The regard for that occupying force diminished as the winter wore on.

The indirect rebuff that Washington received (probably without ever knowing it) was reflected in other reports of civilians who refused admission to officers or quarreled with them about accommodations. General Greene, who had been in town for a few weeks and had brought his pregnant young wife Kitty to stay with him, expressed his bitterness in a letter to Washington written on Christmas Day:

> *There is a very different kind of inhabitant in the place to what there was when you were here. They receive us with coldness, and provide for us with reluctance.*

Greene had personal experience with being rebuffed. He had rented rooms for Kitty and himself in The Arnold Tavern facing the green when he and others were evaluating the suitability of the Morristown area for the winter months. Jacob Arnold, the owner, willingly accepted the initial per diem arrangement for Kitty but balked at the thought of his place being used again for the full winter.

Greene wrote Arnold on December 16, "I expected to reward you in the same way as any other traveler." Matters changed when "the plan for hutting the army here was fixt upon…what was intended only as lodgings became necessary to hold as quarters."

There was no mincing of words with the tavern owner. He told Arnold after the fact that "if you had objected, I should have been obliged to apply to a magistrate and if he would not have quartered me and the rest of the officers agreeable to my application, I should have quartered them and myself without the consent of the people."

True enough, Greene agreed, that would have been "a disagreeable circumstance and an alternative which I never wish to be reduced to; but you may depend upon it that the officers of the Army will not lodge in the open fields for fear of putting the inhabitants to a little inconvenience." The line had been drawn; Greene allowed no room for negotiation if it meant hurting the army in any way.

Washington's thoughts were with the troops marching to Jockey Hollow day after day. They would be made as comfortable as possible but first they had to fell the trees, clear the ground, and build the lodgings they would occupy.

Enlistment periods were beginning to run out for many of the soldiers. There was little incentive to stay in the army for the low pay, which, more often than not, was months behind schedule. And why should anyone in his right mind shiver in the close quarters of the huts and freeze on the parade grounds? Each night, men slipped away into the darkness to return home.

Within the first week of his stay in Morristown, Washington warned Congress that if substantial moves were not taken to strengthen and supply the army, the British, "if they keep their present collected force, will have it in their power to take such advantage of our situation as may be fatal to our affairs."

Clinton was still in New York, despite rumors that he was about to depart to strengthen the already powerful British army forces in the South. For his part, Washington had already sent North Carolina soldiers south to help the desperate situation there. Soon, Virginia detachments would follow them.

The shadow of Clinton's army in New York overlay all thinking in Morristown; he was expected to make the first move. Washington warned on December 15: "Sir Henry Clinton may be induced shortly to undertake an operation in this state."

The third winter encampment in the shelter of the Watchung Mountains was underway. As the winter unfolded, Clinton would be the least of Washington's worries.

A depiction of the medal honoring General Wayne for his success in reconquering Stony Point on July 16, 1779. A similar medal was struck to commemorate Major Henry Lee's raid on the fort at Paulus Hook on August 19.

The Key to the Continent

British General Henry Clinton persistently agreed with George Washington that control of the Hudson River would lead to victory. English control would split the northern and southern states and link British troops in Canada with those in New York, where the English capital remained during the war except for the 1777-78 stay in Philadelphia.

Conversely, American control would maintain the flow of commerce and the movement of troops between New England and the Middle Atlantic states. It would also help pin down British troops in New York City.

After Clinton became second-in-command to General William Howe in 1777, he continually pressed for a strike northward on the Hudson. Howe opted to shift his headquarters to Philadelphia. Clinton succeeded Howe in the spring of 1788 and brought the army back to New York. Except for the successful capture of fortifications at Stony Point, well south of West Point, he never made a serious foray on the river.

West Point became the American center of concern. It was greatly strengthened and additional fortifications were added. The ultimate strategy — to forestall a possible British armada attempting a move toward Albany — was a mighty chain stretched across the Hudson between the west shore and Constitution Island to the east.

The British quickly destroyed a light chain extended across the River in 1777. Washington immediately ordered 800 new wrought iron links, each weighing about 125 pounds, to be hastily forged at nearby Sterling Furnace in New York State. The finished chain weighed sixty-five tons. Merely getting it from the furnace to the West Point site was a daunting journey.

Finally, the 1500-foot-long chain was stretched across the river, held in place by forty heavy log rafts. Forty men completed the monumental task in four days, on April 30, 1778. Within a few days, word came that the chain and its supportive log rafts had to be dragged out of the river, lest the rising waters created by annual river floods snap some of the links and sink the chain.

Each winter for the next four years of the war, the mighty chain had to be stretched eastward, and each spring it had to be taken ashore. American troops dubbed the barrier "George Washington's watch chain."

The chain was never directly challenged by a British ship. Benedict Arnold, commander at West Point, failed in an attempt to sabotage the links, but when he fled to join the British, Arnold insisted the chain could be easily breached. Recent studies indicate that Arnold may have been right. Fortunately the British never put the chain to the test. If the invulnerability were merely psychological, it served the purpose.

Lincoln Diamont, in his book *Yankee Doodle Days,* states that the only authentic links surviving are the thirteen chain links surrounding a mortar at West Point. The other 787, according to Diamont, were taken to the West Point Foundry near Cold Spring, N.Y., where they were melted down and used for other purposes.

The illustration of the West Point cannon and its thirteen chain links, below, was drawn by Benson J. Lossing in about 1850.

The thirteen chain links preserved around a mortar at the U.S. Military Academy at West Point are all that remain of the 800 wrought iron links that were forged at Sterling Furnace, just north of the New Jersey-New York boundary. Soon after the war, the other 787 original links were melted down at the West Point Foundry for other uses. Many bogus links have been forged and sold as the real thing.

Chapter Six

AT HOME *in* LOG HOUSE CITY

Day after day, hour after hour, in the last days of November and early December 1779, American troops straggled over snow-covered roads leading into and through Morristown. They evoked close attention but few, if any, fanfares of appreciation. The ragged, hungry regiments had come from the north by different routes, lest the men fight among themselves for any food stored in barns or flour stashed away in mills and other farm buildings.

Well aware that it would be "difficult to procure the necessary supplies of forage" along the way, Washington authorized his commanders to "impress [seize] the necessary forage on the march of the army through the States of New York and New Jersey to their winter stations, when this warrant is to cease." Fairness must be observed, said the general: the army must "take as equally as possible from each according to what can be spared."

North Carolina troops entered Morristown first, hastening south after leaving West Point. They would not linger in town, for they were headed off to bolster troops in the rapidly deteriorating American situation in South Carolina. Washington told General Greene that more soldiers would be sent to the Carolinas, but cautioned him to "say nothing of the further reinforcement southward."

Anyone in Morristown naïve enough to expect a briskly marching, healthy, brightly uniformed, and proudly victorious army was in for a shock. These tough, hardened, fighting men were mostly extremely thin; months and even years of lean diets had taken a toll. Many had been in the ranks for four years or more; If they ever had been issued distinctive uniforms showing state affiliation or regimental pride, that had been reduced to dirty rags

"A Truly Motley Effect"

Harold L. Peterson, whose volume, *The Book of the Continental Soldier*, is the yardstick for measuring Continental soldier life, said it "was almost impossible to differentiate" between ranks. "At any given time," according to Peterson, "a review of the Continental Army would produce a truly motley effect, with coat colors varying from battalion to battalion and from company to company. Because officers were responsible for buying their own uniforms, they often appeared in attire which differed from the men under their command."

General officers wore colored sashes across their chests; other officers wore cockades; non-commissioned officers wore epaulettes or strips of cloth on their shoulders. Enlisted men could also point out that generals were easy to recognize: they rode horses.

Most of the men wore some kind of head covering, usually the familiar cocked hat adorned with a rosette or cockade worn on the left side as a distinguishing feature. Evergreens were attached to all soldiers' hats on special occasions. Officers sported feathers or cedar twigs in their cockades to distinguish themselves from foot soldiers. Some of the men wore leather or woolen caps.

---

by constant wear.

Eyewitnesses wrote of men being "naked," meaning, in eighteenth century terms not fully clothed, rather than nude. The word was used often enough in written accounts to emphasize that many soldiers were wrapped only in thin garments rather than wearing the neat woolen uniforms they had been promised upon enlistment.

There was no exaggeration or innuendo, however, when great numbers of the men were described as "shoeless." Washington observed "the deficiency in shoes is so extensive that a great portion of the army is totally incapable of duty." The often-used term, "bloody footprints in the snow," was a plain truth.

The nearest approach to uniformity was the "hunting shirt," a practical, inexpensive, garment that reached almost to the knees. It was made of linen or any other homespun cloth that could be dyed almost any color. Thus it was almost impossible to differentiate between ranks or regiments.

Beneath the hunting shirts, men usually wore an overall article of clothing that covered the lower part of the torso and the legs. This generally was homespun, but some of the men wore leather trousers, which were long lasting but could become extremely uncomfortable in cold weather.

Headgear was essential in the cold certain to grip the Morristown area, even in the mildest of winters. Many men sported the traditional cocked hat turned up on the left side, some wore "round hats," similar to what farmers wore, or woolen caps, but significant numbers had no head covering.

General Anthony Wayne wrote a fellow officer, in a mood both whimsical and bitter:

> *I must confess that they [soldiers] would make a better appearance had they a sufficiency of hats, but as Congress don't seem to think that an essential part of the uniform, they mean to keep us uniformly bare-headed — as well as bare-footed — and if they find we can bare it tolerably well in the two extremes, perhaps they may try it in the center.*

The chief exception to the otherwise motley army was General Henry Knox's artillery brigade, the best-disciplined and most meticulously commanded component in the army. Knox, who had earned a reputation for fastidiousness, constantly badgered his men to keep themselves and their artillery weapons as fine looking as possible.

Strong horses pulled the artillery's big and small cannons Knox had beguiled Congress into providing. The brass fittings on the horses harness and on the weapons were polished; the cannons were scrubbed to perfection. Surely Morristown's inhabitants liked the artillery and its general, especially when they marched out of town headed not for Jockey Hollow but westward on the road to Mendham. They camped in a region now called Burnham Park.

Originally, plans had called for the artillery to occupy the barracks and other substantial buildings they had erected the previous year in Pluckemin — if the structures could be "sufficiently covered" or reinforced by the main army in case of a major attack. But Pluckemin was too distant to permit easy rallying of the cannoneers if the British struck from New York City or orders came to speed to the defense of West Point. The artillery buildings became an army hospital for that winter.

There was no attempt in Morristown to replicate the impressive structures at the Pluckemin Artillery Academy; time and deep snow precluded such careful construction. The artillerymen built their cabins, as did every other segment of the army. Knox lived nearby in a small farmhouse, which was, as usual, soon brightened by Lucy.

Most of the rest of the army would be "hutted" in Jockey Hollow, a tree-covered, hilly area about three miles south of the town center. The derivation of the name is not known, but one tale holds that part of the woodland once had been the bargaining and selling center where area horse traders gathered to inspect, trade or sell their steeds. The term "jockey" also meant a bargaining tactic. The area was dotted with several distinct hills, each about 600 feet above sea level.

As the brutal winter closed in on Morristown, arriving soldiers felled trees, trimmed and cut them into logs for their huts, which they built to very precise standards issued by Washington.

The men built in Jockey Hollow what would be called Log House City, a name bestowed by a visiting Connecticut schoolmaster. He fancied the huts to be "tabernacles like Israel of old." The analogy was far-fetched.

The "city" contained more than 1,000 buildings erected in about two months. Its exact planning and conformation to standards set at Valley Forge and duplicated at Middlebrok were superior to nearly any town from which a soldier might have come. Few of the family dwellings they had built or helped to build back home were fashioned to such rigid standards as those in Jockey Hollow.

The encampment became New Jersey's largest municipality, both in number of buildings and in approximate population. Its approximately 10,000 army residents ranked Log House City sixth nationally in population behind Philadelphia (40,000), New York (25,000), Boston (16,000), Charleston (12,000) and Newport (11,000). (All are pre-1776 figures rounded to the nearest thousand.) The populations of all the cities fluctuated during the war as troops and residents moved in or out. At one point after 1776, it might even have been said that Log House City was the nation's fourth largest city, when populations plummeted in New York, Boston and Newport.

Log House City was not a city, of course. It had no taverns, stores, craft shops, smithies, churches, barns, stables, orchards, gardens, marketplaces, centers of entertainment or any other urban amenities.

A Soldier's Best Friends

Infantrymen on both sides depended heavily on one of a soldier's best friends, *Brown Bess,* the nickname for a type of short-barreled musket that had been in use for nearly seventy-five years when the American Revolution began.

The "brown" apparently came from the color of the wooden stock, while "Bess" is said to be a corruption of the "buss," or box, in blunderbuss. The musket became the weapon of choice because it could be loaded and fired quickly; soldiers were drilled to deliver a sustained fire of one bullet every fifteen seconds. In the few seconds between shots, powder was placed in the barrel, a round bullet and wadding were injected, all were tamped down, and a new charge went into the flint box. The musket could be fired again.

The caliber of most muskets was .75 — three quarters of an inch in diameter. The lead ball weighed about an ounce, enough to put a significant hole in an enemy at 100 yards or less. The ball could be effective up to 300 yards, but a hit would be random. A musket could not be accurately aimed at that distance.

Each musket had a fourteen-inch bayonet for close fighting if the volleys of musket balls were inadequate and the enemy closed in. The musket with bayonet attached weighed about fourteen pounds. (Modern army rifles weight about eight pounds,)

Riflemen had a distinct edge in accuracy over muskets, but were not as effective in close combat. The rifle had a slow reloading time and was not supplemented by a fixed bayonet. Riflemen were specialists, not necessarily infantrymen.

Officers did not carry muskets or rifles. Their weapons were pistols carried in their pockets or saddles. The weapon was detonated by the usual flintlock mechanism.

Cavalrymen fought with heavy sabers and most officers and sergeants carried traditional swords, lighter and easier to use than sabers. Officers also carried spontoons in battle. The spontoon was a long spear with an axe-like attachment near the pointed end of the spear.

Three types of artillery were used: the gun (cannon), the howitzer and the mortar. Guns could be either iron or bronze. Iron guns could be used more effectively in stationary roles, such as sieges or from fortifications. Bronze guns were best for campaigning because they were lighter and easier to tow from place to place. Howitzers had shorter barrels and were fired at a higher angle of elevation to throw projectiles over such obstacles as ramparts or small hills. Short, stumpy mortars, with a fixed elevation of forty-five degrees, pitched explosive shells set to drop shrapnel directly on enemy troops.

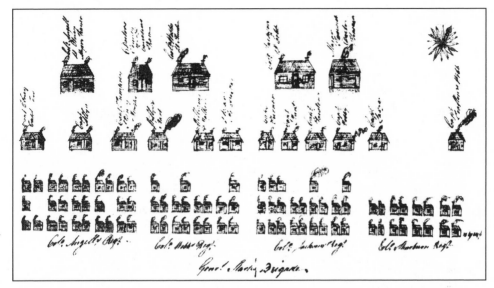

This drawing of the hutting arrangement of Stark's Brigade at Jockey Hollow in 1779-80 shows the placements of the regiment's four brigades, their colonels, and the the other officers of the brigade. The regimental colonels named at the bottom of the huts were Angell, Webb, Jackson and Sherburne.

Each hut had to be fourteen feet wide, sixteen feet long, and six and a half feet high at the eaves. If clay could be found, it was packed between the logs; more usually the caulking was a mixture of mud and clay. The roof shakes were installed without nails; small logs kept them in place. Huts had to be erected in a straight line and set apart from one another at exact intervals.

Washington directed Quartermaster General Greene to furnish only one plan to every regiment. It set forth the intended exact dimensions of each building, "in the construction of which it is expected that minute attention will be paid to the plan." Soldiers and their officers paid heed. Felling hardwood trees, trimming them, and cutting them to length, then placing the heavy logs exactly in position was not an activity to be repeated needlessly. Few, if any, huts had to be pulled down and rebuilt.

Much of the encampment area was on the property of a prosperous farmer named Henry Wick, who owned about 1,400 acres in the area. He and his family lived in a fine wooden Cape Cod-type house, surrounded by outbuildings, orchards, gardens, and grazing areas. The Wick house still stands as evidence that some colonial settlers erected substantial, permanent dwellings despite their lack of training, their self-drawn plans and the crude tools that were available.

The New York Brigade and Hand's Brigade were the first permanent units to arrive in the incipient Log House City, perhaps reaching Morristown a day before Washington arrived at the Ford Mansion. The First Maryland, hurrying in from West Point, also reported being in Jockey Hollow on November 30.

Connecticut's two brigades received notice the next day that they would leave their temporary camp in Parsippany to head for Morristown. They were assigned sites on the property of William Kemble, along the road that led into Jockey Hollow from Mt. Kemble Road.

General William Woodford's Virginia Division reached Jockey Hollow in the first week of December and immediately began felling and trimming trees for their huts. They were on borrowed time. Washington had written Congress on November 29 that he planned to "put the whole of the Virginia troops in motion" to South Carolina, although he complained they really "could not be spared." Congress approved the movement on December 4. Word did not reach Jockey Hollow until two days later.

The Virginians promptly stopped work and departed on December 7, leaving their logs neatly piled on the site they had been assigned. Washington issued a special order warning troops that the materials for the proposed Virginia huts must not be touched by any other soldiers, on pain of severe punishment. There was always the possibility that the Virginians would return, although they never did.

Dr. James Thacher, arrived on December 14 with his Massachusetts outfit, part of Stark's brigade, which included soldiers from Connecticut and Rhode Island. Thacher likened Jockey Hollow to "a wilderness," where "the snow on the ground is about two feet deep, and the weather extremely cold; the soldiers are destitute of both tents and blankets, and some of them are actually barefooted and almost naked."

Adding to the suffering, Thacher wrote, "the whole army has been for seven or eight days destitute of the staff of life (bread); our only food is miserable beef, without bread, salt or vegetables." The young doctor could not have foreseen a condition that would develop almost immediately: the food they deemed sparse on December 14 would, by Christmas Day, seem to have been ample.

Joseph Plumb Martin's Connecticut Brigade reached Morristown in mid-December. His description of the march and his subsequent settling in for the winter is the only known detailed common soldier's remembrance of the winter of 1779-80.

Martin's outfit crossed the Hudson River in mid-December, marched southward, headed for what he called "Basking Ridge," likely the campground on the Kemble land at the southern end of Jockey Hollow. Follow him on his journey:

The snow had fallen nearly a foot deep. Now I request the reader to consider what must have been our situation at this time, naked, fatigued and starved, forced to march many a weary mile in winter, through cold and snow, to seek a situation in some (to us, unknown) wood, to build us habitations to starve and suffer in.

The men would of course build their huts, and until the job was done they would sleep on the snow. Their "mattress" (a Martin term) if they could find it, was straw as insulation from the snow and as a preserver of body heat. The fortunate among them had a blanket, the luckier were able to erect tents on the frozen ground, the truly blessed had both a tent and a blanket.

The Connecticut Brigade began, "like the wild animals," to build their huts. They decided not to wait for tools to be issued, but "found" crosscut saws, handsaws, augers and other tools on their own. In Martin's view, "it is no business of the readers by what means they procured their tools." If anyone made "a shrewd Yankee guess" about the method, Martin urged readers to remember the soldiers were in distress, and that "a man in that condition will not be overly scrupulous how he obtains relief."

Rules for by-the-book handling of tools had been established at Valley Forge. Tools were to be "justly allotted" to Regimental overseers, who kept "an exact account of the men's names into whose hands they are placed." They were also supposed to be returned with the same exactitude. How Martin and his cohorts obtained their tools will never be known; the art of "scrounging" or "midnight requisitions" is an army custom as old, as enduring, and as mysterious, as warfare itself.

Martin naturally penned an on-the-scene report describing the building of a hut, including the finding of toads after the workers cleared away more than a foot of snow, leveled the ground and dug into the loamy soil. The private liked his find; at least he "knew where toads take up their winter quarters,"

"The last thing," wrote the indefatigable private, "was to hew stuff and build up cabins or berths to sleep in, and then the buildings were ready for the reception of *gentleman soldiers* (italics by Martin)." There, in the richness of Martin's imagination, he and eleven other Connecticut men lived out the horrible winter of 1779-80 in fanciful splendor. The hut interiors were everything to each dozen men who occupied them — sleeping quarters, laundry room, recreation hall, mess hall, group discussion center, game room, a place to live, and, for some, a place to die.

A reproduction of the interior of a soldier's hut is displayed at the Jockey Hollow visitor center, complete with bunks and a fireplace. The odors and claustrophobic nature of an actual room can only be imagined. A quick glance makes one wonder if Major General Johann Kalb's use of the word "shanties" to describe the buildings might have been closer to the truth than even the accepted term, "huts."

All enlisted men eventually moved into their completed huts, in groups of twelve,

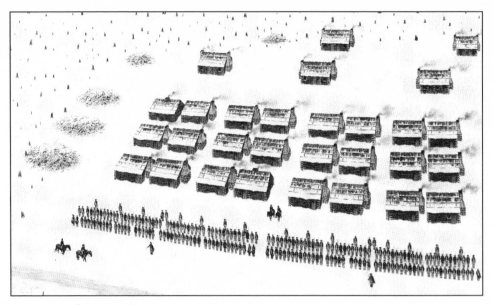

This view of neatly built huts is from a large mural in the Jockey Hollow Visitor Center.

before the worst of the winter. They then turned to the doubtful pleasure of clearing a large parade ground near each group of huts for the purposes of daily duties.

Officers up to the rank of colonel lived adjacent to their brigades in one- or two-room huts (built by their enlisted men, of course), with considerably more room. Officers followed strict orders that their winter quarters would not be built until all enlisted men were housed. Most of the officers suffered the same kinds of physical discomfort as their men, and in the late completion of quarters, they fared far worse. A soldier wrote in his diary on February 11 that "a number of officers are still in tents." In some cases, officers moved into huts built for non-commissioned officers or shared another officer's quarters until their own huts were ready.

General officers received housing in area homes in the order of their reporting for duty in Morristown. Thus, by arriving first with his First Maryland brigade, Brigadier General William Smallwood was assigned rooms in the fine mansion owned by avowed Loyalist Peter Kemble on the road to Vealtown (Bernardsville).

Physically closest to the Jockey Hollow encampment was Major General Arthur St. Clair, who occupied rooms in the small, albeit comfortable farmhouse of Henry Wick. The house was nearly in the center of the encampment.

Many residents of the area resisted the placement of all generals and a few colonels in private or public facilities. Washington was "extremely concerned" about this attitude; if officers were treated with scorn, enlisted men could expect worse if they ventured into town. Many officers chose the period of being without a hut to ask for furloughs to permit them to return home. That created major problems, too. Washington wrote on January 22:

> *There are, in some of the Regiments, too many officers absent on furlough, so that they* [the troops] *are left without a sufficient number* [of officers] *to preserve order and perform the common routine of service.*

Most officers also endured dreary lives in their huts, although there were places and occasions where an officer might find warmth and recreation. Some officers also used their huts for impromptu parties. Although their cabins were larger, more comfortable and shared by, at most, four men, officers had to suffer the smoke, the poor light, the smells, the empty stomachs, and the dread of the brutal winter that closed in on the camp — and on nearly all of the eastern seaboard.

Contours at Jockey Hollow

The long lines of soldiers passing spectators on their way into Morristown during early December 1779 probably all looked alike in their ragged, non-matching clothing. But each man in the line of march was accounted for. Each company, each regiment, each brigade was assigned an area.

The drawing below shows the final destinations. Each brigade had its own "mountain" in Jockey Hollow, assigned as a regiment's soldiers reached the campground. A favored place was near the Kemble mansion that overlooked the main road to Morristown. Connecticut's First and Second Brigades held the presumed place of convenience. The radiating lines are rough indications of contour lines, drawn to designate on which slopes a brigade was stationed.

This map, used to instruct area teachers at Jockey Hollow orientation sessions, was compiled by National Park Service employees. Three documents were used: A rough survey of Morristown completed in December 1779; a map by Washington's mapmaker, Robert Erskine; and a map of the Jockey Hollow area drawn by Captain Etienne de Roche-fontaine.

Each company at full strength (which very few were) comprised seventy-six pri-

vates, a captain, two lieutenants, one ensign, four sergeants, four corporals and two fifers or drummers. Eight companies made up a regiment, and four regiments formed a brigade. There were eight brigades in Jockey Hollow for the 1779-80 winter camp. Each brigade was commanded by a brigadier general, each regiment by a colonel or lieutenant colonel, and each company by a captain. Two or more brigades comprised a division, headed by a Major General.

The map below, showing accurate contour lines, was drawn in the late twentieth century for an ecological study of the campground. Four of the hills have names: Mt. Kemble, Tea Hill, Fort Hill and Sugar Loaf Mountain. Note that the hills rise gradually from the surrounding terrain, which averages about 380 feet above sea level. Sugar Loaf Mountain is the tallest, about 720 feet above sea level, followed by Mt. Kemble, about 680 feet high, whose rise is more precipitous that any of the others.

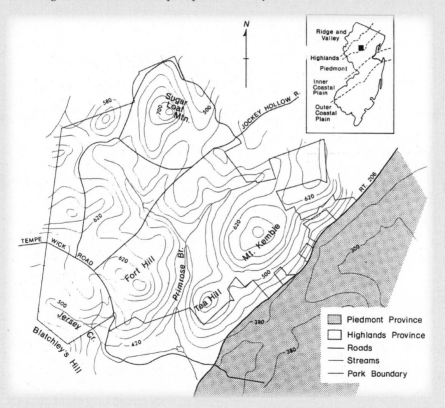

This contour map, drawn for a National Park Service study, shows several prominent hills in Jockey Hollow, each between 650 and 700 feet above sea level and easily defended postions. Sugar Loaf Mountain, the tallest, rises nearly 750 feet. The entire area was mostly covered with trees.

Chapter Seven

WINTER *of the* WOOLLY BEARS

Without daily newspaper weather reports, much less television and radio weathermen predicting snow and falling temperatures, early Americans relied on such long-range prognosticators as the "woolly bear" caterpillar, the thickness of a goose's breastbone, or the direction of a church weathervane at noon on St. Thomas' Day, December 21. If the woolly bear had wide brown rings in its thick hair, the goose's breast bone was thick and white, and the weathervane showed the wind from the north, it was time to batten down.

All of the above and every other augury known to man came into conjunction in late 1779 when it snowed during the first week in November, when the Hudson River began to freeze in the coves by November 15, and winds blew steadily out of the north by December 1. There was no need even to look at the weathervane on St. Thomas' Day; the worst winter of the Revolutionary War was by then in full swing.

Soldiers at Jockey Hollow understandably might have considered themselves the only victims of the weather, but the civilians who surrounded their camp knew the same frostbite and frozen toes, as did the British army and the non-military residents of New York City. A mere river, and a solidly frozen one at that, was no barrier against the snows and winds that affected nearly all of the East Coast. Actually, New York City residents might have suffered more than New Jerseyans: their forests had been felled decades before and there was almost no firewood in the city. Logs had to be imported from Long Island.

David Ludlum, the respected weather historian, summarized the widespread effects of that winter in his book, *The Weather Factor:*

An accurate depiction of the huts on a Jockey Hollow hillside, drawn by John W. Barber.

During one winter only in recorded American meteorological history have all the statewide inlets, harbors and sounds of the Atlantic coastal plain, from North Carolina northeastward, frozen over and remained closed to navigation for a period of a full month and more. This occurred during what has been called "The Hard Winter of 1780."

The only major American exodus to the relative warmth of the south that winter were North Carolina and Virginia regiments detached from Washington's army in November and December to aid in the defense of the Carolinas. In New York, General Henry Clinton, commander of the British army, was dispatched to spend the winter where British troops seemed likely to enjoy major success — at Charleston, South Carolina.

True to his capacity for delay and his indecision about the French fleet that might

When Day Became Night

The sun rose on May 19, 1780, as the almanacs had predicted, but by noon the day had become as dark as night. Joseph Plumb Martin reported on the impact at Morristown:

> "*It has been said that the darkness was not as great in New Jersey as in New England. How great it was there I do not know, but I know it was very dark where I then was in New Jersey; so dark that the fowls went to their nests, the cocks crew and the whippoorwills sang their usual serenade.*"

George Washington recorded "heavy and uncommon kind of clouds – dark & at the same time a bright and reddish kind of light intermixed with them."

In Connecticut, when "none could see to read or write," the state legislature adjourned its morning session. In Providence, Rhode Island, an observer said some saw it "as the dark day predicted by our savior" that would bring "the desolation of the world."

Fears evaporated when the sun came out. A few days later a Massachusetts observer attributed the phenomenon to "smoak and vapor" carried by the wind from forest fires in the western part of New England. Modern meteorologists likely would spell it smoke and term it an atmospheric inversion.

---

attack New York — or his flotilla in open Atlantic Ocean waters — Clinton nearly lost the chance to depart before the ice thickened and completely closed the Hudson River. Finally, on December 26, Clinton sailed south; he would be no threat to New Jersey that winter.

Behind the departing general, the Hudson River froze ever more thickly. On January 30, Johann Dohla, a Hessian soldier stationed in New York, made this journal entry: "The North [Hudson] and East rivers were frozen solid. The ice was checked and found to be 18 feet thick. All ships were frozen in." Three weeks passed before Dohla wrote on February 22 that "Today the North River began to break."

The thickening ice crept southward and westward, until the Arthur Kill became "a bridge of ice" connecting Staten Island and Essex County in New Jersey. Farther west, the Hackensack, Passaic, and Raritan Rivers were frozen almost to their bottoms. The Delaware River was so solidly frozen that horse-drawn sleighs could travel on the ice from Trenton to Philadelphia. Ice in Jockey Hollow's brooks and springs had to be chipped away each day to provide drinking and cooking water.

Quartermaster General Greene added a dimension to what he called "the most ter-

Drawn to depict the misery at Valley Forge, this image of Washington surrounded by winter perils far better depicts Morristown, where the winter of 1779-80 is now known to have been much worse than the corresponding months at Valley Forge two years earlier.

rible winter that ever I knew." All living things, he wrote, were affected: "Almost all the wild beasts of the fields and the birds of the air have perished with the cold."

The frozen rivers offered rare opportunities for Americans and British alike to undertake extraordinary military movements. Washington worried constantly that the British and Hessian forces left in New York would storm across the ice-formed Hudson River "thoroughfare," hoping to reach Morristown quickly. English fears in the city were a mirror image, with Americans as the invaders.

Increasingly heavy snowstorms during December created a far greater immediate problem, bringing operations in Morristown and Jockey Hollow almost to a standstill. The "very severe storm of hail & snow all day" that welcomed Washington to Morristown on December 1 lasted through a second day. A two-day storm on December 5 and 6 piled up knee-deep snow and on December 14 the snow reportedly was about two feet deep. More snow fell on December 15, 16, and 18.

By then, most of the men in Jockey Hollow had been sleeping in the snow beneath scant cover for a week or two while they finished building their huts. Very few soldiers, whether privates or generals, would have slept well had they known what was coming.

In the last week of December and the first week of January, three storms swept through the Middle Atlantic states with a fury that earned them a place in weather annals. Ludlum declared that the merging of the three storms "rank with the greatest such combinations in our meteorological history."

Johann Dohla, the storm-preoccupied Hessian, wrote a colorful description of the frightening storm that enveloped the area surrounding New York on December 28 and 29:

> An astonishing wind arose, accompanied by rain, which was almost like an earthquake and lasted twenty-four hours. It severely damaged ships in the Hudson Bay [upper New York Bay] and New York Harbor. Many ships, which had put out two or three anchors, broke loose and were wrecked. Many old houses in the city collapsed, and the best and sturdiest buildings suffered noticeable damage. The inhabitants of New York remembered no such storms, and it was believed that the world and the city were sinking and that it would be the day of final judgment.

Even that fright paled beside remembrances of the blizzard that struck Jockey Hollow on January 2 and 3, 1780, the worst storm of the century. Dr. Thacher composed his own dramatic, emotional description:

> On the 3d instant [January 3], we experienced one of the most tremendous snowstorms ever remembered; no man could endure it many minutes without danger of his life. Several marquees [tents] were torn asunder and blown down over the officers' heads in the night. And some of the soldiers were actually covered while in their tents, and buried like sheep under the snow.

Dr. Thacher saw a silver lining, however dubious: "We are greatly favored by having a

The "Lost" Brigade

The four regiments of the New Jersey Brigade commanded by General William Maxwell were well enough known to George Washington, although when they finally reached Jockey Hollow for the winter of 1779-80 they were assigned a camp site about three miles awau from the other brigades by the existing roads.

Their remoteness was acknowledged in an order from Washington on February 23, 1780, excusing the brigade's soldiers from duty at the army's parade ground. Communications were maintained and the camp grounds were positioned in maps drawn for the command.

The New Jerseyans built their huts on a hillside overlooking "Eyre's Forge" on Hard Scrabble Road. Construction was according to the same standards used at Jockey Hollow.

After the war, the huts deteriorated and disappeared and by the early 1960s the campground's existence persisted only in local traditions and on a map drawn by Washington's map maker, Robert Erskine. Even as dedicated a National Park Service historian as Melvin Weig had to guess at the New Jersey Brigade's exact location. The brigade was, in essence, lost in history.

Clayton Smith of Madison discussed the camp's location in a talk he gave in 1961. That induced Fred and Isabell Bartenstein to begin a serious quest. Using Erskine's maps, modern aerial maps, contour drawings, road commission records, diaries and other sources, they found the brigade's exact location. The Bartenstein research was published in a definitive pamphlet in 1967.

Shortly after publication of the Bartenstein document, comprehensive archaeological digs followed the clues, and fully confirmed the location of and the extent of the once-lost brigade's campground.

---

supply of straw for bedding; over this we spread all our blankets, and with our clothes on and large fires at our feet, while four or five are crowded together, preserve ourselves from freezing."

The surgeon reported, "The snow is now four to six feet deep; which so obstructs our roads as to prevent our receiving a supply of provisions." Thacher's estimate probably included drifts, but it made little difference; three days later, the third howling two-day storm in eleven days struck.

Washington himself reported that third storm. On January 6, he noted: "The snow which in general is eighteen inches deep [probably meaning just the new snow] is much drifted — roads almost impassable." The next day, he wrote, was "very boisterous…sometimes snowing, which being very dry drifted exceedingly." A New Yorker on the same day declared, "We had such a terrible storm last night that we thought the house would be blown down."

The war took a back seat while civilians, soldiers, and militiamen worked to clear passages through New Jersey's main roads, chiefly to seek food for the army. While it is a matter of record that the men were to open the roads, it is not known exactly how they accomplished this. It is believed that the men walked up and down the roads, packing them down sufficiently so that sleighs or wagons could be driven over the "cleared" passageways.

The ordinary daily routine for the army in Jockey Hollow also went on despite the deepening snows: morning assembly, assigning guard duty, turning out for lashings administered to lawbreakers, and twice during the winter parading before the hanging of a deserter. Presumably, soldiers tamped down the deep snow to create access to the parade grounds and to make executions easier for spectators to reach.

Each day, fifty or sixty soldiers assigned to guard duties and other routine tasks in Morristown had to push their way through drifts as high as their heads. At day's end, they reversed the arduous trek, totally worn out. They shed their icy cold, wet clothing as soon as they were inside their huts, and hung it up to dry, then tried to get some warmth from the hut fireplaces or their straw "mattresses" and thin blankets.

As the enlisted men and Jockey Hollow officers struggled to survive in the snow, Washington with his staff secretly hammered out a daring plan that would take advantage of the extreme winter conditions — an attack on the British garrison stationed on Staten Island. The thick ice on the narrow Arthur Kill, which separates New Jersey and Staten Island, should have made the attack quite easy. The plan would require stealth, speed, proper timing and a heavy element of surprise.

On January 9, the commander asked Brigadier General William Irvine to determine whether the Arthur Kill was sufficiently frozen to support a full-scale assault on British positions on Staten Island. The execution had to be perfect, but Washington told Irvine, "I cannot relinquish the idea of attempting it." He asked Irvine to examine every aspect of an attack, underscoring the urgency by concluding, "We shall hope to see you in the course of tomorrow."

Washington ordered Major General William Alexander of the first New Jersey Regiment to lead the audacious foray. In his order to Alexander, the commander addressed him as "My Lord," acknowledging Alexander's insistence that he was the Earl of Stirling.

Washington set the operation in motion on January 12, ordering Colonel Moses Ha-

Soldiers clustered wherever a fire blazed. Some had only a ragged blanket to protect themselves from the incessant cold.

zen to lead 1,000 men toward the Arthur Kill. That contingent, and all the others who would join later, were told this was a military operation, not an act of vengeance; anyone caught plundering would be "shot on the spot."

Joseph Lewis, a well-connected Morris County quartermaster and a son-in-law of the noted Morristown Presbyterian minister Timothy Johnes, was ordered by General Nathanael Greene to provide men, 300 sleds and teams of horses to move Alexander's group to Staten island. The army had no sleds and most of its horses were in Pennsylvania, where the forage was better. Lewis told farmers who agreed to participate that the expedition would fan out through the country to the west, seeking provisions.

On January 14, the day the operation would begin, 500 farmers drove their horse-drawn sleds into rendezvous points in Morristown and Jockey Hollow — an amazing response. Stirling loaded his 900 troops and as much armament as possible aboard the sleds.

The armament was an assorted lot. Several sleds carried cannons and two howitzers. An eighteen-pounder, capable of wreaking great damage, was said to be on one of the sleds, but unfortunately no ammunitition could be found to feed the giant weapon and Washington was doubtful that General Henry Knox would find any. It is unlikely that the cumbersome weapon actually was given sled room.

Some of the sleds carried 2,000 board feet of planking supplied by Allen and Hathaway's Morristown sawmill. The planking was vital: it would provide the firm footing necessary to move the sleds and artillery as the attackers descended from the banks of the Arthur Kill to the ice that covered the waterway.

Lewis saluted the departure of the expedition, vowing and boasting that it would "remove all Staten Island, bag and baggage, to Morristown." It was said that the quartermaster's gleeful words were in anticipation only of the military supplies and cattle that would be confiscated, signifying that Lewis was not promulgating civilian plundering.

Among the throng leaving Morristown were many non-military men, some along just for the excitement. Others in towns along the way joined the increasingly large and boisterous operation as it surged toward the Arthur Kill. The American soldiers and their non-military followers spent the early hours of January 15 on the banks of the Arthur Kill, then tramped down over the Morristown boards to cross the waterway at daybreak. The 2,700 soldiers were followed by a horde of civilians, whose only possible reasons for joining the expedition were sightseeing or looting.

Futility overlay the high-risk, daylight adventure. The Staten Island defense, composed largely of New Jersey and New York Loyalists, should have been easy to overcome if the exploit were conducted in the ordered silence, but the islanders day of reckoning was not to be that January 15. The defenders were almost as well-informed of the coming assault as if they were on the communications pipeline of the American command. Hugh Gaines, publisher of *The New York Gazette,* wrote on January 13 — two days before the invasion — that "the rebels meditate an attack in Staten Island." If Gaines knew it, all of New York and Staten Island shared the alleged secret.

The invaders spent the night on the island, trying to keep warm in front of roaring fires. In the morning, Alexander called a retreat after assumptions swelled that reinforcements were on the way from New York to bolster the defendants. (Actually, the reinforcements could not be sent for a day or two.)

Joseph Plumb Martin was among the frustrated soldiers. He left his usual eyewitness account:

> We took up our abode for the night on a bare, bleak hill, in full rake of the north-west wind, with no other covering or shelter than the canopy of the heavens and no fuel but some old rotten rails that we dug up through the snow, which was about two or three feet deep. The weather was cold enough to cut a man in half. We lay in this accommodating spot till morning, when we began our retreat from the island. The British were quickly in pursuit; they attacked our rear guard and made several of them prisoners, among who was one of my particular associates. Poor young fellow! I have never seen or heard anything from him since. We arrived at camp after a tedious and cold march of many hours, some with frozen toes, some with frozen fingers and ears, and half-starved in the bargain. Thus ended our Staten Island expedition.

Surgeon James Thacher offered a more precise medical report on the foray: "About 500 were slightly frozen and six were killed by a party of horse, who pursued our rear guard."

The Staten Island adventure was over for Martin and his fellow soldiers, but severe criticism was about to explode over reports that the civilians who crossed the ice with the army plundered the homes of non-combatants.

Washington was furious. He angrily ordered that all stolen goods, estimated to be worth $10,000, be returned to the Reverend James Caldwell, a noted Elizabethtown Presbyterian pastor and an American quartermaster, for return to the owners. The minister took most of the loot back to Staten Island under a flag of truce, but he wrote Washington the day after the ill-fated adventure:

From the vast majority who greedily rushed to plunder, our country has received such disgrace as will not easily, I may say possibly, be wiped off.

Worse, the raid inflamed British anger and insured enemy retaliation. It was swift, brutal, a well-kept secret, and far more effective than the futile American effort on Staten Island.

A precise two-pronged attack was launched on January 25 from Paulus Hook and Staten Island. About 500 British and Hessian soldiers crossed icebound marshlands under cover of darkness and swept into Newark at about 10 p.m. They posted guards on every street corner and surrounded Newark Academy, which had been pre-empted by American troops as a barracks. Simultaneously, detachments of British soldiers and Tories marched across the frozen Arthur Kill to attack Elizabeth. The mission in both cases was the same: plunder and destroy, burn and kill.

The attackers in Newark burned several barns and private homes, then set the torch to the Newark Academy building after killing seven or eight defenders, As the invaders moved southward on Broad Street, the sky across the marshlands in the direction of Elizabethtown glowed red from a British-set fire roaring through the First Presbyterian Church. The Newark raiders beat a hasty retreat to Paulus Hook, herding before them thirty-five soldiers captured at Newark Academy.

On the way out of Newark, the Redcoats paused at the home of Joseph Hedden, Jr., justice of the peace and confiscator of Loyalist estates. Though he was ill, Hedden was ordered out of bed and forced to march at bayonet point to Paulus Hook, clad only in his nightclothes. Along the way, a friend passed him a blanket, and that kept him alive through the intense cold. Later, desperately ill, he was returned to Newark, where he died.

The fighting had all but ceased for the winter, but nature continued to deliver its own telling blows. Five snowstorms struck in March. The last, on March 31, dropped ten inches of snow. Finally, on April 1, the final flakes of the season fell on Morristown. It brought to twenty-eight the number of recorded snowfalls of the winter. Spring was greatly delayed; budding trees and warmer days would not come until a week into May.

Filled with resentment, their stomachs growling in hunger, the New Englanders, like all their fellow soldiers, began felling oak and chestnut trees for their huts, cutting the felled trees into logs the proper length. Thacher eloquently expressed both their despair and their fortitude:

> It is a circumstance greatly to be deprecated, that the army, who are devoting their lives and everything dear to the defense of our country's freedom, should be subjected to such unparalleled privations, while in the midst of a country abounding in every kind of provisions. The time has before occurred when the army was on the point of dissolution for the want of provisions, and it is to be ascribed to their patriotism, and to a sense of honor and duty that they have not long since abandoned the cause of their country.

Weather's cruelty had eased, but greater, man-made problems remained — inflation, food shortages, lack of clothing, desertions, increasing dissatisfaction among the troops, falling enlistments, and perhaps most demoralizing, the court martial in Morristown of Benedict Arnold, second only to George Washington in the hearts and minds of most Americans. Private Martin harkened back to Thomas Paine's "a time to try men's souls." Martin wrote bitterly: "I often found that these times not only tried men's souls, but their bodies, too; I know that they did mine, and not effectually."

But the most ironic footnote to the winter came from Bavarian-born Major General Johann Kalb, a seasoned soldier who had come to America with the Marquis de Lafayette in 1777. As he was preparing to write in his journal, "the ink in my pen froze," despite the fact he sat before a lit fireplace that was supposed to warm the room. Kalb unfroze the ink and wrote:

> Those who have only been to Valley Forge or Middlebrook during the last two winters but have not tasted the cruelties of this one know not what it is to suffer.

Transporting supplies between states, difficult in good weather, was a winter nightmare.

Lord of Basking Ridge

Major General William Alexander, the self-titled Earl of Stirling, despite illnesses affected by cold weather, threw himself fervently into the ill-fated attempt to capture Staten Island in January 1780. It became another inexplicable bungling by a man whose passionate desire to merit his British title clashed with his fervent embracing of the American cause.

Who could hope to understand William Alexander? He boasted that he possessed a royal title and lived like a lord of the manor in Basking Ridge — and yet became a fervent revolutionist.

His father, James Alexander, had fled from Scotland in 1716 after supporting the losing side in a rebellion against the Crown. In New York City he became a noted lawyer, married the widow of a prosperous merchant, and won both fame and rebuke for his stout but unsuccessful defense of John Peter Zenger in a celebrated early test of the freedom of the press. He came to New Jersey and became surveyor-general of the East New Jersey Proprietors, a sure step toward wealth and colonial power. His son William was born in 1726.

Well-educated and solidly set in his mother's mercantile business, William succeeded his father as surveyor general and in 1748 married Sarah Livingston, the sister of William Livingston, who would become the Revolutionary War governor of New Jersey.

Young Alexander wanted more. He fretted because his father had never applied to be the Earl of Stirling, a title that became vacant when an uncle died childless. The first Earl of Stirling had received large grants of land in Nova Scotia, Canada, Maine and Long Island, which originally was called the Isle of Stirling.

Alexander went to Scotland, established his claim to the title but failed to convince the British House of Lords that he was their peer. That bothered him not at all. In his own mind, he was the Earl of Stirling, and determined to live as such. He called himself Lord Stirling; his wife became Lady Stirling, and their daughter was called Lady Kitty.

Back home in Basking Ridge he built a manor fit for an earl. Samuel Smith, New Jersey's first real historian, wrote in 1756 that his "taste and expense promise more than anything of the kind hitherto affected in the province."

The manor house, the stables and coach houses all were topped by cupolas and gilded weather vanes. The Earl's carriages displayed his coat of arms. The house and grounds often rang with the sights and sounds of lavish entertainment.

Surely a man with such pretensions could have been expected to remain loyal to the King. Instead, Stirling threw himself passionately into action as an American general. He served with varying degrees of success and bravery at the battles of Long Island,

Trenton, Princeton, Germantown, Monmouth and elsewhere.

Washington valued Alexander's friendship and abilities and addressed him always in some version of Alexander's pretensions: "My Lord," "Your Lordship" or "Lord Stirling". Washington valued Alexander's loyalty, yet wondered why field operations entrusted to Alexander so often went astray, as they did on Staten Island,

Troops occasionally laughed at "His Lordship's" vanity. They repeated the story of a soldier condemned to be hanged. He prayed aloud, "Lord have mercy on me." Stirling, who was standing nearby, allegedly replied, "I won't, you rascal! I won't have mercy on you!"

The vain general lost his wealth through a series of tangled financial deals as the war progressed. When he died in Albany, New York, in 1783, he retained only his hollow title and his abandoned estate at Basking Ridge.

Chapter Eight

The SHADOW *of* DOOMSDAY

T he numbing winds and the paralyzing snows sweeping over Jockey Hollow and Morristown in the three-day January blizzard were only the most evident of the evils that beset the Continental army. Spring, even if delayed, would calm the north winds, melt the deep snow, and send warmth coursing through the bodies of scantily clad soldiers. But that January there was ample reason to believe that the army might not even exist in May.

America stood in the very shadow of a doomsday that threatened to dissolve the American army and to erase even proud memories of Trenton, Princeton, Valley Forge, Saratoga, and Monmouth.

This was the fifth winter of the war, with no great American success in sight or any evidence that victory was near. Except for the scintillating successes at Trenton and Princeton, Washington had not won a major victory. Savannah had fallen and the rest of the South was being swept up by British troops. Widespread dissatisfaction with the progress of the war swept across the nation. Inflation and profiteering were rampant. Desertion was on the rise and re-enlistment was decreasing.

As the year 1779 merged into the year 1780, the United States of America was virtually bankrupt, even if Congress failed to admit it. The American dollar was so nearly worthless that it took more than ninety Continental dollars to equal a dollar in gold or silver. The military's supply system, poor enough when Congress controlled it, fell into worse disarray when Congress handed the job over to the states.

The concept of state supply verged on fantasy. The states were not united, despite the declaration of unity: Massachusetts was as different from South Carolina as Pennsylvania was unlike Georgia. The geographical terrain varied markedly from state to state, as did the climate and the seasons, and the time element of delivery in an era of crude transportation was not conducive to quick supply.

Teams of horses were scarce throughout the colonies and a persistent amount of forage to feed them was impossible during the winter. Wagons were in short supply and wagon drivers were in demand. Quartermaster General Greene said driving a supply wagon was "disagreeable in itself," an overly mild assessment.

The driver was always at the mercy of weather, cold and snow in winter, excessive heat and rain in summer. He had to drive thirteen to fourteen hours each day, seven days a week, and each night slept on a wooden floor in a barn or in grass on the edge of a farmer's field. He was always at the mercy of thieves, including both soldiers and civilians. By 1779, the pay was $15 a month plus a promised bounty of a suit of clothing.

The fall of the Continental dollar was meteoric. As 1779 began, a dollar in specie was worth $6.94 in Continental currency, a reasonable discrepancy. By the end of the year, one gold or silver dollar equalled forty-two Continental paper dollars. Within a year, in December 1780, one dollar in hard money would be worth about ninety-nine Continental dollars. By then, a Connecticut congressman would say that the nation's currency was fit for little more than making "the tail of a kite."

The nation in fact had no official currency; after printing $201 million in paper dollars, Congress stopped the presses in the waning weeks of 1779. A flood of counterfeit bills into Philadelphia followed. It was easy to spot counterfeit currency: the bills were of a much better printing quality than the American bills.

Few, if any, of the soldiers cared about the details of the money problems. They were hungry. It was possible to escape the cold, if only for a little while; but body-weakening, gut-numbing hunger could hang on for days and weeks without relief — and most of the time during December and January there was little or nothing in the larder. Joseph Plumb Martin wrote in January 1780:

> We were absolutely, literally starved. I solemnly declare that [during one period] I did not put a single morsel of food into my mouth for four days and as many nights, except a little black birch bark which I gnawed off a stick of wood. I saw several men roast their old shoes and eat them. And I was afterwards informed by one of the officer's waiters that some of the officers killed and ate a little dog that belonged to one of them.

No mess wagons followed Martin's Connecticut Brigade, or any other brigade. No giant mess tent was erected when the regiment stopped. Eating, for the Continental army, was constantly a catch-as-catch-can arrangement, even in the best of times. Many plans for feeding the army were proposed but there seldom was, in reality, enough provisions to feed the troops on a regular basis.

The quest for what Martin called "belly timber" did not begin in Morristown. It had been his major preoccupation from the time he entered service in 1776. Along the way he ate anything he could acquire and acquired it by any means possible. He seldom joined campfire arguments about whether what the company had just eaten was "horse beef," "mule beef," or no kind of beef at all. He simply ate whatever was available and appreciated even the most meager fare.

Washington was as aware of the food shortage as his soldiers, although the richness of his daily table could not possibly have made him know the horrible ache of starvation in the huts. But in writing to Joseph Reed, president of Congress, on December 16, the commander foresaw a monumental calamity on the horizon:

> The situation of the army, with respect to supplies, is beyond description, alarming. It has been five or six weeks past on half allowance, and we have not three day's bread on hand or anywhere within reach. When this is exhausted, we must rely on the precarious gleanings of the neighboring country... We have not experienced a like extremity at any period of the war.

Two days before Christmas in 1779, Colonel Clement Biddle was instructed to grind all Indian corn in storage, then give the flour to the solders in camp. Indian corn normally was considered fit only for horses. Some steeds likely starved in the diverting of the corn; it was for a good cause, at least in the eyes of the soldiers.

The situation gradually worsened. Washington noted on Christmas Eve that the soldiers were on half food allowances "and that only of rice." Far more tellingly, the general pointed out to Congress, "as you observe there is by no means a real scarcity of grain." He knew, and Congress knew, that by the winter of 1780 nearly all farmers saw their crops as prosperity for themselves and devil take the soldiers. And not for the first time, he expressed a thought that provisions might have to be seized if civilians made no effort to help.

Nathanael Greene expanded on the theme of starvation in the midst of plenty: "A country overflowing with plenty is now suffering an army, employed for the defence of everything that is dear and valuable, to perish for want of food."

The three-day blizzard that began to roar across the area on January 2 brought the matter to a head. Impassable roads created an emergency food situation beyond compare. Greene ordered area magistrates to call out men and teams of horses to aid soldiers in opening a road to Hackettstown, where some food had arrived.

After the blizzard, ragged and destitute soldiers began plodding through the drifting snow, trudging painfully as far away as Mendham to the west and Chatham to the east,

The Fighting Quaker

Nathanael Greene, often cited as a strategist and an inspiring leader in battles, was raised as a member of the Society of Friends (Quakers), who are opposed to war. On September 30, 1773, Greene was "put from under the care of the [Quaker] meeting" for watching a military parade.

Greene recognized the possibiity of a war with England and in October 1774, helped organize a Rhode Island militia company known as the Kentish Guards. Because of a chronic stiff knee that limited his movements, he was accepted only as a private. Seven months later, when Rhode Island raised three militia units in May 1775, he was put in command as a brigadier general.

On June 22, shortly before his thirty-fourth birthday, he took his state troops to Long Island to join the emerging army and was made a brigadier general in the Continental Army, the youngest of the army's first brigaidier generals.

After distinguishing himself in the battles outside Philadelphia before the Valley Forge winter, Greene served with distinction in the Battle of Monmouth. He

became quartermaster general of the army in February 1778, and brought considerable order to the almost impossible job of securing supplies. Washington appointed him commander of West Point and the Hudson Highlands when Benedict Arnold's treason was exposed in late September 1780. On October 14, 1780, Washington put the general in charge of the southern army. Greene managed to rescue the failing campaign in the months before the Battle of Yorktown — although he did not fight there.

Greene left Charleston in August 1783 and made a triumphant return to Rhode Island. He was in serious financial trouble, having invested most of his money in a bankrupt venure. He had no assets in Rhode Island and returned south to occupy a confisticated estate given him by the State of Georgia. He died there of sunstroke at age forty-four.

seeking food and clothing. Nearly every neighbor gave them bits of food or a bit of clothing, but these were pittances in the face of the overwhelming need.

The pace of understandable begging, by any name, stepped up, then spilled over into bold-faced stealing. By mid-January, many soldiers had taken matters into their own hands, "going out of camp and committing every species of robbery." Washington felt helpless; while he deplored the wanton thievery, he fully understood and sympathized with the reasons why hungry soldiers stole whatever food they could find:

> *The men have at last been brought to such an extremity that no authority or influence of the officers, no patience or virtue of the men themselves could any longer dictate their obeying the orders.*

However, Washington wrote in General Orders that any man found outside the camp at night could be whipped on the spot. Yet, in the midst of what verged on anarchy, the commander temporarily laid aside the floggings and other punishments promised for law-breakers: "I have not in my power to punish or repress the practice [of thievery]." It was a major bending of the accepted morality of the day.

There was food aplenty beyond the camp and neighborly farmers were willing to sell it to Army buyers — provided they could show hard specie or pay wildly inflated prices if Continental currency were the medium of exchange. The sight of fat cattle, grain-filled barns, well-fed pigs and sheep, and plump geese waddling across farm yards made it inevitable that starving soldiers would ignore the harsh army orders against stealing.

Most farmers sold readily when civilian speculators from Philadelphia and other parts of Pennsylvania rushed into the state to buy at any price. The buyers would then hold the provisions, awaiting still higher prices. Provisions often changed hands four or five times before a final sale, with each exchange boosting the price further beyond the army's woefully slim budget.

A quart of meal in January sold for $8 and wheat cost $69 a bushel. An ear of corn sold for 50 cents. A quart of rum commanded $40 to $50. Rye was $29 a bushel, corn $39, and oats, $20. Speculators readily paid such prices — in gold or silver.

A blatantly open practice, called "the London Trade," intensified the increasingly bitter quest for food. "The Traders" were a well-organized, anonymous group that roamed the countryside with bags of gold and silver coins jingling at their sides. A farmer would ask no questions; the ultimate purchaser might well be British but even allegedly patriotic farmers preferred not to know.

The Traders boldly herded their cattle or loaded their grain wagons within the American lines — a practice entirely within the law. No legal or military action could be taken unless the produce crossed the line into enemy territory. By then it would be too late to

Continental currency was first issued by Congress in June 1775. Bills were printed in varying quantities and denominations, from one dollar to as much as sixty-five dollars. By 1780 more than 200 million dollars in paper money had been printed. All were easy to counterfeit, which hastened the depreciation, as did the printing of more bills.

stop the practice. The State of New Jersey required a pass to travel outside one's county but the illegal trade persisted. The army simply did not have enough manpower to end the flagrant trading.

Sandy Hook, occupied by the British through most of the war, was a particularly lively place for the London Traders. It was reported from Monmouth County that "there are always considerable quantities of cattle brought from West Jersey, and lodged near the shore to be handy to send off to New York as a good opportunity serves." Inevitably a perfect night for surreptitious sailing would come; the cattle would be herded aboard boats hastily and shipped to a British-controlled area.

On January 5, Washington wrote to Congress, reiterating the extreme hardships in Morristown; but he did not fill Congressmen in on two harsh measures he was about to take in an attempt to ease provision shortages. First, he ordered brigade commanders to discharge all men whose enlistments expired on January 31. That would mean fewer mouths to feed. Secondly, he decided that food must be impressed from farmers.

Despairing of Congressional quotas of food and supplies that states were requested to supply for the army but did not deliver, Washington placed the matter of supply squarely in the hands of New Jersey's citizens in January 18. In an "address" to magistrates in the several counties surrounding Morristown, he advised them that specific quotas of food must be supplied, as well as wagons and manpower to transport the supplies to army storehouses.

The choices for the populace left no room for negotiation: they could have their goods seized by the army with no chance of recompense, or they could deal immediately with the army, with an assurance of pay — no matter how inflated the American dollar. Waiting for food to be delivered as ordered by Congress would end, temporarily replaced by a program of impressment that firmly fixed the role of civilians in supplying the army.

Washington's address to the magistrates began with a patriotic plea to appreciate and understand the plight of starving soldiers, who bore "their sufferings with a patience that merits the approbation and ought to excite the sympathy of their Countrymen." True enough, he admitted, there had been thievery but soldiers "had been so stricken that they had been impelled to the kind of marauding that in good times would have been punished with exemplary severity."

But, Washington wrote, stealing had become "an unfortunate necessity" created by miseries beyond human capacity to bear. A "worse evil" could be averted only by an unusual effort within New Jersey. Failure would bring "fatal consequences that must unavoidably ensue."

Washington continued the gentle, fatherly tone for another paragraph. He implied that civilians were not really to blame: if it had not been for the unusually difficult winter and the blocking of highways by snow, there might not have been any emergency.

Then he turned harsh: the time had come for each county to assume responsibility for army supplies. It was impressment, no matter how sugarcoated, and each county's responsibility was carefully spelled out in exact bushels and pounds. Bergen County, for example, was to provide 800 bushels of grain and 200 head of cattle. Quotas were to be delivered to a specific site within four days after each county magistrate had received his notice. The counties were to provide, in total, a combined 12,150 bushels of grain and 2,200 head of cattle.

There would be payment by the army, of course, not equal to what profiteers or London Traders might offer, but exactly what the army decreed. Each seller would receive a certificate that could be redeemed at the market price of that time, or at the market price at the time of redemption.

Officers who delivered Washington's "address" were ordered to report back promptly. At that point the transaction acquired its steel backbone. If any magistrate refused or even hesitated, the quotas were to be taken forcibly by army detachments, a blunt warning that this was not a voluntary, charitable contribution.

Whether compliance was voluntary or forced, Washington insisted to his soldiers that the quotas be acquired "with as much tenderness as possible to the inhabitants." No milk cows were to be taken and no family was to be completely stripped, leaving it without food.

Weights of grain and counts of cattle were judged jointly by county magistrates and army representatives. Some adjustments had to be made, particularly in rounding up sufficient numbers of cattle. Counties, on request and explanation, could contribute specific amounts of grain for each cattle allotment if there was a proven shortage. For example, when Hunterdon County reported that it could meet its quota of 150 cattle only by including oxen needed for fieldwork or hauling, Washington permitted the county to substitute grain for each ox held back.

Washington particularly stressed that the episode must be conducted with full regard for citizen rights. His officers and men assigned to the quota enforcement were ordered to comply fully with his instructions:

> *I am persuaded that you will not forget, that, as we are compelled by necessity to take the property of citizens for the support of the army on whom their safety depends, we should be careful to manifest that we have a reverence for their rights, and wish not to do anything which that necessity, and even their own good, do not absolutely require.*

Congress knew nothing about the food impressments in New Jersey until January 27, when Washington reported the unauthorized venture had been such a success "that the Army in a great measure has been kept together." Congress responded by adopting a resolution expressing gratitude for the patriotism of New Jersey's citizens.

Strangely, restoration of reasonable amounts of food to Jockey Hollow seemed to accelerate the plundering of area neighborhoods by soldiers. Morris County magistrates wrote Washington on January 25 that they had understood the prior need of starving soldiers to get food by any method, but how could continued plundering and insulting behavior be explained or tolerated after the quotas of food placed on counties?

The general responded swiftly. He wrote on January 27 that he appreciated the aid of the people and vowed to protect their property and their persons. If offenders were identified, they "shall be subjected to the most condign punishment."

The next day an order over Washington's signature was posted. He condemned stealing and "insulting" behavior as "intolerable and a disgrace to the Army." Also, any soldier found outside of camp after retreat would receive "One Hundred Lashes on the Spot." Any soldier committing a robbery, in camp or in a civilian area, would "receive from One to Five Hundred Lashes at the Discretion of the Officer." If, viewed in terms of today's standards of punishment, that seems excessive or even an abrogation of civil rights, it was effective and customary for the time. The day after the order was posted, one Private Jack Miller of a New York regiment received 100 lashes for the thievery of some mutton. No thief could plead hunger as a defense.

Dr. Thacher, the peripatetic Massachusetts physician/diarist, wrote a long, brutal account of the Jockey Hollow punishments and something of an apology for them. Every man beaten had been convicted by a court martial, he said. Whipping, wrote the doctor, was "humane" because it enabled the bloodied thief to return to duty rather than being condemned to death, a possible alternative. As for the severity of 100 lashes, Dr. Thacher pointed out that the British army code of punishments allowed 1,000 lashes.

The whippings diminished the thievery but they did nothing to solve the constant specter of hunger and the incessant cold of a vicious winter. Many farmers returned to their old habits, the London Trade continued to flourish, and shortages of food in Jockey Hollow eased only for short occasions during the winter.

Still, after the successful impressment in January, life for a short time was back to the normalcy of the enlisted men's huts, where a full belly, a hardwood fire roaring in the fireplace, someone twanging on a Jew's harp, a less-than enlightened argument about women, and once in a while, a rare gill of rum made life tolerable, if not wholly comfortable or warmly satisfying.

It was all customary and familiar. Problems abounded for the army, particularly the ever-mounting inflation. But few, if any, soldiers were concerned about the plummeting value of the Continental dollar. Most of them had no dollars: they had not been paid in months, or even years.

A Washington Life Guard, depicted in bronze. The Ford Mansion is seen beyond the flag.

Washington's Life Guard

Aware that he was an obvious target for enemy kidnappers or assassins, Washington formed a special unit in 1776 to guard his person as well as his papers and baggage. The unit has been known as Washington's Life Guard but it also bore such names as "His Excellencies Guards", "the Commander in Chief's Guards" or just "the Guards". The Guard's motto was "Conquer or Die," leaving no doubt as to their mission.

Washington's personal Life Guard marched under this white silk banner, showing one of the guards accepting a flag from "the Genius of Liberty."

Initially there were only fifty men in the guard. Each had to be a native-born American; five-feet, nine inches to five-feet, ten inches tall. These were elite troops, better dressed and better drilled for the task of protecting the chief. For all their vaunted prestige and responsibility, members of the guard were paid the same meager wages as all other officers and soldiers. They were not all well educated; several are known to have signed their payrolls with an "X".

Occasionally as many as 300 men were posted to the guard, although about 150 is a more likely average. A rotating picket guard was sent from Jockey Hollow each day to augment the Life Guard.

When the guard arrived in Morristown in 1779, three days after Washington began living in the Ford Mansion, members built their own huts on property about 200 feet south of the mansion. Later, they cut and trimmed logs and built the walls and roof of a new kitchen for the Ford Mansion. They may also have built the log office attached to the west side of the mansion.

Many other guard tasks were menial. At least six of them worked for Washington as servants. One was a steward and another worked as a cook. Three men worked as hostlers (stable hands). As many as fourteen could be assigned to pick up supplies and many served as messengers. Major Caleb Gibbs, commander of the Guards, was responsible for keeping the headquarters expense accounts and overseeing the general's household. The Guard's prime duty, however was to protect Washington. In times of a possible British incursion, guards were placed on roads surrounding Morristown. In February 1780, Ensign Jeremiah Greenman of the Second Rhode Island Regiment, a picket guard temporarily attached to the Life Guard, wrote:

> This day we went on his Excellencies Piquit (Picket) Guard, were continued till the 22nd. Hear [sic] we posted a small guard in the room & a serjt & 6 men at the head of the stairs.

In March 1780, British intelligence estimated the strength as between 350 and 400 men. A month before, on February 11, an attempt to kidnap the general was aborted.

On December 1, 1932, Morristown Mayor Clyde Potts dedicated a plaque memorializing Washington's Life Guard. Schoolchildren attended the ceremony on the site where the guard camped across from the Ford Mansion.

Chapter Nine

LIFE *in* CAMP: *The* SOLDIERS

Awaken at dawn to the boom of the morning gun. Stand in knee-high snow for roll call. Hear the day's assignments. Eat a meager breakfast, cooked by a hut mate. Police the campground, clean out old latrines or dig new ones, serve officers, run errands to Morristown and back, a six-mile round trip. Eat dinner (the supposed big meal), a midday time to relax and eat whatever is available. Supper, not much. Beating of tattoo, 8 p.m. bedtime.

Easily reconstructed from orders of the day, that was the bare bones life of the common soldier at Jockey Hollow in the winter of 1780 — every dreary day, seven unfulfilling days a week, month after boring month. An unexpected skirmish or orders for a general preparation for battle came as welcome relief and a stirring change from parade ground tedium.

Private Martin believed "fighting the enemy is the greatest scarecrow to people unacquainted with the duties of the army." He argued, "I tell a simple truth that I felt more anxiety, undertook more fatigue and hardships" away from the battlefields "than I ever did in fighting the hottest battle I ever engaged in."

A very high percentage of enlisted men were illiterate or only slightly schooled, but education and ability are not synonyms; these men were skilled with tools, knew how to hunt and fish, could plow straight furrows, deftly cut wheat with scythes, load a musket quickly, and fire with deadly accuracy.

Those who could read and write might stand a slim chance of becoming a sergeant when the army became continental rather than local. Far more likely, they would be in the ranks as long as the war lasted, until they were discharged or until they decided to desert. The enlisted men at Jockey Hollow were the nearly forgotten, unranked soldiers who bore the brunt of combat duties — the very symbol of an under-equipped army that responded well when called to action.

Though in succeeding wars, the "ordinary" soldier became as familiar to the non-combatant public as the boy next door, the lives of Revolutionary soldiers are little known. Except for the celebrated and much-quoted Martin book, there was almost no comprehensive writing by any other enlisted man during the war. It is not surprising for a time when most people had little formal education. In an agricultural economy there was little need to read or write more than fundamental ledger entries.

Not even Sundays gave surcease from the menial lives the soldiers led. All of the daily chores had to be accomplished and guard duty had to be performed. One day ran into another without end, with constant harping on cleanliness — of the musket as well as the self.

Despite the reiteration to the troops and their officers that a soldier's weapon was a fighting man's best friend, and despite threats of punishment, many, if not most, soldiers failed to give their weapons basic care. There are numerous mentions in regular orders of ill-treated, rusted muskets.

In February 1780, a report told of men carrying dirty or rusted muskets to the Grand Parade ground for guard mounting and other formal occasions. Any soldier caught with an improperly cleaned weapon was given thirty lashes immediately. His sergeant was reduced in rank and ordered to wear a piece of cloth on his jacket as a mark of failure and shame.

Enlisted men were supposed to be at least as clean as their muskets and well shaven, with no facilities for bathing, much less any kind of shower or sink. Each brigade was supplied with fat for making soap. Clothing was expected to be neat and clean, a feat not easily achieved because the rags worn on parade were the same rags worn to dig latrines, or to sleep in for a bit of warmth.

Army regulations about cleanliness and a neat appearance were in large measure based on the fiction that, from September 1777, every soldier would be supplied annually with a new suit of clothes, including a warm regimental coat. If there were a soldier at Jockey Hollow who had ever been so supplied, he would have been as conspicuous as a prince among paupers.

Despite the reality of public neglect of the army, an order from Washington insisted that "those who appear in Contrary Order [not up to accepted standards] will not [only] merit but actually receive immediate punishment." A starving, freezing, unshaven, unclean, improperly uniformed private could not hope to escape with a mere warning.

When the National Park Service acquired the Henry Wick house in 1933, its siding was white clapboard. Later, shingles were cut by the Civilian Conservation Corps to encase the building. Below, the interior was essentially as it had been during the Revolution.

This contemporary drawing by artist Bil Canfield depicts the misery, suffering and despair that overwhelmed soldiers at Jockey Hollow.

Each day was lived by rote, punctuated by seemingly incessant drum rolls. Snare drums played the role that bugles or recorded sound play today. Reveille was the most agonizing of calls. It came in the pre-dawn darkness, shrilly calling men out of the sleep they so desperately needed. The natural inclination was to wish the drummer dead.

Each drum call had a different beat, a rat-a-tat code that summoned men to duty or released them from a commitment, such as completed guard duty. In emergencies or even for simple orders, a designated drummer beat a call for other drummers to prepare for bigger and more general drumming.

The "reveille roll" awakened the camp, a "retreat roll" brought the regiment together at sunset for roll call and assignment of guard duties. "Tattoo" drumming ended each day, warning soldiers that they must be in their huts by 8 p.m. — where they must stay until reveille. As the winter of 1780 moved along, requiring that men be in their huts after tattoo increased the difficulty for any deserter hoping to slip away from camp in the darkness.

Between the early morning and early evening drum rolls, there were such drum beatings as the "troop roll," alerting all men to pay attention to an upcoming drum message (quite like the navy's later distinctive call, "Now Hear This"). Law breakers received the "Rogue's March" on their way to punishment and prostitutes were drummed out of camp

Food Fit for a King

Despite the differences that might have divided them, all soldiers were united in the never-ending quest of securing and preparing food. The drumbeat that announced delivery of rations struck a resonance in even the most tone-deaf ears. Officially, men were supposed to receive regular weekly rations, as per the guidelines issued in Boston early in the war:

1. One pound of bread

2. Half a pound of beef and half a pound of pork, and if pork cannot be had, a pound and one quarter of beef, and one day in seven they shall have one pound and one quarter of salt fish, instead of beef.

3. One pint of milk, or if milk cannot be had, one gill of rice.

4. One pint of spruce or malt beer.

5. One gill of peas or beans, or other sauce equivalent.

6. Six ounces of good butter per week.

7. One pound of good common soap per man per week.

8. Half a pint of vinegar a week, if it can be had.

If Private Martin (or any common soldier) had seen that list, he would have considered it a cruel joke or a fantasy. Martin never saw that much food nor did he ever see the promised variety.

Drawing rations was usually a distressing experience. An allotted half-pound of salted meat was as often as not spoiled. Each hut was assigned a large iron kettle for cooking stews, in the unlikely event meat and vegetables were available at the same time. Preparing the food over flames in the hut fireplace, or out-of-doors, required skills that are little known today.

Cooking meat on an improvised skewer was possible, and both available time and ravenous appetites made it certain that any such meat was cut into smaller pieces and cooked individually and quickly on the end of a stick or long iron pin. Some soldiers used the ramrods of their guns as skewers.

Bread or its equivalent was the staple of every food plan. There were army bakeries in Morristown, although the exact locations are not known. In camp, men could fashion fire cakes from the flour they were issued. A recipe of a sort existed: "One pound of turkey wheat (corn), grounded or pounded into rough flour. Add water to create thick dough. Spread on a board (or flat rock) to about a half-inch thick. Place close to fire, turn frequently to cook both sides." The baked fire cake had to be taken off the board as soon as it became brown all over, and handled very carefully lest it fall apart. Quick eating was recommended; within a day such a morsel became so hard that breaking off a piece was like trying to break off a piece of oak board.

by the "Whore's March." Muffled drums accompanied a dead soldier to his grave.

There was no drumbeat to announce recreational time; there were too few spare minutes in a day to waste them in play. Even if there had been time, there were no organized sports (such as baseball or soccer) for the masses.

Sport competition was as simple and direct as a challenge for a foot race from one end of the camp to the other or bare-knuckle boxing matches. The latter were most often the kind of spontaneous "fights" common wherever young, vigorous men gather. These would attract a crowd that lent support to either of the candidates. Such "bouts" were usually quickly ended by an officer, a sergeant, or a bloody nose.

Sometimes a spontaneous parade ground fight would bring a challenge for an unsanctioned, after-duty meeting that would be promoted by word of mouth. Occasionally a bout for bragging rights might be sanctioned by brigade officers. The bare-knuckle combatants would meet in an open "ring" formed by supporters for each man. Rules were adopted, chiefly one that forbade the combatants to "strike each other in the face." A bout could last only a few minutes or could go on for hours as the bloodied contestants battered each other. The rivals sat down four or five times during a five-hour bout to rest and savor a cup of water. A fighter's victory was considered a triumph for his brigade as well as for himself.

Impromptu fighting was common, as might have been expected where thousands of overworked, underfed, and bored soldiers were crowded together in crude huts. One memorable hut fight in January 1780 led to a murder, and to one of the strangest legal decisions ever made at Morristown.

The fight began when an innocent bystander named Richard Savage broke up a fight between a William Loudon and an unknown soldier. After roll call, Loudon berated, then punched, Savage for stopping the first fight. As they scuffled, Loudon picked up a knife from a shelf and stabbed Savage twice. A witness said Savage cried out, "You have murdered me! I am a gone man!" Savage was right; within minutes he was dead.

Without explanation, Washington turned Loudon over to civil authorities for trial. He was found guilty of murder. A local jurist intervened to ask Governor William Livingston to declare Loudon guilty of manslaughter rather than murder. The governor complied. Loudon was permitted to ask for "benefit of clergy," an old custom that allowed a first time offender to avoid a death sentence. Loudon was branded on the hand and returned to the military and apparently escaped further punishment.

During the winter of 1779-80, Washington ordered the building of a two-room building between the New York and Pennsylvania lines for courts martial and use as an orderly room. Major trials were also held in Morristown taverns. Officer huts were pressed into service when the numbers of cases ran high.

With the daily tedium and sense of deprivation, it was no wonder that some, if not many, men turned to drinking, gambling, and "immoral" women (if such could be found near camp). All such behavior was illegal and considered by those on high to be the most common and the most pernicious of evils — for enlisted men. What happened in officers' huts was not subject to such judgment.

Alcoholic beverages were not entirely banned for enlisted men; when rum was available in sufficient quantity, it was doled out to the soldiers as part of their rations. It could also be used as a reward for stellar achievements or for special celebrations. Excessive, unsanctioned use of alcohol was the target of warnings against alcohol use.

Despite stern warnings and prohibitions, drinking continued in the ranks, although the men's known lack of money makes it difficult to imag-

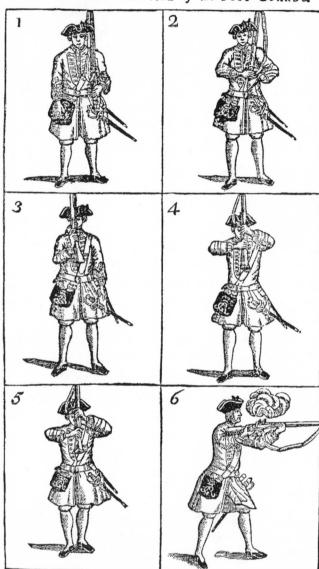

The MANUAL EXERCISE of the FOOT GUARDS.

1 Take Caro.   2 Join your Right-Hand to your Firelock.   3 Poife your Firelock.
4 Join your Left-Hand to your Firelock.   5 Cock your Firelock.   6 Prefent. Fire.

Important to army discipline and for soldier readiness, handling arms had to be practiced no matter how deep the snow. This "Manual of Exercises" was British, but American soldiers were drilled in much the same way.

ine how they could afford the high-priced, illicit alcohol. No matter how the liquor was obtained, drunkenness was a serious concern. As one consequence, men were sometimes found drunk while on guard duty, or worse, were found to have left their posts because of excessive alcoholic intake.

A most unusual situation linked to drunkenness centered on one Edmund Burk of the Third New York Regiment, who in the winter of 1780 attacked a fifer and an ensign while besotted. A subsequent court martial found him guilty and ordered that he be executed, the most severe penalty ever given for behavior emanating from drinking. Surprisingly, in light of his frequent preaching about the evils of drinking, Washington issued Burk a reprieve on February 20, 1780, using the occasion to provide an example of how the "pernicious Crime of Drunkenness will frequently betray soldiers."

While gambling had been banned by general orders for several years, playing cards is known to have been common in the huts. It is difficult to believe that the men played only the innocent game of loo or wagered only acorns in friendly games. The limiting factor in gambling for money had to be the scant pay the men received, if they received any at all.

There is no written evidence of prostitution in Jockey Hollow, but prostitutes likely were near the camp. Their existence would have been admitted only if one of them was arrested and drummed out of camp. A prostitute's greatest official sin, from a practical standpoint, might have been getting caught.

In a setting devoid of mass amusement, there was little question that whippings, hangings, and other punishments attracted spectators. Witnesses were assigned from each regiment to witness the punishment, presumably in the belief that seeing a fellow soldier brutalized in public provided a lasting lesson about the evil of sinning. Civilian spectators attended the executions, perhaps to be dissuaded from sinning, more likely to revel in the hangings. An execution might draw thousands of spectators to view the drama and the excitement. Dr. Thacher wrote of a girl who "walked seven miles, in a torrent of rain, to see a man hanged, and returned in tears, because the criminal was reprieved."

On June 19, 1780, Thacher wrote of three British spies who were executed in Jockey Hollow. They had been caught hiding in a barn, dressed in civilian clothes. Their leader refused to surrender and was shot. The others were given a court martial and were found guilty. On hanging day, when the two spies faced their executioner, "their mournful cries and lamentations were beyond description." The crowd undoubtedly enjoyed the live theater.

Drummers beat the way to punishment areas. Those found guilty of crimes other than the most serious, such as desertion, were led to what soldiers called 'The Adjutant's Daughter," the place where a convicted man stood while a drummer or fifer lashed him — thirty times, fifty times, or 100 times.

Whippings, however cruel by twenty-first-century standards, were not the worst of punishments. Nothing exceeded the brutality of the "wooden horse" with a sharply ridged top rail. When a man was placed on the fiendish contraption, supported by the end of his spine, he quickly fainted. That punishment was soon abandoned; a man so emotionally and physically degraded was almost certain to be useless for any kind of work.

Desertion was among the most serious of army crimes and the most severely punished. At least eight of Washington's most trusted men, his Life Guard, deserted during the course of the war. The public humiliations and fierce punishments of deserters were considered the underpinning of camp discipline.

It must be questioned whether that severe approach worked: more than 1,000 Jockey Hollow men deserted during the winter of 1779-80, about one in ten if the numbers for the original encampment in December are reliable. The percentages by the beginning of spring increased because of the numbers of troops who also went home legitimately when their enlistments expired.

Some deserters crossed the Hudson River and joined the British army, where they would be paid in real money rather than in nearly worthless Continental dollars. They would be better fed and certainly far better clothed. Desertion to a Loyalist regiment in New York must have been a powerful incentive. From a British standpoint, each American deserter who came over was a coup.

Hanging was the worst punishment, and seldom used. Only murders, multiple crimes, or continued desertions commanded the death sentence. Intriguingly, the first Continental hanged in 1777 was a member of Washington's elite Life Guard. He had been found guilty of engaging in a plot against the commander in chief.

Only two soldiers were sent to the gallows in Morristown during the 1779-80 encampment. Several others were sentenced to hang but Washington remanded their sentences, nearly always at the last minute.

On February 18, James Hammel and Samuel Crawford, both members of the Fifth Pennsylvania Regiment, were given death sentences for robbery. The hangings were scheduled for the next day.

Crowds of soldiers and civilians gathered for the executions; each regiment sent 200 men to witness the executions and the Corps of Artillery band was on hand for the musical portion of the ceremonies. As Hammel and Crawford were about to mount the scaffold, a messenger brought word that Hammel's sentence had been delayed. (Washington later remitted Hammel's death sentence, with the expressed hope that such leniency would "Operate in ye minds of Offenders, to the Improvement of their Morals.")

Crawford was beyond the improvement of his morals. He mounted the steps, alone and quaking to the point that he could scarcely move without assistance. Within minutes he died, dangling from the noose.

The months of February and May in 1780 were times for multiple death sentences, mass reprieves, and the emergence of a peculiar kind of folk hero named James Coleman, a repeated deserter and forger and an all-around bad man..

A mass execution of eleven convicted deserters, including Coleman, was set for 11 a.m. on May 25. Eight were to be hanged, the other three would face a firing squad. The convicted men, from the New York, Pennsylvania, and New Jersey Brigades, rode to the execution site in carts. As they entered the parade ground, they passed eleven freshly dug graves where all of them believed they were to lie forever.

Just as ropes were about to be placed on eight necks, a messenger arrived with reprieves for seven of those awaiting the noose and for all three who were to be shot by fellow soldiers. The eleventh man, the designated example of proof that crime did not pay, was James Coleman, a multiple deserter himself and a leader in helping many others to flee the camp.

Coleman coolly addressed the crowd, admitting all and demanding that the hangman get on with his job. As the rope was being draped on his neck, Coleman objected to the noose and complained about the thin rope — it would break, he insisted, if it were used for the hanging. He was ignored.

True to Coleman's prediction, the rope broke as he was suspended. He leaped up from the ground, exclaiming "I told you so.' He remounted the scaffold, helped pick out a properly strong rope, placed it around his neck, and died without protest. It was prime time live theater, but the hangings at Jockey Hollow ended with Coleman's performance.

The crimes, the courts martial, and the punishments continued, day after day. If the punishments and the justifications often verged more on the pleasures of the Marquis de Sade than the rule of mercy, there was no arguing against them — even when the victims were often described as naked, shoeless, and starving. It is difficult to imagine a victim of the beatings being grateful enough to renew his "service to the public."

There was mounting dissatisfaction and distress in the camp as the numbers of men present for duty thinned. Replacement of the young retirees — and the deserters — became an arduous and perplexing situation that aggravated those who had to stay in the huts because of long enlistments to which they were committed.

Soldiers who reenlisted might return to camp flashing cash or boasting of large bonuses they had received for reenlisting. It was no secret. Washington addressed the subject in a letter to New Jersey Governor William Livingston on February 19:

> Those soldiers, who are truly engaged for the war, are dissatisfied at seeing others, returning home, and having it in their power to obtain new bounties and new encouragements for their services, while [those who] held to their original engagements, are deprived of those privileges.

The wonder was not that men slipped out of their dark, quiet huts some time in the night, listening for sounds of a sentry, then vanishing into the deep Jockey Hollow woods, racing toward desertion. The wonder was that anyone bothered to stay.

Imagination must replace written, on-the-scene knowledge about life in the huts when a day's service was done. After the sounding of tattoo, the men were in effect walled in from the world, far from home and wives or sweethearts, with no kind of economic independence, no regular postal service, and not even desks on which to write home, much less quills and ink to use in writing.

Fires roared in the fireplaces; wood was about the only commodity in ample supply. Nearly as much smoke filtered through the huts as went up the chimneys, creating a murky, unhealthy smell of smoked humans. Like soldiers in every war, these revolutionists cherished "sack time," the precious few minutes when they could lie in their bunks, enjoying, or agonizing over, their memories.

They played cards to relieve the tedium, drank the occasional ration of liquor they were given, and devoured whatever scraps of food came their way. There would be talk of bygone days. About one-fifth of the soldiers were married; and a letter from a wife or sweetheart was most often a plaintive plea for help, detailing the sufferings at home because of a lack of money, or at worst, no money at all. Such a letter would cast a pall inside the hut; there was nothing any soldier could say in answer that would be either helpful or comforting.

Mutiny or desertion slipped into discussion on those worst of days, on those days when officers displayed unreasonable temperaments; when a hut mate might be mercilessly flogged; on days when food was not delivered or when warm clothing promised by officers never appeared. Surely there was contemplation of mutiny, in the heat of bunk talk, in the abstract or even in the first stages of planning.

The army rolls dropped as May ended. But how — or why — could any of them stay in the hills of Morris County, willing to face another year of discouragement, futility, despair, and lack of accomplishment?

Perhaps they stayed because of inertia, the continuance of camaraderie and friendship in the huts, a precious bond among men, something that any former serviceman understands. Perhaps they had no better place to go, particularly if they were single. Few had been the big fish in their village ponds before the war. The army offered food, clothing, pay, and land when the war ended. Soldiers quickly learned the promised food, clothing and pay were pies-in-the-sky. The prospect of land was an incentive to remain.

Historians' studies point to "unit cohesion" as a reason for not deserting. New recruits might leave because the army was not what they expected or because they could desert and collect another bonus for enlisting in another army company. Men who stayed had bonds with fellow soldiers. They had come this far, through Bunker Hill, Trenton, Princeton, Brandywine, Valley Forge and Monmouth, and wanted to see how it would all come out.

Certainly many stayed because they believed in the cause, believed in the emerging nation, and sensed that no great social experiment in all history to that point matched the American Revolution. They liked the idea of being Americans.

J. P. Martin let posterity know why he stayed: "We were unwilling to desert the cause of our country when in distress; we knew her cause involved our own…"

A Soldier's Home

Soon after the National Park Service acquired Jockey Hollow in 1933, it built this replica of a soldier's hut (top, opposite page). The replication was not difficult, since clear directions, written by Washington and dating back to Valley Forge, have survived. This replica was destroyed, but six newer huts have since been built in a line atop one of the Jockey Hollow hills.

Plans and specifications for "hutting" date to Valley Forge, where the structures were built in such desperate haste that some allowances had to be made in exact specifications if buildings or locations were slightly out of line with orders. Huts had to be completed swiftly, lest the absence of clothing cause the army to perish for want of protection from the elements. However, no deviation from the basic plan of the sixteen-by-fourteen huts was allowed at Middlebrook in the winter of 1779-89, or at Morristown a year later.

Each regiment had precise written instructions on where and how to locate and build each hut, based on Washington's plan. His model was "the form of the Penna. (Pennsylvania) Huts and the mode of placing them at Rariton (Raritan) last winter." That meant Middlebrook, but the plans had actually begun evolving at Valley Forge, the

The inside of a hut (above) in an exhibit in the Jockey Hollow Visitor Center. A replica of a hut at Jockey Hollow (facing page) built by the National Park Service was torn down many years ago.

first year the soldiers were in log huts.

The general left no doubt in Morristown concerning his insistence that the buildings follow the established plans: "The Commander in Chief takes the opportunity of assuring that any hut not conformable to the plan, or the least out of line, shall be pulled down and built again agreeable to the model and its proper place." Ignoring of the edict meant increased work and hardship.

Slight variances might be allowed. The door could be at either end of a building, as could the inside fireplaces. A hut might have one window, two, or none at all, depending on the whim of each builder. Windows generally were not cut into the logs until spring, the better to keep heat inside during the winter. Finally, a huge stone fireplace, for heat, cooking and light, was built into an end wall.

Living inside the huts meant the sharing of nearly every facet of a soldier's wintertime existence, from cooking food over a hot fire in the fireplace to writing letters home before the fire or reading whatever might be available. The crude, crowded style of living in a hut is demonstrated in the interior of a hut (opposite page) that is a major exhibit in the reception center near the Wick House.

The demonstration room suggests a time when the men might have just left the hut. Laundry hangs from hooks beside bunks, a musket leans again one bunk and several articles of clothing can be seen. On the far right, a large tree stump, smooth on top, served as a checkers board or, tellingly enough, the site of a card game that has just ended. Playing cards are on the game "board" surface. Washington banned gaming of all kinds. It might be presumed that soldiers followed the order, meaning that there was no money on the game board when the soldiers laid down their hands.

Chapter Ten

LIFE *in* CAMP: *The* OFFICERS

Lieutenant Erkuries Beatty stumbled into his Jockey Hollow tent on the afternoon of Christmas Day 1779, determined to write a long-overdue reply to the three letters his brother Reading had written him within the last month. Beatty's only family news was that their brother John "is now gone to Princeton to eat his Christmas dinner." As for himself, he was deep into his own rum-tinged holiday celebration:

> *I am just down from dinner about half drunk; all dined together upon a good roast and broiled, but in a cold hut; however grog enough will keep out cold for which there is no desiring. Tomorrow we all dine with the Colonel. Which will be another excellent dinner and I think you may call that fair living…*

It doesn't take a literary sleuth to figure out that Beatty was an officer, as were all three of his privileged brothers. The rum that sparked the revelry cost about $50 a quart — roughly eight times the monthly income of a private. Enlisted men had no holiday on Christmas Day, would not have had "a good roast," much less enough grog to ward off the cold.

It is often argued that officers also suffered that winter, perhaps "worse than enlisted men," because officers had to buy their own uniforms, food and whatever luxuries they wanted. That might be true except that the clothing, including shoes, and the adequate food promised each enlisted man, were virtually missing from Jockey Hollow that winter.

Certainly there were many officers who felt very deeply about the welfare of their men. Officers, by regulation, received extra money to buy extra food in lieu of rations,

This sketch of a mournful George Washington was intended to portray a bitter day in the 1777-78 winter at Valley Forge. It far more accurately depicts Morristown in the brutal winter of 1779-80, as the corresponding months at Valley Forge were quite agreeable.

General Arthur St. Clair (pronounced Sinclair) was born in Scotland in 1737 and came to America to fight in the French and Indian War. He joined the American Army in 1775. He spent the winter of 1779-80 in the Wick house in Jockey Hollow.

and Brigadier General William Irvine wrote that "many officers have lived on bread and water rather than take any of the scanty allowance from the men."

If good times occured with any regularity for enlisted men at Morristown, they have escaped the attention of the many researchers and writers who have discussed the American Revolution. Common soldiers were not welcomed or expected in town, nor did they have much reason to frequent the streets except traveling to and from work assignments in town. Even if they saw coveted goods in the fine shops near the green, soldiers had no money in their pockets.

Officers frequented taverns, for meals or drinking and for the conviviality of townspeople and officers from other regiments. Here they learned the names and addresses of young women who might accept invitations to social affairs — and human nature being what it is, possibly some young women who might not be too particular about decorum. All was not serene on the tavern front; in January 1780 several officers faced charges of attacking another officer and throwing him out of a Morristown tavern.

Erkuries Beatty, who was "half drunk" on Christmas Day, seemed to be as non-stop a party man as can be imagined. One of his letters briefly discusses "a half whore dance I was at two nights ago when we kicked off a Hell of a dust." Unfortunately for modern readers, Beatty ended the letter abruptly by writing a brusque "But stop" immediately after the word dust, not explaining what, or whom, a "half whore dance" involved. In another letter, Beatty emphasized his persistent love of dancing:

Afterwards I was at two or three dances in Morristown (and) I have been at a couple of dances at my Brother John's quarters at Battle Hill [Bottle Hill, now Madison] where I spent the evenings very agreeable, and when I can frolick nowhere else, I do it at home with some of my friends. I am determined to drive all care away."

The files of officer life in Morristown during the winter are filled with tales of high jinks, dances and parties, all with bevies of reportedly lovely young women from northern New Jersey. The women came from long distances for special affairs, as far away as Raritan (near Somerville) and Mount Hope (about twelve miles north of Morristown).

None of this is to demean the officer class, but rather to emphasize that such a privileged group was accepted by Congress, the public, and the rank and file of the army. It was generally agreed, that officers were of a higher caste and that enlisted men must be kept subordinate for their own good.

National Park Service historian Eric Olsen, who has studied the 1779-80 Morristown encampment for many years — more closely than anyone else — has pondered the accounts of the suffering in the huts and the tales of officer parties. "Somehow," he has written, "these two pictures don't seem to go together. " He adds: "There was another side to the story of the winter camp."

Although Quartermaster General Nathanael Greene worked unceasingly to acquire the necessities of life for the enlisted men, he accepted and promoted the high level social life. His young, vivacious wife, Kitty, was in town for the winter, as were the spouses of most officers who could afford it. In February 1780 Greene wrote to his friend, Colonel Samuel Webb: "I hope you will come and partake of our diversions." A month later Greene wrote "We are very merry at camp!"

Washington attended many dinners and other social gatherings in Morristown, including small parties that he hosted in the exquisite Ford Mansion. But his letters — ranging from his intense sorrow at the suffering in Jockey Hollow to his dealings with the French government — prove that little escaped his attention, or was done without his approval, during his long working hours.

Each day was arduous for the commander in chief and his aides. Each of his letters required careful preparation and careful wording. Official correspondence permitted little latitude and no off-hand trivializing or insults, even in answers to letters that deserved such. A man with his burdens could have been excused for his social life.

Additionally, and not surprisingly, since they fashioned the regulations governing such things, officers expected privileges above and beyond common practice. The privileges depended on rank, starting with the commander in chief and working downward, with lessening perquisites to lieutenants and finally, ensigns. Thus, as was his due, Washington was expected to live far beyond the means of his subordinates.

Washington's spirit of *noblesse oblige* was in startling contrast to the bleakness and deprivation of Jockey Hollow. He always ate and drank well, even lavishly. He entertained in high style. He was well supplied with everything, including whatever quantities of food or fine wines that he desired. He could buy stylish and well-tailored uniforms. He put nearly everything on his expense account, in accordance with an agreement he reached with Congress. He would not be paid a salary but would be reimbursed for recorded expenses.

In December, Washington ordered Quartermaster General Greene to start work on one of two major additions to the Ford Mansion. The first one, a greatly enlarged kitchen, led to one of the very rare piques that Washington allowed himself. Because the chief had told Greene to finish hutting the men before considering the new kitchen, little had been done on the headquarters addition.

When Washington's personal Life Guard finished their huts (eleven enlisted men's and three officers') directly across the street from headquarters, the general asked them to start on the new kitchen. The guardsmen raised log walls and affixed a roof, but construction stalled because flooring boards were not available.

On January 22 — at a time when most of the officers huts in Jockey Hollow had not been finished — Washington dispatched a tart letter to Greene, including an often-quoted statement:

> *I have been in my prest. Quarters since the 1st day of Dec. And have not a kitchen to cook a dinner in, although the logs have been put together some considerable time by my own Guard…Eighteen people belonging to my family and all of Mrs. Ford's are crowded together in her Kitchen and scarce one of them able to speak for the colds they have caught… [Washington was referring to his servants and those of Mrs. Ford, not his professional aides.]*

Greene responded quickly and with obvious ill feeling, pointing out that in December that floorboards were scarce and that he had been busy. (Part of Greene's being busy was because he was adding a kitchen to his own quarters in The Arnold Tavern.) But Greene soon found about 2,000 square feet of white pine for the floor in the new kitchen. The amount of floorboards suggests that the new kitchen would have been about forty-by-fifty feet, allowing ample dining space for servants.

The second addition to the mansion was a large temporary room affixed to the northwest side of the mansion to provide space for receiving military personnel and visitors and to provide working space for the general's busy staff. It was not a luxury; the stream of aides

The army storehouse, on the site where Epstein's department store was later built, became the hall where three officer-sponsored Assemblies (formal balls) were held in the winter of 1780.

and visitors through the building was constant.

Mrs. Washington was on her way north from Virginia in late December. She had not arrived by Christmas Day, but some kind of affair was held in the Ford Mansion. The only clue is in Washington's expense book, dated December 15: "Band of Musick, $15." Nothing is known of the kind of music played, but instruments in other such bands of the day included drums, fifes, French horns, trombones, bassoons, and oboes.

A member of Washington's staff took a sleigh from Morristown to Philadelphia in late December to pick up Martha Washington. They returned to Morristown on New Year's Day. At the time, the commander also was seeking a coach [known as a chariot] for his wife. He ordered Colonel John Mitchell to find "a genteel plain Chariot with neat harness for four horses and to go with two postilions [positions for riders who drove the team of horses]."

First consideration was given to a vehicle seized from a Tory, Captain Archibald Kennedy of Bergen County. Washington rejected it as "old-fashioned and uncoath [uncouth]." A suitable coach finally was custom-built in Philadelphia, with "painting well done, and in a tasty stile (sic) with respect to color, in which I have no particular choice." Although he said he preferred "a plain Chariot," Washington believed it "may not be amiss to ornament the moldings with a light airy gilding." This would "add little to the expence and much to the appearance." There would be no difficulty in paying for the carriage. The maker could have specie in gold or silver or he could have "paper money at the difference of exchange then prevailing, be it little or much."

Mrs. Washington's arrival picked up the social pace. Based on numerous letters and diary entries for the first months of 1780, parties, dances, or other kinds of entertainment or celebration were often available for officers. Not all of them partied every night but some of them at least made the effort.

A usual place for officers to entertain three or four friends was in their huts. While far from luxurious, these buildings had several major differences from the housing that the enlisted men had created for themselves. The floors were wooden, compared with mud or dirt floors in the men's quarters, and the windows had real glass in them. Most important, only two or three bunks were in a shared officers' quarters, compared with the twelve that rose in tiers along the walls of enlisted men's huts.

With a fire roaring in the fireplace and candles glowing from holders on tables or walls, the officer quarters probably were at least as attractive as the average town tavern. There is little question that some, if not many, officer huts often resounded with music and the welcome echoes of female voices.

Young Colonel Ebenezer Huntington, who had run away from his classes at Yale to join the army in 1775, two days after the Battle of Concord, showed his youthful anticipation when he wrote his regimental commander on February 16. He fantasized about the quarters that soon would be his:

> My hut — ah, my hut! — it is building and will be till nearly the first of next month,
> Then sir, I expect to open the doors and welcome every guest that comes with stores,
> doubly to pay for what he eats and drinks while with me. I expect to have a dozen fine
> girls to drink tea with me the first afternoon.

A dozen fine, tea-drinking girls was not beyond possibility, if officer letters are to be trusted. Simeon De Witt, an army surveyor and map maker who was on Washington's staff, sought to entice an officer friend to visit him in Morristown by writing, "I wish you would come and see us. You don't know what pretty girls there are about this place." Captain Samuel Shaw, an artilleryman and an aide to General Henry Knox, was amazed that "the circle of pretty creatures is so engaging there seems to be no quitting it."

Quite naturally, the "pretty creatures" had to be entertained between dances and dinners. The deep snow that overlay the area was perfect for taking eager young women for long sleigh rides. Cuddling together under heavy blankets in horse-drawn sleighs racing across open fields — at speeds as exhilarating as twelve miles an hour — likely was at least as satisfying as a minuet on a crowded, closely chaperoned dance floor. There were no chaperones on sleds.

Sleigh riding at top speeds had its hazards, however. Erkuries Beatty remembered one sleighing party as "a pretty clever Kick-up," suggesting an overturned sleigh filled with screaming, excited young women. A sudden turn, a frightened horse, or some unexpected obstacle might tip any sleigh, even with the most careful driver. Simeon Dewitt, who urged friends to visit him to enjoy the area girls, also recalled sleighing and its mishaps:

We have noble slaying [sic]. The other day (I mean night) we tumbled over two slay [sic] loads of ladies helter skelter, head over heels, into the snow.

One sleighing incident drew Washington's wrath. Several officers, accompanied by female friends distributed in four sleighs, stopped at a Rahway tavern to do some dancing. British soldiers surrounded the tavern, took the officers as prisoners, seized the sleighs and nine horses, and left the young women to find their way home. The general exploded in anger and let his feelings be widely known in General Orders:

The late capture of some officers on the lines who were not there on duty ought to be a caution against the like practices in the future. Gentlemen taken in this manner may ensure themselves they will not be exchanged in turn [for British officers], but will be postponed as long as possible.

Although Simeon DeWitt had written of Morristown's pretty girls, he was not totally committed to females, sleigh riding and dancing. For one thing, as an officer on Washington's headquarters staff, he became acquainted with eighteen-year-old Tim Ford, son of the late Jacob Ford, Jr., and Mrs. Theodosia Ford, in whose home Washington was quartered. DeWitt described the friendship in a letter to a friend:

You know Tim Ford. He and I have got accidentally acquainted with each other and amuse ourselves by speaking, composing, playing on the flute, smoking together, walking &c, &c, &c, &c.

Tim Ford also became friendly with Major Caleb Gibbs, commander of the general's Life Guard. Tim was allowed to accompany the major on a dangerous assignment and was wounded in the Battle of Springfield. Tim told his mother and friends that he had "a couple of Clever Marks" to show for his patriotism.

DeWitt bought a fiddle to broaden his diversions, and within three weeks had taught himself to play "two or three tunes." He intended to "become perfect in it if I can, but I have so much upon hand between amusements and business that my thoughts are never at a stand or languish for the want of exercise. With musick [sic], drawing, drafting, writing, reading, walking, conversing, sometimes dancing, singing, &c, my hours insensibly slip away."

Talk of a major officers' assembly (a formal ball) had circulated in camp since mid-December. As the winter progressed, an assembly became the anticipated hope for fine entertainment. with each passing week. All of the January dancing, sleighing, and dining became secondary passions as officers discussed the great First Assembly scheduled for February 23. Thirty-five officers, including Washington, had each pledged $400 for a series of three Assemblies.

Another evidence of officer anticipation was cited in a letter written by Colonel Huntington. He wrote, "The colonel likely was overly optimistic, but there is no question that the assemblies set the officer class on fire."

Excitement heightened as the great night approached. Some officers did not waste time in preparation. With whatever ladies they might find, they indulged in what might be considered training for the first assembly. Four days before the big dance, Captain Samuel Shaw wrote to a friend that he and some fellow officers had been kept busy dancing for three consecutive nights with certain unnamed ladies.

The Assembly would also mark the debut of Morristown's newest building — a huge wooden structure built as an army storehouse. Later, it became George O'Hara's Tavern. (The M. Epstein department store occupied the site in the twentieth century.) Partygoers on the first Assembly night could be excused for believing the building was intended only as a setting for their pleasure.

General Greene created an unpleasant stir when he announced, the day before the Assembly, that if necessary the affair might have to give way to a court martial or even to yield space for making tents for the army, two of the original purposes of the building. Neither happened. A postponement of the Assembly might have caused a roar that could have been heard in the halls of Congress in Philadelphia.

By late afternoon on February 23, falling snow made it evident that the numbers attending the Assembly would be thinned; Royal Flint, assistant Commissary of Purchases, observed "the weather is bad and the roads shocking." His anticipation of a small attendance was right. Only twenty-three ladies and sixty-five officers attended the evening affair.

Washington stepped on the floor to begin the first Assembly. Lucy Knox, the "lively and meddlesome but amiable" wife of Brigadier Henry Knox, joined him in the opening dance. The Knoxes were foremost among those who loved the good life.

Two more Assemblies were held that season, the second on March 1 and the third on April 24. Both were well attended, A day after the March affair, General Greene wrote that he "was at the assembly last night and feel a little fatigued and cloudy." Captain Samuel Shaw, writing about the same Assembly to a friend stationed at West Point, opined that the Point "must be very disagreeable contrary to the diversions of Morristown."

One social event that season simmered in officer gossip circles for a year before it broke into a public exchange of letters that verged on scandalous. Sometime in late March 1780, according to the gossip, Colonel and Mrs. Clement Biddle entertained the cream of officer society in their rented quarters. Guests included the Washingtons and the Greenes and several other notables, including civilians Mr. and Mrs. George Olney.

No official word ever was spoken about the party at the time but whispers in the camp alleged that Mrs. Olney screamed at Washington that "if he did not let go her hand, she would tear out his eyes, or the hair on his head, and that 'tho he was a General, he was but a man.'"

The talk became so pervasive and lasted so long that a year later Washington's aide-de-camp, Tench Tilghman, issued a formal explanation (which presumably Washington had approved). Tilghman said the affair was little more than a playful scuffle that occurred when George Olney refused to drink with the officers, including Washington, and went to talk with the ladies. The slighted officers then "rescued" Olney and took him back to where other officers were imbibing. Mrs. Olney witnessed the scuffling and took offense.

According to Tilghman's long-delayed explanation, it was just a happy rumpus, as "any good natured person must suppose." As for Mrs. Olney, Tilghman said she used "no expressions unbecoming a lady of the good breeding." It was a clever semantic trap; Mrs. Olney dared not deny her good breeding.

At the very least, the raucous happening had to be viewed in official circles as the consequence of far too much alcohol consumed in an effort to ease the harsh winter for a group of selected officers. It was a fitting, if disturbing, end to a very pleasant winter — for the officers. It was also time to get back to the business of war.

The mansion, completed in 1774 by one of Morristown's most distinguished citizen, Jacob Ford, Jr., was Washington's headquarters during the brutal winter of 1779-80. The wing on the right side of the house was added that winter.

The Finest House in Town

The Ford Mansion, better known locally as Washington's Headquarters, is much as it was in the winter of 1779-80, when the commander in chief, Mrs. Washington, and the general's aides were quartered there. It is furnished as the National Park Service believes it appeared, but as an occupied home rather than a colonial mansion showcasing antique furniture.

Colonel Jacob Ford, his wife Theodosia, and their four children moved into this fine home in 1774. Two hundred acres surrounded the mansion and sloped away toward the Whippany River.

The house was built in the Georgian style, with four large rooms on each floor, divided by spacious hallways on each floor. The home's classic architecture features the front doorway. It is fashioned in the Palladian mode, a style named for Italian Andrea Palladio, who won his fame in the sixteenth century. His work featured ancient Roman ideals and harmonic proportions.

Georgian homes all had long central halls reaching from back to front. When doors at either end of each hallway were opened on hot summer days, the slightest breeze sent cool air coursing through the hallways. The Ford halls were wider than usual, to allow for larger gatherings as well as to provide storage space for the firewood needed to supply the many fireplaces, the only means of heating the large house.

The army took over six of the rooms, two on the first floor and four on the second, for use as offices as well as sleeping space. Mrs., Ford and her four children occupied the other two first floor rooms. The spacious kitchen was shared. Soldiers plastered two second-floor rooms when the army moved in.

After Mrs. Washington arrived in town on December 31, 1779, she and the general occupied the main chamber on the second floor. Officers slept on folding cots in shared rooms. Cots were folded during working hours to provide desks or tables. Later in the winter, a temporary office building was attached to the west side of the building. It provided sleeping space by night and office space by day. Washington's eighteen servants, including his cook, as well Mrs. Ford's household servants, spent their days in the warm kitchen. In time, Washington built a kitchen annex to provide more space.

For all its grandeur, the mansion had none of the amenities considered necessary today, such as central heat, running water or bathrooms. Outside wooden buildings, called "necessaries" accommodated toilet needs.

The wing of the mansion contained the kitchen and its imposing fireplace It was built after Washington complained on January 22, 1780 that "eighteen belonging to my family, and all of Mrs. Fords, were huddled in the old kitchen, all suffering from colds."

Chapter Eleven

THE WOOING *of the* GREEN

A day off for the eleven brigades at Jockey Hollow was as rare as a brand new uniform, a full course meal, or furloughs for all sergeants. Joy swept through the ranks when a general order read to all the troops on March 16, 1780, specified that "all fatigue and working parties cease for tomorrow the 17th."

The order came directly from the top, from "The General", as he identified himself in the first paragraph of the order. He paid tribute to his troops and indirectly laid a burden on them: Irishmen in American uniform were to be part of a bid for major support from Ireland, whether the soldiers knew it or not.

Washington declared that "very interesting proceedings of the Parliament of Ireland, and of the inhabitants of that country," made it likely that the ancient nation was ready "to remove heavy and tyrannical oppressions" intended "to restore to a Brave and Generous People their ancient Rights and Freedom."

It is doubtful anyone in the ranks fully understood the weight of that paragraph, much less understood why the American army deserved congratulations for what was said to be happening in Ireland. Actually, the message was meant for the eyes of the political leaders in Ireland rather than the men at Jockey Hollow.

What Washington wanted to convey, cautiously disguised, was that word had reached him of major political changes in Ireland, with even a possibility that a revolt was brewing against English rule in the Emerald Isle. The Irish Parliament had demanded an end to the elimination of British trade restrictions, a bold move for a small nation that had long been under Great Britain's heavy thumb. An Irish uprising was good news for the American cause.

More easily understood by every soldier, however, was that Washington had declared St, Patrick's Day a holiday to commemorate both Ireland's patron saint and that nation's most important day of worship and celebration. Every man, Irish or not, would share in the holiday.

There was a touch of hopeful blarney in the closing words of the Order; "He [The General] persuades himself that the celebration of the day will not be attended with the least rioting or disorder." Deserved or undeserved, the sons of Erin had a reputation for a bit of high-spirited, and sometimes downright disorderly, conduct, if a touch of the drink happened to be handy.

Colonel Francis Johnson of the Second Pennsylvania Brigade sent a hogshead [slightly more than 250 quarts] of rum to his men. He warned that they must conduct themselves "with the greatest sobriety and good order," as if rum were a sedative.

Based on accounts of the day, the Irish soldiers met the general's and the colonel's every hope. The day began with band music, followed by a spontaneous parade under a regimental flag on which the men had drawn an Irish harp and printed in capital letters the words, THE INDEPENDENCE OF IRELAND. Then the rum was consumed, slowly, sip by sip, lest the solemnity be sacrificed on the altar of dissipation.

English propagandists in New York City pooh-poohed the glowing reports from Morristown. The *New York Mercury*, a leading New York City newspaper and dispenser of British propaganda, reported that Irish soldiers in Morristown, smarting under the alleged pain of being "seduced" to join the Continentals, actually were on the verge of deserting.

According to the *Mercury*, the Irish vented their Hibernian spleens by threatening on March 16, the day before their national holiday, that if any attempt were made to stop a celebration there would be a hot time in old Morristown.

"It was a day of apprehension to some who looked for bloodshed and murder," claimed the *Mercury*, "but American policy outwitted Irish good humor." The reason there was no bloodshed or murder was that the prospect (or perhaps hope) for such excesses existed mainly in the *Mercury* editor's imagination. The British editor also printed a rumor that "seventy thousand men in arms" were "scattered through the camp" to preserve order. If this had been true, the keepers of the peace would have outnumbered the celebrants by more than ten to one.

Mercury editor Hugh Gaines admitted in later fanciful articles that "the simple-hearted Teagues [presumably intended as a slur], charmed with the sight of the harp forgot their sufferings, controlled their complaints and seemed perfectly happy for the moment, though not a drop of whiskey or taffie [West Indies rum] was seen in the camp." He saw it as "a dry and unusual way of celebrating the tutelary divinity of England's fair and jolly sister, the Kingdom of Ireland." Obviously he had not learned of Colonel Johnson's gift of the hogshead of rum.

Whether the day was to be judged by Gaines' imaginative tales or by reports of those Americans who were at the scene, the Irish soldiers behaved as well as Washington desired. Whatever his ulterior motive was in creating the unexpected holiday, Washington had reason to be grateful for the sober role played by the Irish enlisted men and their officers on that St. Patrick's Day.

One of the commander-in-chief's hopes for a reasonably sober holiday was to get across at least a subliminal message to the troops. He wanted them to see their potential value in linking the American cause to Ireland's current national restlessness with Great Britain's restrictive policies against the troubled island.

The United States had been openly wooing Ireland since July 1775, a year before the Declaration of Independence, and, of course, before there was even a United States of America. In 1775, supporters of vigorous action against England asked for support from Ireland and suggested that the Irish themselves were not "without grievances," a gross understatement. Then, in 1778, when Ireland was vigorously opposing English laws that were ruining Irish industries, and British landlords who were heartlessly exploiting Irish farmers, Benjamin Franklin sought to fan the embers of revolt. On October 4, 1778, he wrote and printed a tract directed "To the good people of Ireland" and had it smuggled into the distressed nation.

Franklin expressed sympathy for the "misery and distress to which your ill-fated country has been so frequently exposed," reacting to British anti-Irish provocations as he saw them. Franklin summarized America's desire to help:

> *I have it in my commission to repeat to you, my good friends, the cordial concern that Congress takes in everything that relates to the happiness of Ireland; they are sensibly affected by the oppressive pensions on your establishments; the arbitrary and illegal exactions of public money by King's letters; the profuse dissipation by sinecure appointments with very large salaries, and the very arbitrary and impolitic restrictions of your trade and manufactures, which are beyond example in the history of the world.*

It was classic Franklin. It was also blatant subversion. If Ireland could be induced to rebel against its English masters, it would in effect set up a second front on England's doorstep. With France ever threatening across the English Channel, and Americans stubbornly battling them across the sea, the British would be in an almost impossible bind.

Restlessness and anguish in Ireland, by the late 1760s, were neither hyperbole nor imagination. Ireland had at last begun to awaken from the torpor created by centuries of

British rule. By the time the American Revolution began, Irishmen had lived so long under Great Britain's cruel and repressive government that it had become a way of life.

Evidences of British cruelty were spread across the sad nation. Ruins of Roman Catholic churches and cathedrals were cruel mementoes of Oliver Cromwell's efforts to stamp out Catholicism everywhere in Great Britain during his reign after the Civil War of 1640. Possessing absolute power from the end of the Civil War in 1642 until his death in 1656, Cromwell savagely attacked any religious group that opposed him. Irish Catholics were a particular target.

The Stuarts, Great Britain's ruling family from 1603 until 1714, except for the Cromwell interlude, continued the anti-Papist hatred. They savagely

In 1778, Benjamin Franklin lent his writing talents and international popularity to the cause of Irish independence, thereby increasing trouble for the British on another front.

attacked Roman Catholic rights in the so-called Penal Laws enacted between 1692 and 1704. By then, the laws had reduced Irish Catholic land holdings to ten percent of their country's area. Catholics could not carry arms, own a horse worth more than five pounds, teach in a school, send children abroad for an education, sit in Parliament. vote in a Parliamentary election, take part in local government, sit on a jury, hold any government office, or become lawyers or doctors.

By 1770, the English program to eliminate Irish Catholics, as fiendish in purpose as Hitler's intention to eliminate Jews during World War II, had reduced Ireland's Catholic population to abject poverty. They now paid exorbitant rents for lands they once owned but that were now in the hands of Protestants. As another form of humbling, Irishmen were expected to tithe to the Protestant churches. On a domestic level, the Irish diet was mainly their share of the potatoes that they laboriously planted and harvested for their English masters.

Understandably, most Irish leaders had eagerly supported the prospect of rebellion in America, from the emerging days of rebellion to the strong resistance to taxation. The most dramatic show of support, however unintended as such, came from the 33,000 Irishmen, mostly Presbyterians, who voluntarily migrated to America between 1770 and 1773. Another 10,000 Irishmen were exiled to Maryland as convicts, nearly all of them labeled as English criminals merely because, in Great Britain, it was a crime to be Catholic.

The exodus deeply troubled large English landowners in Ireland who were exploiting Irish families as cheap labor. The "dispeopling of Ireland" appalled Lord Hillsborough, a secretary of state for colonial affairs. Not incidentally, his Lordship's huge estate in Ireland depended on the toil of thousands of poor Irish Protestant tenant farmers. Their departure for America, he feared, would eliminate a measure of security against possible rebellious Catholics, not to mention what might happen to his huge crops if not tended by Irish peasants.

By 1778, Irish militants in the homeland were demanding that His Majesty eliminate the trade barriers that prevented Irish manufacturers from sending their wares to any nation other than England. In November 1779, Dublin mobs rioted against restrictions on free trade.

A month later, Lord North introduced "free trade" legislation, a decision bolstered in February 1780 by a still stronger measure. There never was the full-scale rebellion that American leaders hoped for — but it underlay Washington's intention in proclaiming the St. Patrick's holiday in 1780 and for congratulating the army for "the very interesting proceedings of the Parliament of Ireland."

The day of St. Patrick celebration in Morristown also was a deserved tribute to the numbers of Irish immigrants in the American army. By 1780, about twenty-five percent of American soldiers were Irish or descended from Irish immigrants. In the Middle Atlantic States, Irish-American soldiers accounted for about forty-five percent of all men on the rolls.

Seven of the eleven American brigades were commanded by generals who were Irish born or of Irish descent: Edward Hand, Hand's Brigade; William Irvine, First Pennsylvania Brigade; General William Maxwell, New Jersey Brigade; General John Stark, Stark's Brigade; Anthony Wayne, Second Pennsylvania Brigade; Henry Knox, Artillery Brigade; and George Clinton, New York Brigade.

One of Washington's aides, James McHenry, a medical doctor, was born in County Antrim, Ireland, and came to Baltimore in 1753. His family followed him a year later and established a prosperous import business.

The Irish rank and file were not universally loved in the American army. They were ridiculed for their short stature (on average, five-feet, three-inches tall) and their way of speaking ("he has the brogue on his tongue"). Even Maryland, once the bastion of Catholicism in the New World, had accepted the Anglican Church as its established religion.

In time, it also became evident that Irish recruits deserted the army at a higher rate than those who were native-born.

General Henry Clinton, commander of the British forces in America, fancied those deserters. He wrote to his superiors in England that "it would be a powerful temptation to the Irish" if he could offer them His Majesty's pardon "for all crimes heretofore committed by them in Ireland, except murder." Irish deserters from the American army, he thought, thus could "return home without apprehension to their families." There is little evidence for the theory that pardons tempted deserters to flock into New York.

There was also an English celebration of St. Patrick's Day in New York on March 17, 1780, considerably more elaborate and better organized than the observance at Jockey Hollow. The organizers did not fret about the status of Ireland, or for that matter, the standing of the Irish in the British army.

The Irish had their own organization within the English forces, the new Volunteers of Ireland, composed only of Irishmen. Their commander, Colonel Francis Rawdon, was born in Ireland, although he was far removed from the peasant class that was migrating to America. Rawdon came from a noble Irish family and was educated at Harrow and Oxford, which automatically made him officer material.

Rawdon was young (only twenty-five when he took command of the "Volunteers of Ireland,") and was described as tall, strong, and vigorous, although he had "a curious reputation as being the 'ugliest man' in England." After reaching a maximum enrollment of 612 in March 1779, the Volunteers fell back to 286 in uniform in 1780; desertion was a two-way street. Lord Rawdon decided that his "natives of Ireland" must have their own 1780 celebration of the Saint's day in New York.

The Volunteers of Ireland, led by their own band, marched into the city from their camp in Jamaica, Long Island, on March 17, and formed ranks before the house of their colonel. He took his place at the head of the formation and marched the Irishmen to a greeting from Hessian General Wilhelm Knyphausen, acting commander of New York while Clinton was away in the Charleston Campaign. The incongruity of a German general giving British greetings to Irishmen in an American city was lost on the reporter who covered the occasion for *The New York Gazette*.

The Irish soldiers then marched to the Bowery for a "noble banquet." Lord Rawdon and the officers left the men at the banquet door, marched back to Rawdon's house and "dined with his Lordship." This was not, after all, a democracy.

"The soldierly appearance of the men," according to *The Gazette* on March 22, "and their order of march, hand in hand, being all NATIVES OF IRELAND, had a striking effect; and many of their Countrymen have since joined them."

Remarkable, too, The *Gazette* editor said, was the fact that such natives of Ireland, "however long they may have remained in the Haunts of Hypocrisy, Cunning, and Disaffection" [his version of American life] remained "gallant and loyal," and would "crow with Ardor to stand forth in the Cause of their King, of their country, and of real, honest, general Liberty, whenever the Opportunity offers." To that list of noble sentiments might have been added the bonus (in hard cash) that recruits (including American deserters) received, the new uniforms, and the reasonably good food that would be served.

In New York, at least for a day, the Volunteers of Ireland stood tall. However, considerably different treatment was accorded another Irish group in British uniforms — the oldest and most prestigious Irish Royal Irish Artillery. Major General James Pattison, who hated Irishmen, commanded the unit during part of the Revolution.

Lord Francis Rawdon, a British officer who distinguished himself at Bunker Hill, was an Irish aristocrat chosen in 1778 to command England's newly recruited Volunteers of Ireland.

Elite was a proper word for the Royal Irish Artillery. Founded in 1755 as The Artillery Company of Ireland, the English recruited and trained the company's men in Dublin Castle and later in Woolwich, England. Some of the group's units were sent to America to fight with General John Burgoyne, the British dandy who fared so badly at Saratoga. Other gunners were shipped directly to General Pattison in New York City.

Pattison went out of his way to label what he called his "bare breeched, diminutive warriors" as "incorrigible, ill mannered, unkempt" and "lower than serpents." He asked that England send him only Englishmen and Scots for his Royal Irish Artillery. When large numbers of new Irish gunners deserted him in New York, Pattison wrote "it was bad enough that they deserted but what was worse was that the rest didn't go with them."

Pattison's intemperate remarks about what was generally considered to be a crack unit of the British army, led the Royal Irish Artillery to regress badly under his leadership. None of his superiors seemed to care.

Success to the shamrogue, and all those who wear it.
Be honour their portion wherever they go
May riches attend them, and store of good claret,
For how to employ them sure none better know.
Every foe surveys them with terror,
But every silk petticoat wants them nearer,
So Yankee keep off, or you'll soon learn your error,
For Paddy will lay prostrate every foe.

This day, but the year I can't rightly determine.
St Patrick the vipers did chase from this land.
Let's see if like him we can't sweep off the vermin
Who dare 'gainst the sons of the shamrogue to stand.
Hand in hand! Let's carol tis chorus,
"As long as the blessings of Ireland hang o'er us,
The crest of the rebellion shall tremble before us,
Like brothers while thus we march hand in hand!"

St. George & St. Patrick, St. Andrew, St. David,
Together may laugh at all Europe in arms.
Fair conquest her standard has o'er their heads waved
And glory has on them conferr'd all her charms!
War's alarms are to us a pleasure.
Since honour our danger repays in good measure.
And all those who join us shall find we have leisure,
To think of our sport ev'n in war's alarms!

The Royal Gazette of New York hailed the attention given to the Volunteers of Ireland Regiment on St. Patrick's Day in 1780. Part of the entertainment was an original song rendered by regiment piper Barny Johnson, sung to the tune of Langolee, an old Irish ballad.

James McHenry: Warrior Doctor

Fort McHenry in Baltimore preserves the memory of James McHenry, an Irish immigrant whose Revolutionary War exploits ranged from active fighting to service as a member of Washington's inner circle of advisers.

Though Irish-American General John Sullivan, a noted Continental Army field officer, and British Colonel Rawdon, who commanded the enemy's Volunteers of Ireland, were better-known, McHenry's services topped the deeds of both.

McHenry was born in Ballymena, County Antrim, in the province of Ulster, Ireland, on November 16, 1753, the son of a prosperous merchant. His classical education in Dublin prepared him for a

This portrait of McHenry, attributed to James Sharples, Sr., hangs at Independence National Historical Park in Philadelphia.

life in business but he immigrated to Philadelphia in 1771, settling in Baltimore a year later, when his family followed him and established an import business there. James continued his education at Newark Academy [now the University of Delaware], and then was apprenticed to Philadelphia's famed Dr. Benjamin Rush to study medicine.

When the war began, McHenry suspended his studies and hastened to Cambridge, Massachusetts, to volunteer for military service. McHenry "followed his idol [Washington]." On August 10, 1776, he was appointed surgeon of the Fifth Pennsylvania Battalion and soon after was assigned to Fort Washington in New York City. The fort surrendered to the British on November 16, McHenry's twenty-third birthday. McHenry was captured and placed in a British jail until his parole on January 27, 1777.

While on parole, McHenry wrote Washington of his captors' cruelty. He wrote that "the insufferable impurity" of one house for prisoners "made up altogether a scene more affecting and horrid than the carnage of a field of battle."

After his exchange on March 5, 1778, McHenry became a senior surgeon at Valley Forge. Senior surgeons did not hold any rank, wear a uniform, or receive any pay. He was in essence an unpaid civilian. Washington chose McHenry on May 15, 1777, to be one of his aides, as an assistant secretary. The commander found his new staff member possessed "an easy and cheerful temperament." McHenry became a favorite of Washington's, and a life-long friendship began.

McHenry saw action at the battles of Monmouth and Springfield and became a strong member of Washington's immediate "military family," along with such officers as Henry Knox, Alexander Hamilton and the Marquis de Lafayette.

After the war, he served in the Continental Congress and in 1787 represented Maryland at the Constitutional Convention. In 1796, President Washington appointed McHenry Secretary of War. As secretary, McHenry helped establish a strong standing army. Despite a belief that such an army might endanger civil liberties, Congress approved the creation of twelve new permanent regiments.

Although McHenry opposed the war of 1812, he encouraged his son to follow in his footstep by becoming a wartime volunteer. His son participated in the defense of Fort McHenry, named for his father, the most notable Irish-American of the American Revolution.

The Continental Army had large numbers of Irish-Americans in its ranks; seven of the eleven brigades at Jockey Hollow were commanded by Irish-American officers, including John Sullivan. Born in New Hampshire, Sullivan fought in most major battles and led a major expedition against the Iroquois in 1779.

Chapter Twelve

The RELUCTANT GENERAL

A s the winter of 1779-80 intensified, General Henry Clinton's concerns about his short supplies and the physical suffering of his men were almost a mirror image of what was happening in Morristown. The cold, the incessant winter storms, and the depth of the snow on the city streets were little different from the terrible conditions in the Morris County hills.

The British commander had frittered away the summer of 1779, just as he had squandered nearly all the months since the Battle of Monmouth. He had made no threatening move at Washington's winter camp in Middlebrook during the previous winter of 1778-79. Except for the credible dash up the Hudson River to capture the forts at Stony Brook and Fort Lafayette across the River on June 1, 1779, Clinton had not taken the offensive. Indeed, as the winter of 1779-80 approached, the general served the Americans well by engaging in bouts with his usual uncertain self.

If that winter is to be fully understood, it is important to know of Clinton's incessant self-abasement, mixed with constant intemperate outbursts. He was frozen in place, not by the increasingly cold weather moving in on New York, but by the recurring despair and indecision that marked his career in America.

He feared Washington would send troops storming eastward from Morristown, to cross the icebound Hudson River and attack the British headquarters in New York. He fretted because promised reinforcements had not arrived from England. He stewed about the thousands of Loyalists crowded into the city, and above all, had qualms about the French fleet that he thought might attack New York.

General Henry Clinton was the self-doubting, querulous, and bombastic leader of the British Army in America from the spring of 1778 until after the Battle of Yorktown.

Despite his agonizing fears and persistent procrastination, Clinton became a lightning rod for American perplexity after he assumed command of the British army in the spring of 1778. His strength in New York constantly dictated American strategy, and his continuing indecision was to his benefit as Washington wasted time and effort trying to determine what the quixotic Clinton might do.

A self-labeled introvert, Clinton was able to confide his deepest resentments and recurring doubts in copious notes he kept throughout the war. Those writings were not revealed until the late 1920s, when the William L. Clements Library of the University of Michigan released the Clinton papers. His own words brand him as at least strongly neurotic and possibly borderline manic-depressive.

He should have been joyful and proud about his rise to commander of the powerful British forces in America in the late spring of 1778. If his dark thoughts left any room for nostalgia, he was returning to the city where he had spent his formative years, from age thirteen to nineteen, when his father was Royal Governor of the Province of New York.

Young Henry sailed to England in his nineteenth year to seek fame in the British army. He performed well in the war with Germany, yet even as he succeeded on battlefields, his inability to appreciate and communicate with his fellow officers became increasingly evident. When he sailed for Boston in the spring of 1775, he found it difficult to talk with fellow generals on the same ship — John ("Gentleman Johnny") Burgoyne and Sir William Howe.

When Howe became commander of the British forces in America after the Battle of Bunker Hill in 1775, Clinton became his second in command. Howe assured his subordinate that he would welcome his advice. Clinton took that at face value, peppering his chief with querulous, bickering suggestions, opinions, and doubts until Howe bluntly ordered Clinton to keep his thoughts to himself. The generals persisted in their disagreements on nearly every problem or opportunity that faced them.

The debacles at Trenton and Princeton in the last days of 1776 and the early days of 1777 prompted Clinton to lash out at Lord Cornwallis, who commanded the botched Trenton-Princeton campaign. As usual, Sir Henry was harshly impolitic, terming Cornwallis guilty "of the most consummate ignorance I ever heard of [in] any officer above a corporal."

Less than a month later, Clinton sailed back to England, angrily swearing never to return to America and vowing *absolutely* never to serve again under Howe. A knighthood soothed his feelings and prompted withdrawal of his resignation. Clinton returned to New York, accepted renewed service under Howe, and resumed his vigorous disapproval of Howe's generalship.

The British army was nearly ready to head for Philadelphia by sea when Clinton returned. He heartily disagreed with the expedition. It made no difference; London's warlords had agreed with Howe's strategy. The troops were already aboard the ships. It was too late to turn back. Clinton fumed as Howe's fleet headed south, likely wishing that he had never returned to America. He told anyone who would listen that Howe had condemned him to a "damned starved defensive."

When Howe was recalled to London in the spring of 1778, Clinton was at the top of a very small list of possible successors.

He permitted himself only minimal joy in his elevation to the most powerful post in the British forces in America. (His taking command in Philadelphia, the well-planned evacuation of the city and his satisfactory performance at Monmouth are recounted in Chapter 3.)

However, if Clinton had any capacity for pride, most, if not all, of it evaporated when it became common knowledge on both sides of the ocean that the Lords of London picked him more for his presence on the scene than for any admiration of his qualities as a leader or tactician.

There is no question that Clinton was pleased to see the last of Howe. His constant disagreements with his former superior were summed up in an anonymous, acidulous, second-guessing account found when the Clinton papers were revealed and probably writ-

A Life of Ease

Joshua Loring, who attained attention by lending his wife to General William Howe to be the general's mistress in New York and Philadelphia, became Commissioner of Prisoners as his part of the agreement. Loring hoped he would achieve a life of ease.

It worked. Loring appropriated "to his own use nearly two-thirds of the rations allowed to the prisoners," sold them, and pocketed the money. It was said that his actions starved to death 300 of "the poor wretches" before an exchange was made. Hundreds more who were alive at the time of release died on the road to home "and many lived but a few days after reaching their habitation."

William Cunningham, provost marshal, also prospered handsomely. On his deathbed he confessed starving to death at least 300 of the 2,000 emaciated men in his "care."

Some have disputed such tales of British brutality, but 8,500 Americans died in British captivity. Many prisoners lived to tell stories of callous starvation, lack of adequate clothing, foul water and cramped quarters.

All of that — for lives of ease.

ten by Clinton after Howe was recalled:

> Had Sir William fortified the hills around Boston he could not have been driven from it; had he pursued his victory on Long Island he had ended the rebellion; had he landed above the lines at New York, not a man could have escaped him; had he operated with the Northern army he had saved it; or had he gone by land to Philadelphia he had ruined Mr. Washington and his forces; but as he did none of these things, had he gone to the D---l before he was sent to America, it had been the saving of infamy to himself and indelible dishonor to his country.

Clinton quickly returned to self-pity and his foolish custom of discussing his plight with junior officers. Shortly after he assumed command of the British army, he confided to Lieutenant Colonel Charles Smart, "with tears in his eyes," that his work now "oppressed him," and that he felt "incapable of his situation." Smart committed his superior's tale of despondency to his diary, where future generations would read the general's words, supposedly spoken in confidence:

> Believe me, my dear Colonel Smart, I envy even that grenadier who is passing the door, and would exchange with joy [our] situations, No. Let me advise you never to take command of an army. I know I am detested — nay hated — in this army. But I

In this drawing of Broadway in New York during the Revolution, General Clinton's headquarters was probably the house on the left.

am indifferent about it because I know it is without cause. I am determined to return home; the minister has used me so ill that I can no longer bear with this life.

As the winter of 1779 impended, the general was at the apex of power and ease. His day-by-day physical comforts were well accommodated in the handsome Archibald Kennedy house at One Broadway, and when bored with city life he could find solitude at the Turtle Bay country seat owned by James Beekman. As many as five farms kept the corpulent general's tables very well supplied.

Kennedy's in-town mansion was typical of the half dozen or so splendid homes that faced the city's esteemed Bowling Green, with the classical features favored by the wealthy: a Palladian front entrance, ornate cornices, spacious rooms, elaborately decorated walls and ceilings, an opulent banquet room, and a staircase as grand as any in the city. This was a neighborhood where loyalty to King George could have been expected.

The general called himself "a shy bitch" to explain his inability to get along with others, but shyness never fully explained Clinton's surly attitude toward nearly all officers in his command. Never genial, he often went as many as two or three days without talking (in public at least) to anyone. Between sulks he entertained frequently and lavishly and more often than not was ridiculed behind his back for his affectations. He confided his deepest resentments in the copious notes he wrote throughout the war, later published posthumously in 1926.

An especially nasty exchange with New York Governor James Robertson saw Clinton imprudently accuse the governor of "smelling after every girl who will let him come nigh her." Robertson retaliated that "Clinton has not the understanding necessary for a corporal; he is inconsistent as a weather cock and knows nothing."

Clinton often secretly planned future military operations, but almost always lacked the will to put his plans into action. He argued constantly with his superiors, often placing them in nearly impossible situations. He never assumed blame if things went wrong.

The general's headquarters took on the flamboyance — and the expense — of a perpetual open house. A staff of twelve waited on the swarms of guests; Clinton's partying ate voraciously into his £12,000 annual expense account. The funds yielded original plays and an orchestra in which Sir Henry played the violin. Clinton feared he faced financial ruin, but tended to ignore the costs of his frivolity, preferring to emphasize that fuel alone cost him £2,000 annually.

During good weather, the general indulged in regular afternoon siestas in the large garden that overlooked the Hudson River in the rear of the Kennedy house. Washington seriously entertained a plan by Captain Henry Lee of the Virginia Light Dragoons, who believed that if soldiers waded ashore at low tide, a napping Clinton easily could be kidnapped and brought to Morristown. Alexander Hamilton scotched the scheme with a terse observation that summed up the accepted American view of Clinton's ineptitude:

New York circa 1780 — as seen by a shipmaster entering the bay — had no formal docks for larger ships, which anchored and loaded troops or supplies in small boats.

It would be our misfortune, since the British government could not find another commander so incompetent to send in his place.

Loyalist transients became an increasingly difficult problem as thousands of them poured into New York from surrounding states. They needed — and expected — protection, food, clothing, and housing as the winter of 1779-80 became every bit as brutal in New York as it was in Jockey Hollow. If anything, the large numbers of non-military Tories in the city on occasion created greater pressures on British resources than the hardships endured at Morristown.

While the food supply ordinarily was not as pinched as in Morristown, the British relied on shipments from England for staples. The ice-clogged river often hampered docking for several days, cutting deeply into food reserves. Attempts to augment the food supply by incursions into New Jersey seeking cattle and other provisions were met by vigorous American militia units.

Fuel for cooking and heating was a far bigger challenge in New York than at Morristown. When the Continentals wanted wood for their fireplaces they cut up limbs discarded during hut building or merely felled more trees. The British had to buy and haul in wood from outside the city, usually from Long Island or Staten Island.

Profiteering in wood brought price controls to New York in the autumn of 1778, Clinton's first year as city commander. Two years later, many impoverished people froze to death in their unheated homes. Judge William Smith declared, "many reputable people lay abed for days for want of fuel."

The judge noted in October that the town was destitute of firewood, with winter coming on. By mid-January, as temperatures plummeted, the shortage became a dire emergency. Garden fences, split rails, old sheds, rotting hulks in the harbor, and anything else that could provide firewood were chopped into fireplace size. One vessel, loaded and ready to sail, had its cargo taken off and the ship was hacked into firewood. Residents were told to burn fat to keep warm or to cook their food.

Housing both the Loyalists and His Majesty's troops, always a pressing problem in the city, reached the point of desperation as more and more Loyalists poured into New York. Jockey Hollow soldiers felled logs to build their own log house city, an arduous task, but it could be done. Finding quarters for an army in established New York buildings became a continuing crisis after the fearsome fire that destroyed a large part of the city on September 21, 1776.

The fire held the city and the army in a dire emotional grip. Residents and officers worried constantly that an arsonist would strike again. Another raging fire on a windy evening could sweep through the wooden buildings, making much of the city close to uninhabitable. Residents were asked to "inspect all parts of the city to apprehend incendiaries." Any stranger in town was to be reported to authorities.

Early in the morning darkness of August 3, 1778, the worst fears seemed about to become reality when "a most dreadful fire broke out in the store of Mr. Jones, ship chandler, on Cruger's wharf." The blaze spread quickly, feeding on the wax used to make candles and other flammables such as ship's sails.

Flames were consuming the wharf and all its buildings by the time city firemen reached the scene. There, a colonel from the Thirty-fifth Regiment told the firemen that he would direct all efforts to quell the fire. As the jurisdictional dispute warmed, flames leaped from the wharf to adjacent streets. Residents of the area accused the colonel of compounding the disaster.

Sixty-four houses and many stores were destroyed before the fire was checked. Arson was suspected and a reward of one hundred guineas was offered for detection of anyone guilty of "aiding in so horrid a crime." However, careful investigation by the authorities convinced them that the cause of the fire was accidental.

Less than a week later, the jittery city again approached panic when 248 barrels of gunpowder blew up on the sloop *Morning Star*, tied up on the East River. The ship's crew perished, the sloop and the dock were destroyed, and windows were shattered in the adjacent area, but the flames were quickly checked. The cause was obvious: lightning had struck the sloop.

Clinton was beset with increasing belligerence by Loyalists who questioned his lack of any plans to press the war during the summer of 1779. In fairness to the general, the whereabouts of the French fleet increasingly preoccupied him.

An old nemesis, Lord Cornwallis, had arrived in New York in April 1778 to be Clinton's second in command. If both remembered Clinton's vicious assessment of Cornwallis after the stunning defeats at Trenton and Princeton, neither spoke of it.

Cornwallis had been in London for three months and had acquired a new stature. He secretly carried a "dormant commission" that would place him in command if anything incapacitated Clinton. The commission was not intended as a threat to Clinton; in essence, it was issued chiefly to insure that a British officer, not a German, would be in charge if Clinton could not fulfill his duties.

Clinton, for his part, harbored the welcome notion that Cornwallis might speed his request to be relieved of command. He greeted Cornwallis cordially and wrote:

> *I flattered myself that every objection to my request of being relieved from my very arduous and unpleasant situation must now cease, since His Majesty had on the spot an officer of rank and experience on whom to confer the command of his army.*

On the surface, the relationship between Clinton and his second in command was pleasant. Yet, after the health of Cornwallis's wife in England deteriorated and the well-traveled general again returned to England in December 1778, an undercurrent of official dislike and mistrust manifested itself. Clinton's aide, Captain William Sutherland — who probably wrote nothing contrary to the thinking at the top — declared in an insensitive letter that included an insulting reference to Cornwallis' cocked eye:

> Lord Cornwallis is gone back home to cock his eye in the House of Lords, [he is an] insipid, good-natured Lord & the worst officer — except in personal courage — under the Crown.

When Cornwallis returned, Clinton believed more than ever the return provided a proper reason to resign his command. He shared with Cornwallis every move as the second Charleston campaign neared, on the grounds that his strategy should be clear to his successor if his request for resignation were accepted. Seven months passed; Clinton's request was denied, making the British leader increasingly bitter, frustrated, anxiety-ridden, and self-doubting. He dispatched streams of openly bitter and indiscreet letters to his government in England.

The entire spring and summer of 1779 slipped away with Cornwallis still on hand and nothing to indicate Clinton had any plan for ending the war, or even any plan to subdue the country immediately surrounding New York City. Raids into the New Jersey countryside, most of them impromptu rather than planned by the high command, did little more than produce a few cattle for food and a few prisoners.

In late summer, a fleet landed the expected British reinforcements for the winter of 1779-80. To Clinton's rightful dismay, only 3,400 troops marched ashore, scarcely half of what had been promised. Worse, more than a hundred men had died in the 116 days it took for the fleet to travel from England to New York. Many of the other new arrivals were ill and by the beginning of October, most of them were in hospitals.

Early in December, Clinton was ordered to put the New York scene into second position. London had decided that he must get the expedition against Charleston into full swing. Clinton and Cornwallis took the fleet out of New York harbor on the day after Christmas. Any action against the hungry, freezing troops in Jockey Hollow had to be in someone else's hands until Clinton returned.

Two nagging problems were left unanswered. First, Hessian General Wilhelm von Knyphausen would be the top-ranked officer in the British command in America if both Clinton and Cornwallis were to perish at sea or in the fighting in or near Charleston, South Carolina. More immediately, the Hessian was about to become the top-ranked officer and decision maker in New York.

Charleston as it appeared in 1780, after Clinton's massive victory. About 5,500 men were killed, wounded or captured in the worst American defeat of the war. Clinton returned home, leaving the city in strong hands.

Secondly, British well-advanced dealings with a mysterious American, "Mr. Moore," had to be left up in the air. The American had volunteered the previous summer to spy for the British — a remarkably good offer if it were true, as Mr. Moore claimed, that he was a highly placed officer in the Continental Army.

To this point, Clinton had trusted the details of dealing with Mr. Moore to his bright young, highly capable aide, Major John André, who had been handling early stages of the promising deal. It could no longer work: André sailed with the expedition. Mr. Moore had to be put on hold.

Unmasking Henry Clinton

No one understood General Henry Clinton's vague, peculiar and often insulting ways when he was living; it was 130 years after his death that he finally defended himself.

Clinton was unmasked by his own hand, when in 1925 collector William L. Clements, founder of the University of Michigan's celebrated Clements Library, gave Clinton's voluminous, wartime papers to the university. The collection included a three-volume manuscript, blandly titled *Historical Detail*, as well as 200 folders of letters, official reports and other documents.

The general's manuscript finally appeared in 1954, retitled *The American Rebellion*, with Henry Clinton as the author. This work, along with five other major collections, forced the rewriting of Revolutionary War history.

"In the familiar story of the American Revolution, Sir Henry Clinton is inconspicuous," William Wilcox wrote in his introduction. "Yet Washington is the only general on either side who held a crucial position so long." Wilcox calls Clinton's obscurity puzzling. Indeed, for nearly two centuries, much of the Clinton story was told in the words of his opponents or his enemies in New York City.

The 1925 letters did little to lessen Clinton's reputation for brashness and neurotic behavior. The death of Clinton's beloved wife in August 1772, after five years of marriage, contributed to his peculiar personality. It is said that he went "virtually out of his mind" after her death and only gradually regained composure.

After Clinton was named second in command to General William Howe, he was rebuffed with infuriating regularity, further upsetting his mental balance. When Howe was recalled to England in the spring of 1778, Clinton excoriated him in a diatribe that verged on cruelty.

Wilcox summarized the British general:

He had, in summary, solid military virtues but his generalship did not last the course. He was intelligent. He understood the map and the importance of sea power, and had a better than average conception of the war's true character.... In his later campaigns he became so addicted to the bread of carefulness that he lost what taste he had for audacity, and at the same time he was increasingly alienated from the two men [Admiral] Arbuthnot and [Lord] Cornwallis, upon whom he chiefly depended for implementing a slow, methodical strategy. Months before the final crisis burst upon him in Virginia, his leadership was bankrupt. The underlying causes of bankruptcy were in him. He was utterly self-centered. But the center was out of focus; he never attained the ruthless egoism that often makes a general great.

His nemesis was *himself*.

S^R HENRY CLINTON.

General Clinton's knighthood in 1777 earned him the coveted right to be called "Sir".

Chapter Thirteen

WAR *within a* WAR

P hilip Van Cortlandt, a wealthy New York merchant who moved to Whippany (East Hanover), New Jersey, with his wife and nine children in 1772, considered himself a moderate in the rebellious turbulence sweeping through the colonies. He sought to convince his neighbors near Morristown not to relinquish "that happy constitution which is the birthright and boast of Englishmen."

Patriots tried to win him to their cause by offering him the rank of colonel in the militia. He refused. He also would not change his pearl ash works into a gunpowder plant to serve the army. He and his philosophy finally were brought to trial in 1774 when he was charged with having negative thoughts about the Continental Congress. It was a clear violation of the civil rights he thought he could enjoy as a British citizen in America.

A huge crowd of spectators gathered to hear the trial in Morristown. Van Cortlandt freely admitted the charge against him was true, but a sympathetic jury acquitted him. He was still held in high regard by people who knew him. Yet, in December 1775 he mused on "the contrast" his neighbors presented "to the happy and contented people of but a short time ago."

Van Cortlandt and his wife serve to demonstrate the indignities heaped on Tories in Morris County and elsewhere. He fled to New York in December 1776, after refusing to take an oath of allegiance to the Continental Congress. He took one son with him, leaving his wife Catherine and their other eight children at the mercy of Patriots. He later wrote

In a mood of spiteful vengeance and humiliation, crowds parade a suspected Loyalist through the streets.

that they were treated "in a manner that would disgrace the most savage barbarians."

Left alone, Catherine found herself constantly harassed by soldiers who entered her home demanding food and lodging. Soon soldiers of a New England unit were housed

TEUCRO DUCE NIL DESPERANDUM.

First Battalion of PENNSYLVANIA LOYALISTS, commanded by His Excellency Sir WILLIAM HOWE, K. B.

ALL INTREPID ABLE-BODIED

HEROES,

WHO are willing to serve His MAJESTY KING GEORGE the Third, in Defence of their Country, Laws and Constitution, against the arbitrary Usurpations of a tyrannical Congress, have now not only an Opportunity of manifesting their Spirit, by assisting in reducing to Obedience their too-long deluded Countrymen, but also of acquiring the polite Accomplishments of a Soldier, by serving only two Years, or during the present Rebellion in America.

Such spirited Fellows, who are willing to engage, will be rewarded at the End of the War, besides their Laurels, with 50 Acres of Land, where every gallant Hero may retire, and enjoy his Bottle and Lass.

Each Volunteer will receive, as a Bounty, FIVE DOLLARS, besides Arms, Cloathing and Accoutrements, and every other Requisite proper to accommodate a Gentleman Soldier, by applying to Lieutenant Colonel ALLEN, or at Captain KEARNY's Rendezvous, at PATRICK TONRY's, three Doors above Market-street, in Second-street.

General Howe, commander of British forces in America, issued this broadside in 1777, seeking recruits for "the First Battalion of Pennsylvania Loyalists." A recruit would receive a signing bounty of $5, arms, clothing, and everything else needed by "a gentleman soldier." After the war, every volunteer was promised fifty acres of land, where he might retire and "enjoy his bottle and his lass."

there. Farmers refused to sell her food. Her children became ragged and shoeless.

She went to Morristown to plead her case with Washington. She did not see him but received a message that no help would be forthcoming unless Van Cortlandt returned. Soon after, her house became an emergency hospital, filled with soldiers who had been inoculated for smallpox.

Forced out of her home, Mrs. Van Cortlandt pleaded with Washington for a pass to join her husband and son in New York. The pass was granted. Mrs. Van Cortlandt and her children left Whippany on horseback during a late afternoon sleet storm. They were in New York about three days later.

In their earlier years in Morris County, the Van Cortlandts represented views common throughout the colonies. Before 1775, few leading Americans wanted, or even seriously imagined, a war with Great Britain. Their protests against taxes or other indignities were lodged as Englishmen, not revolutionaries. Benjamin Franklin believed in July 1773, that "every encroachment on rights is not worth a rebellion." Thomas Jefferson could write on August 25, 1775 — three months after the battles of Lexington and Concord — that he was still looking with fondness toward reconciliation with Great Britain.

Revolt against one's long-accepted country is civil war. While America did not split into sections, as it would do in the Civil War, it is generally estimated that when the war became reality, about one-third of Americans eagerly welcomed a fight, another third clung to their allegiance to the King, and the last third sat on the fence, ready to jump to the winning side.

New Jersey aptly reflected that divisions by thirds. Wherever there were Presbyterians — as in Newark, Elizabeth, Princeton, and Morristown — there was powerful support for a break with England. Where Church of England congregations prevailed — such as in Perth Amboy and Burlington — Loyalists were strong. Bergen County's predominantly Dutch population generally either opposed the war or remained neutral. The predominantly Quaker population in southern New Jersey wanted no part of the hostilities.

Within that formula-of-thirds lay the seeds of Loyalist-Patriot strife whose cruel violence at times exceeded the harshness of the armies. Loyalists became hated Tories and Patriots were despised by Tories as Whigs.

The enduring link to England remained strong in the thirteen colonies even after the first shot was fired at Concord. Of the twelve generals besides Washington who were appointed by Congress in June 1775, all but one — Nathanael Greene of Rhode Island — had held commissions under the Crown, even if only in the militia.

Morristown and its surrounding communities, founded and nurtured by largely Presbyterian inhabitants, had few resident Loyalists as the war approached. However, in 1777, the town became the central point for both jailing and trying Loyalists rounded up in surrounding New Jersey counties.

As the early war clouds thickened, it is unlikely that any other colony had a confused political situation exceeding New Jersey's. The colony's American-born, American-educated, Royal governor, William Franklin, the illegitimate son of Benjamin Franklin, was firmly loyal to the British government. Yet, as an American, he understood and sympathized with the temperament and yearnings of an emerging nation. More than any other colonial governor, Franklin combined wisdom, charm, patience, and tact to keep his subjects close to England.

Born in Philadelphia in 1731, William accompanied his illustrious father to England at age twenty-six. There he studied law and was admitted to the British bar. His six years in England gave him an awareness of the problems in governing colonies from 3,000 miles away.

Young Franklin returned to America in 1763 to become New Jersey's Royal Governor at age thirty-two, bringing with him a young bride. The handsome couple was heartily welcomed at his inauguration in Perth Amboy, one of the state's two colonial capitals. The other was Burlington on the Delaware River. The governor divided his residence between Perth Amboy and Burlington until 1774, when the Franklins moved into the handsome fourteen-room Perth Amboy mansion that the East New Jersey Proprietors had built to entice the governor to live in their thriving town on the Arthur Kill.

Franklin carefully and patiently pursued his thirteen-year reign as New Jersey's governor from 1763 to 1776. Nevertheless, he remained what his father called "a thorough government man" as England tightened the reins on its American colonies. Franklin held New Jerseyans together for more than a decade with a thin cord of allegiance that tied his constituents as much to him as to the mother country.

The cord frayed in the winter of 1776, after publication in January of Thomas Paine's vigorous pamphlet, *Common Sense*. Its clear call for revolution prompted Governor Franklin to express a "hope" that the tract would open the eyes of "people of sense and property" to awareness that dangerous words of anger fouled the colonial air. By people of property, the governor essentially meant the fellow Loyalists who surrounded him in Perth Amboy.

As the home of the Board of Proprietors of the Eastern Division of New Jersey, Perth Amboy was New Jersey's prime Loyalist breeding ground. Founded in 1684 — in London — the main, if not official, purpose of the Proprietors was to insure that the approximately three million acres of land they owned in eastern New Jersey would gradually be sold to a severely restricted upper class establishment as defined by the Proprietors. Few "American" economic ventures reeked more of direct ties to England than the East New Jersey Board of Proprietors.

A similar proprietor group, composed largely of Quakers and therefore professedly neutral in political beliefs, was founded in 1685 to own and control the 4,500 square miles of land in western New Jersey. Although its members had a political and financial stake in the outcome of the war and leaned toward England, there were few openly avowed Loyalists or Patriots among the Quakers.

Both boards of proprietors had almost complete economic and political power and, through their land ownership, expected guaranteed high-income levels. They were, in fact as well as in theory, a government in themselves. They controlled all transactions in unoccupied land, an opportunity for tremendous wealth. To be a proprietor was to be rich, socially superior, and aware that power stemmed from the freedoms granted them by the lords of London.

More than half of the proprietors stayed loyal to the king or walked the thin line of neutrality. Astonishingly, therefore, because of his avowed belief that he was a proper claimant to the English title of Lord Stirling, the first proprietor to commit himself openly was William Alexander, the board's surveyor general. He accepted an invitation late in the summer of 1775 from the Provincial Congress to recruit and command a regiment of New Jersey militia.

As the board's surveyor general, Alexander surveyed and registered land transfers, the lifeblood and raison d' etre of the proprietors. He devoted himself to the New Jersey militia so completely that confirmation of Proprietor land sales virtually ground to a halt.

The lord of Basking Ridge became the best recruiter of militia in his colony. His men boldly seized royal supplies and weapons, and raided a British ship entering New York harbor and carried away "some hundred pounds of gunpowder as well as other useful supplies."

On the other hand, if ever there was an American family destined to be Loyalists, it was the Skinners of Perth Amboy. Their Anglican heritage stemmed from the first Skinner in America, Reverend William Skinner, rector of St. Peter's Church of England in Perth Amboy from 1724 until his death in 1757. Cortlandt Skinner, one of his sons and a proprietor, became the colony's attorney general at age twenty-nine. As the war impended, he was one of New Jersey's most powerful political bellwethers.

Then, on January 8, 1776, the Colony's allegiance to Franklin ended. Acting on his own volition, Alexander ordered Lieutenant Colonel William Winds to ask Governor Franklin for "your word and honor you will not depart this province." When the governor resisted, Alexander ordered Winds to put Franklin under house arrest in the Proprietary House — a house that Alexander had been instrumental in designing and building.

That same night, troops also broke into Skinner's Perth Amboy home with orders to arrest him. He fled across the Arthur Kill to sanctuary on Staten Island, leaving behind his wife and twelve children. They joined him later in New York City and eventually the family grew to include five sons and eleven daughters.

A dozen other proprietors followed Skinner into Loyalist exile, including a younger brother Stephen, who fled to New York's Loyalist protection in March. He took with him his wife, ten children, a sister, several friends, and forty-four pipes of wine (at 126 gallons a pipe), the better to buoy his spirits in the event of a long war.

New Jersey's Loyalist leaders included, in addition to Franklin and the Skinners, New Jersey Chief Justice Frederick Smyth, the wealthy Kearnys, Rutherfurds and Parkers of Perth Amboy, the divided Ogden family of Newark and the split Hatfields of Elizabeth. Three of the Ogden sons became Loyalists, two became active revolutionists. In Elizabeth, Cornelius Hatfield, Jr. became a Loyalist but his father chose the Patriot cause.

On June 17, 1776, Franklin's tie to New Jersey's government ended. Soldiers dispatched that day by the New Jersey Provincial Congress seized the governor in his Perth Amboy home. The deposed governor lashed out at his captors as "supposed patriots bent on independent Republican tyranny." Soon after, he was marched to Connecticut under guard. In October 1778 he was exchanged for high-level revolutionist John McKinley, president of Delaware and a British prisoner in New York. Franklin went to the city and soon assumed leadership among New York Loyalists.

Franklin's arrest did not signify any overwhelming revolutionary spirit in New Jersey, as proved on July 2, 1776, when the colony's Provincial Congress reluctantly adopted a constitution that would make New Jersey a state in an evolving nation rather than a colony under the rule of King George III. The delegates hammered the constitution together after a mere eight days of debate.

The vote to adopt was far from a resounding cry for freedom. Thirty of the sixty delegates abstained. Of the thirty brave enough to vote, nine declared themselves against the constitution. Thus, only twenty-one of New Jersey's leading citizens (thirty-five percent, or about one-third of the delegation) opted for independence. Even that slender support was tempered in the document's closing paragraph:

> *If a reconciliation between Great Britain and these colonies should take place and the latter be taken again under the protection and government of the Crown of Great Britain, this charter shall be null and void.*

Despite that tenuous endorsement of independence, New Jersey was nevertheless the third of the thirteen colonies to adopt a written, signed declaration for freedom. Only New Hampshire and South Carolina had previously approved independent constitutions. Massachusetts and Virginia leaders, despite their fiery protestations of liberty, had not yet completely cut ties with England.

By July 2, the Loyalist versus Patriot schism was not wide anywhere. Those who abstained or voted against state constitutions, or who had not yet pushed for statehood,

The Proprietary House as it appeared in 1888. It was built between 1762 to 1764, by the East New Jersey Proprietors, to house the Royal governors of New Jersey. Governor William Franklin, the last Royal governor, and his wife moved into the home in 1774. The house later served as a private residence, as the Brighton Hotel, and as a Presbyterian home for disabled ministers and Presbyterian orphans.

certainly were not all Tories. Many saw economic disaster in leaving the comfortable leadership and protection that Great Britain had offered for more than a century.

Two days after New Jersey declared itself a state, the Declaration of Independence was made public in Philadelphia, but signing did not come until August 2. The gauntlet had been thrown down. What Lexington and Concord, or state constitutions, had not brought — an official war — had now been declared.

Brigadier General William Livingston resigned his New Jersey militia commission when he was chosen to be the state's first non-Royal governor on August 30, 1776. He suspected that many of his militia officers had been secretly committed to "the King's Prosperity" rather than to "the health and freedom of this State." Such Tory officers, he feared, "would embrace the first opportunity to cut our throats."

The governor's apprehension was far-fetched rhetoric; his pre-Revolution, Tory-leaning officers were most likely of the same class as he: wealthy, well-connected, respected professionals and politically powerful men. Nearly all of them could be expected to be loyal to the government that had ruled the colonies for nearly a century. Livingston's words

On the night of January 8, 1776, Lieutenant Colonel William Winds put Royal Governor William Franklin under house arrest in the Proprietary House in Perth Amboy.

evidenced, however, that bitterness had begun to replace reason.

The pressure to choose sides intensified in late November and early December as the British and Hessians drove Washington's army southward out of Bergen County, through Newark, across the Raritan River at New Brunswick, and finally into winter camp in Pennsylvania.

The amnesty offered by the invading British to all loyal subjects was observed more in promise than in deed. British and Hessian soldiers ran amok, pillaging the homes of Loyalists, Patriots and neutralists with impartiality. A contemporary account told of the plight of one Newark Loyalist as General William Howe's army swept through Newark:

> *There was one Nuttman, who had always been a remarkable Tory, and who met the British troops with huzzahs of joy, but had his house plundered of almost everything. He himself had his shoes taken off his feet and was threatened to be hanged, so that with difficulty he escaped from being murdered by them.*

Poor Nuttman! He became a quintessential victim of a civil war. The former militia captain, friend of the British and now grown old in service, saw his joy at seeing the British turn to bitter mistreatment. Later, when the fortunes of war swung the other way, American troops arrested Nuttman and clapped him into jail in Morristown. Both sides had served notice that niceties had come to an end.

After informing his troops that the late 1776 push on the Americans was to restore order and to help loyal Americans return to their rightful government, Howe distributed a broadside inviting all Americans in central New Jersey to rejoin the fold. Anyone who did so within sixty days and promised to remain "in a peaceful obedience" to His Majesty would receive a "full and free pardon" for anything he had done. He was also given a certificate that guaranteed his life and property. Significant numbers of New Jerseyans accepted the invitation — about 3,000 according to British sources. Americans disputed the estimate and claimed that the actual figures tended to show a lack of Loyalist strength among middle class Americans.

As Howe unleashed his dove of peace and his guarantees of life and property, his men continued to hammer out a different and ugly message of pillaging, looting and ravishing through the countryside south of the Raritan River. Any recruits gained were more than offset by those who became ardent Patriots after the viciousness of the British and Hessians.

British Major John André, who would find his great war role later, was horrified by the conduct of Howe's army as it pursued the desperate American army across New Jersey to the Delaware River. He asked: "What can be said to vindicate a conduct so atrocious which involves our friends in ruin and falsifies the word of the general?"

Washington's army had only limited reason to fear Tories in Morristown during the winter of 1777. The predominantly Presbyterian population assured strong area support for the cause. There was naturally a continuing fear that an attempt might be made to kidnap or assassinate Washington, but his strong personal Life Guard stationed near headquarters was constantly alert.

Washington tightened the screws on the Tories on January 25, 1777, when he issued a proclamation in Morristown, notifying all suspected Loyalists they must either take an oath of allegiance to the United States or admit they preferred "the interest and protection of Great Britain to the freedom and happiness of their country." In the latter case they were "forthwith to withdraw themselves and their families within the enemy's lines."

The proclamation completely reversed previous conditions of what property departing Loyalists could take with them. Initially, everything — including livestock — was considered acceptable. Now it was ordered that "such as go over to the Enemy, are not to take with them anything but their clothing and furniture. Their horses, cattle and forage must be left behind."

When those choosing American "freedom and happiness" declined in numbers as summer began, New Jersey's Committee of Safety stepped up vigorous efforts to quell rising Tory strength. Loyalists had one of two choices: Take an oath of allegiance immediately or have their estates confiscated. Loyalists who had already fled to New York could return, take the oath, and save their properties.

The response was still sparse in August. The Committee directed Colonel Winds to lead fast-moving militia on continuing Tory roundups in Morris, Hunterdon, Bergen, and Essex counties. Major Samuel Hays led similar raids in Bergen and Essex counties. The militia knocked on targeted doors, burst into living rooms, crashed into meetings, or stomped thoughtlessly through fields of ripening corn. The orders in essence read: arrest first, question later.

Hundreds of known or suspected Loyalists were taken into custody; about half were released when no evidence against them could be found. The rest went to Morristown, where the most belligerent were placed in the tiny jail to await trial. Others were paroled within the town limits. Arresting some less offensive Tories was part of a wartime game of tit-for-tat. The British in New York had mistreated and jailed many Whigs on flimsy pretexts.

In September and October, the trials of twenty-four alleged Loyalists in Morristown belied the belief that most Tories were older, wealthy, and politically powerful men. These prisoners were essentially a young, low-income group. Some were in their teens and nearly three quarters were age twenty-five or younger. They generally said they had no trade or were employed in jobs that required little knowledge or training. Most were sentenced to be hanged in Morristown on December 2, but only two actually died on the gallows. The others escaped death by enlisting in the Continental Army.

The exceptions, James Iliff and John Mee, refused to take the American oath. Iliff had been an officer in a British Loyalist regiment, and Mee had previously been a member of the British regular army. When offered the chance to escape hanging by enlisting in the American army, both said they would rather die than sacrifice their loyalty to the King. Their wish was granted.

In 1777, a foray into Hunterdon County netted James Parker, president of the East New Jersey Proprietors, and board member Walter Rutherfurd. Both had proclaimed their neutrality and lived comfortably in the Hunterdon hills. They were taken to Morristown as hostages for two Americans imprisoned by the British.

Rutherfurd and Parker were at first well treated and even allowed paroles to visit their homes. But, in December, when they returned from one of the paroles, they were cast into what Mrs. Rutherfurd called "the common jail, filled with dirt and vermin." She wrote her husband that "surely the governor cannot mean that horrid dungeon" for distinguished and wealthy neutrals. The governor agreed; the two were placed on permanent parole in February 1778.

Oppressively hot July days and nights, combined with wretched food and a lack of air, caused great discomfort and suffering in the Morristown jail for prisoners less well connected than Rutherfurd and Parker. Three Essex County men begged to be returned to the Newark jail to free them from "the stench and filth of the gaol, the unhealthy state of the air in the town of Morris, and the prevalence of the bloody flux, and camp fever in said town." They added:

> Sufferings in the gaol of Morris have been exceedingly grievous. Sometimes upwards of 50 have been confined with them in one room not exceeding 18 feet square. Frequently water was not to be had from the failure of the public pump. Often they have been obliged to fast 48 hours; unless relieved by the charity of families in the neighborhood they must have starved to death.

The Tory-Whig enmity intensified as a war-within-a-war, particularly in New Jersey's so-called "Neutral Ground" between the Watchung Mountains and the Hudson River, where Loyalist detachments struck often across the river from New York. Usually facing them would be their counterparts, the foot soldiers of the New Jersey Militia.

Americans from New Jersey, Connecticut, and New York's Hudson River valley fled to New York City to join Loyalist regiments. They attacked one-time neighbors with revenge-motivated ferocity — killing, burning, plundering, and turning the neutral zone into a hit-and-run battlefield. The American militia would retaliate with equal hatred.

American-born, American-bred Loyalists seemed to London a likely source for desperately needed new troops. Cortland Skinner, the wealthy New Jersey refugee who had fled to New York to escape arrest in Perth Amboy, stepped up early. He won instant appointment to brigadier general in the New Jersey Volunteers, a regiment of five battalions of Loyalist troops.

Skinner's willingness to muster Loyalist troops won strong encouragement from the Crown, but only if the Americans served in the British army as foot soldiers. Few accepted the low pay, strict discipline and social inferiority of an ordinary British soldier. Their lives as Americans had made them too proud and too accustomed to leadership in whatever enterprise they fostered.

London then decided it would be best to form Loyalist regiments recruited by state or geographic ties. They were to be officered by what the King's officials labeled "natives of America" — but British officers could not be excluded from the Loyalist regiments if they wished to serve.

Skinner found his own soldiers, mostly from New Jersey. He had 517 officers and men in late 1777, and had more than doubled that in two years to 1,101. On December 20, 1777, General William Howe, commander of British forces in America, wrote his London superior, Lord George Sackville Germaine, Secretary of State for the American Colonies, that Skinner's performance merited a commendation.

General Clinton's enthusiasm for Loyalist troops was lukewarm. He wrote Germaine that "many attempts to raise men have always totally failed of success, and some corps which at first were thought to be of importance have remained in so very weak a state that there is little encouragement to undertake anything more in that line."

The major problem, Clinton recognized, was that while potential provincial officers volunteered in such numbers that there was a waiting list, enlistments as privates were few. The British commander mistrusted "the sanguine hopes of gentlemen" whose offer of services included expectations that high rank, uniforms, food, and arms would be supplied.

In the summer of 1779, General William Tryon urged William Franklin to organize what Tryon called the Associated Loyalists, freewheeling groups of refugees who would raid the countryside in Connecticut, New York, and New Jersey as lawless freebooters. Whatever booty they secured would be split among themselves, a kind of reckless, British-approved land piracy.

Tryon's name was associated with brutal savagery. In November 1777, his Loyalists had plundered and burned Tarrytown on the Hudson River. When Tarrytown's defenders protested the wanton plundering, indiscriminate burning, and inhumane treatment of non-combatants, Tryon responded:

> I should, were I more in authority, burn every committeeman's house within reach, as I deem those agents the wicked instruments of the continued calamities of this country.

Tryon also led seven days of Loyalist plundering and burning on the Connecticut coast in July 1779, an operation approved in London. Two thousand of Tryon's invaders burned nearly a thousand buildings and returned triumphantly to New York with several hundred thousand dollars worth of stolen goods.

Clinton vigorously protested the formation of the Associated Loyalists, not because of Tryon's demonstrated brutality but because he feared independent military units might "alarm the enemy when he [Clinton] might wish to lull them into security." Tryon and his followers appealed directly to Lord Germaine and obtained approval to unleash their freebooters. Franklin eagerly accepted command of the disreputable new group, not surprising in view of his bitterness when forcibly removed as Governor of New Jersey. He wanted revenge, a typical Loyalist point of view before and after formation of the Associates.

Raiding was not new for the Loyalists; they had been rampaging through villages in New Jersey, New York, and elsewhere through 1779, burning churches, barns, houses, and anything else available as they drove off cattle and carried away looted goods. The difference was that the marauders now had financial gains from their plundering.

Capturing General Washington was a recurring Clinton dream. Barring that, a second target in British fantasy was Governor William Livingston, who owned a manorial home on the outskirts of Elizabeth, New Jersey. Late in March 1779, Livingston wrote Clinton a furious letter complaining "I am possessed of the most authentic proof of a general officer under your command having offered a large sum of money to an inhabitant of this state to assassinate me in case he could not take me alive."

Livingston gave Clinton "this opportunity for disavowing such dark proceedings." However, if Clinton had "countenanced" the deed, Livingston boasted — perhaps foolishly —"your person is more in my power than I have reason to think you imagine."

Although Clinton seldom resorted to bon mots, he won a decisive edge in sarcastic wit with his reply a fortnight later:

Had I a soul capable of harbouring so infamous an idea as assassination, you, Sir, at least would have nothing to fear; for be assured I would not blacken myself with so foul a crime to obtain so trifling an end.

Nearly all Loyalists remained true to England even after Yorktown, when finally they knew their cause was doomed. They recognized, of course, that they had no place in the rising nation they professed to despise. Fleet after fleet after fleet of British transports carried them to their final destinations. Thousands sailed for England, faithful to the end. Ultimately, most settled for large grants of acreage in Canada, particularly in Nova Scotia, and generous grants of money from the King.

Among the departing throng were about a thousand African-Americans who had joined the British army to escape their slave bonds. When American protests rose that these men were "property," British General Guy Carlton, Clinton's successor, declared that the men had been freed by British proclamation and were sailing as free men. They peacefully boarded a ship bound for Nova Scotia.

One case helps prove the point that a Loyalist could not expect peaceful old age in America. Tory Cavalier Jouett, who had been a prisoner in Woodbridge, New Jersey, returned after the war with his family, hoping to take up permanent residence. Jouett was met with a scorn that nearly erupted into violence. Residents told him he "had no right or title to come here." Some of the town's most bitter men, armed with sticks and whips surrounded him, threatening a "continental jacket" [tar and feathers] if he persisted in his effort to become a citizen of Woodbridge.

"What have I ever done to any of you?" Jouett asked. An angry chorus yelled that he was a traitor to his country. One clear voice rose above the din to give Jouett the farewell message:

No such damned rascal should ever enjoy the benefits of this country again.

One Who Was Loyal

James Moody of Sussex County, New Jersey, wrote that he lived in "the best climate in the best country in the world" — that is, until the Declaration of Independence was drafted. Then he made no secret of his belief that this rebellion was "the foulest of crimes."

According to his own account, Lieutenant James Moody's narrative of his *Exertions and Sufferings*, written and published in London in 1783, Moody took "every possible precaution not to give offense" during the early days of the war. Late in March 1777, an armed mob of former friends attacked him on his farm but Moody escaped. The Sussex Tory returned within a month and convinced seventy-three "loyal" neighbors from Sussex County and lower New York State to join Cortlandt Skinner's Loyalist regiment being recruited in New York. He returned home again in June, seeking more "loyal men." He claimed that this time 500 followed him into the Loyalist ranks, undoubtedly a highly exaggerated estimate. Moody never underestimated his abilities or his successes.

Moody led a daring raid on Tinton Falls in Monmouth County in June 1778 to destroy a powder magazine. He spied constantly on the American army at Morristown in 1779-80, by pilfering mail or examining army records.

The bold Tory led a dash toward Morristown in May 1780 in an effort to trap "someone of note" (probably New Jersey Governor William Livingston). That venture failed before it began when one of Moody's men was captured and revealed the plot. After the aborted attempt to kidnap Livingston, Moody issued a joking proclamation, offering 200 guineas for "a certain William Livingston, late an attorney at law and now a *lawless usurper and incorrigible rebel.*" If *all* of Livingston could not be taken, the proclamation offered half the reward money for "his ears and nose, which are too well known, and too remarkable to be mistaken."

It became difficult at times to know whether Moody was serving as a Loyalist soldier or a British spy. On one run into Morristown, he paused to read and copy troop rosters to determine the army's strength in Jockey Hollow. On other occasions, even when captured and led to prison, he made mental notes of camp locations and general conditions in all areas.

General Anthony Wayne captured Moody late in 1779 near West Point. He was kept under heavy surveillance and then shackled and placed under heavy guard to be taken to General Washington. Along the way that night, he broke the bolt on his handcuffs, knocked down a careless sentry and stole his musket. When soldiers responded to an alarm, he calmly joined them in the darkness without being detected.

Moody's tale of freeing a Loyalist prisoner from a New Town (Newton) jail in Sussex County was based entirely on his autobiography, publsihed in London after the war. Moody also furnished all details for this drawing of the prisoner being released from his chains.

He drifted away in a few minutes and made his way back to New York.

Few, if any, loyalists worked so diligently or so audaciously as Moody. He conducted daring raids in the area between the Watchung Mountains and the Hudson River, usually as a freelance raider without orders. On one occasion he intercepted correspondence between the French general Le Comte de Rochambeau and Washington as the two planned the march that eventually led to Yorktown.

Shortly after, Moody raided the New Town (Newton) jail in his home county and freed a Loyalist prisoner. The accompanying illustration, from Moody's book, portrays that action. After the war, Moody sailed to England to write and publish his memoirs. Eventually he joined other Loyalists in Nova Scotia, where he lived until his death.

Chapter Fourteen

GEORGE WASHINGTON: SPY MASTER

Washington knew as early as the summer of 1776 that he needed an extensive spy system. As he tried to keep the army alive during their escape from New York City, he believed "nothing is more necessary than good intelligence to frustrate a designing enemy & nothing that requires greater pains to obtain." The first winter in Morristown, and the one at Middlebrook — each close to New York and the British Army — intensified the need for a top-flight spy network.

Washington started from scratch, aware that he must be personally in charge of the network, with information always filtering upward to him. He needed perceptive, completely trustworthy and daring agents who could move easily within enemy territory. His spies needed little or no disguise to slip through the countryside or into or out of New York, using legitimate businesses as their cover. Infiltration was a two-sided coin, as useful and as easy for the British as for Washington's men.

Many of the spies were unpaid volunteers. Their information could be faulty, but dedicated professionals weighed and interpreted whatever was passed on to them by those outside the loop. By the time Washington led his army into Morristown for the winter of 1777, the spy system was in rudimentary order. It would face an immediate test.

The war's first major ruse, and perhaps the greatest if viewed from the need to survive, came early that winter. Washington's diminished army of about 3,000 men in the first week of January was losing soldiers at a disturbing rate, through expiring term enlistments, desertions, and disease.

The late arrival in town made it necessary to scatter soldiers in private homes throughout the area surrounding Morristown. Most neighbors estimated the troop strength at about 15,000 men. That "fact" quickly reached General William Howe, the British Commander in New York. Washington confidently advised Congress "we are deceiving our enemies with false opinions of our numbers."

The euphoria was punctured in February, when all Continental Army men were being inoculated for smallpox protection. At one time, a thousand or more soldiers were recovering in homes and makeshift hospitals. Washington feared the British might take advantage of the large numbers of stricken men to launch a major attack on Morristown.

In 1778 Major Tallmadge of Connecticut was twenty-four years old when chosen to head Washington's spy ring, where he established a highly successful espionage service for the Continental Army. Later he played an important role in helping to unmask Benedict Arnold as a traitor.

Howe sent a spy, masking himself as a merchant, to get solid numbers on Continental troop strength. The British agent was easily detected but Washington ordered that he not be arrested. Rather, he was to be quietly befriended. As the pleasant relationships expanded, so did the false information picked up by the visiting spy. Washington ordered every brigade commander to submit highly inflated written lists of troop strength that would total about 12,000 men fit and ready for action.

The spy, making his rounds, became friendly with a high-ranked officer, who deliberately left the false figures in plain sight in his pigeonholed desk. Then, the prying visitor was invited to dine with the officer. During a pre-meal chat, the American received an "emergency call" from his superior. He excused himself, said he would be gone for about twenty minutes, and left the room.

Artist Howard Pyle's interpretation of the hanging of American spy Nathan Hale, in New York on September 22, 1776. Hale became renowned for allegedly declaring his only regret was that he had but one life to give for his country.

The merchant-spy raced to the desk, pulled out the false brigade lists and rapidly jotted down numbers that, sure enough, totaled about 12,000. While very high, it was believable in light of some wild guesses that had set American strength as high as 40,000 men. The Continental officer returned and the two sat down to a pleasant dinner. The spy's detailed, false report rapidly made its way to the British, reassuring Howe that he had acted wisely in not attacking Morristown.

Meanwhile, a Loyalist officer from Elizabeth named William Luce, paroled in Morristown on his promise not to flee, roamed freely, compiling true numbers that laid bare the American misinformation. He violated his parole and fled to New York to present his findings to Howe personally, expecting the glory and praise surely due a man who brought good news.

Instead, Howe rebuked Luce savagely, citing the false reports previously received. He accused Luce of being a double agent, bearing enemy-inspired propaganda. After threatening to "hang him up the first tree," Howe relented and satisfied himself by dismissing

Luce with "contempt & severity."

Apparently enjoying this secret life in the shadows of deceit, Washington encouraged double-dealing, profiting from the lies he fed his enemies, or the truths he stole from them. He gained a defensive edge from misleading the British by any means possible — a hoax, misdirection, or false statistics deliberately leaked to known British agents.

The British also played the spy game expertly, and they had been playing the game for a far longer time. They exploited ardent Loyalists in Morristown and elsewhere in New Jersey who were eager to report American troop strengths, military movements, and the status of supplies.

Washington immersed himself in the tools of the trade — secret meeting places, aliases, double-dealing, codes, ciphers, "invisible" ink, and the art of finesse. He also secretly secured the hard money (gold and silver coins) that most spies demanded; no capable agent could be expected to accept nearly worthless Continental paper money.

Shortly before the Battle of Trenton, Washington sent an urgent letter to Robert Morris, asking for hard specie "to pay a certain set of people who are of particular use to us." (He meant spies, of course.) The money was sent in two canvas bags that reportedly held "410 Spanish dollars, two English crowns, ten shillings and sixpence." Washington recounted the incident seven years later as he was explaining his war expenses to Congress.

Major Benjamin Tallmadge of Connecticut, twenty-four years old, was chosen in 1778 to command the Continental spy network. He was a former schoolteacher, and, as a Yale graduate, a friend of Nathan Hale, the young Yale man who was caught and hanged in New York on September 22, 1776. Hale had attempted a dangerous espionage job that required far more than raw courage. He was judged guilty, and summarily hanged. He went calmly to the gallows.

A few days after the execution, a British officer recalled that he had heard Hale say: "I regret that I have but one life to give for my country." Those bold, defiant words (which may or may not have been exactly what Hale said) spread like wildfire through the American ranks and it is by that phrase that Hale is remembered, particularly in textbooks.

Although his stirring words earned the spy an enduring place in history, Hale in reality accomplished nothing except to spur awareness that the American spy network was virtually non-existent. By turning to Tallmadge, Washington signaled that America's secret espionage network would become fully organized.

Tallmadge had solid military accomplishments to support his demeanor as a suave workaholic; his appointment was not a political plum. He joined Connecticut's State Regiment in June 1776, and fought at Long Island, White Plains, Brandywine, Germantown, and Monmouth before Washington pulled him out of field service to run the army's spy network.

The War's Most Daring Exploit

Colonel John Graves Simcoe, commander of the famed Queen's Rangers, a Tory horse and foot unit, probably was the most successful, most reckless and most disturbing of all British officers.

Simcoe was known for hard fighting and brutal assaults on American troops, but his bravery was diminished by such occasional savagery as the massacre on March 21, 1778, of thirty Americans as they lay asleep in Judge William Hancock's house at Hancock's Bridge in Salem County.

Never one to shrink from duty, Simcoe served in America from the first fighting in the Boston area in 1775 to the battle at Yorktown. His most famous exploit was a spectacular dash across central New Jersey that began on the night of October 27, 1779.

Simcoe led his mounted Queens Rangers of out Elizabethtown and headed for the Raritan River. He paused in Quibbletown (now Rahway) and, coolly passing himself off as an American officer, drew supplies from an American quartermaster. Then he headed for Van Veghten's Bridge (Finderne) to destroy about thirty flat-bottomed boats, each capable of carrying seventy men.

The hard-riding Ranger was not the man to stop with only one job done. He raced on and burned an old Dutch church being used as a storehouse in Van Veghten. The night had just begun.

Simcoe's men pounded through the Millstone River valley in a dash that many historians believe was the most incredible single exploit of the war. Simcoe and his Rangers covered fifty-five miles in that one night. At Millstone, then known as Somerset Court House, they burned the courthouse, the jail, a church and several houses, striking terror throughout the valley.

As the marauders returned toward New Brunswick in the early morning of October 28, they were ambushed near Middlebush. Simcoe and four of his men were injured and captured; the remainder of the Rangers safely reached New Brunswick.

Simcoe was exchanged on December 1, 1779, and returned to fight with the traitor Benedict Arnold in the early January 1781 British attack on Richmond. He was among those who surrendered at Yorktown.

After the war, Simcoe became a member of the British Parliament and was appointed as the first governor of Canada in 1792. He selected Niagara (then called Newark) as his capital. Loyal subjects in Canada named a county, a town and a river for him.

Simcoe was dispatched to India in 1806 but took sick on the way out and died at sea on October 26, 1806, at age fifty-four.

Robert Townsend and Abraham Woodhull became paramount in what Tallmadge called the "Culper Ring." Woodhull assumed the alias Samuel Culper Sr. and Townsend became Culper Jr. in American spy circles. Every agent in the ring had an alias, including Tallmadge, who was known as John Bolton. They were in full readiness when the American Army wintered at Middlebrook in 1778-79 and at Morristown a year later.

Aliases were practical only when the spy rings were small and concentrated. Eventually so many spies were at work in the American system that Woodhull created an expansive code of 763 numbers that could identify by a number any agent, place name, type of mission, and a variety of other information. Washington, for example, was "711," not number "1" as might have been anticipated.

The code was so complicated that agents needed a code dictionary to decipher incoming messages or to compose their own work. Compounding the secrecy, messages were often written in "invisible ink" and allegedly could be read only if a special "sympathetic liquid" was spread over the "disappeared" ink to make messages reappear. Children in the elementary grades can duplicate the simple chemistry feat today, but in colonial times invisible ink was as mysterious and advanced as is a modern coded message from a spy satellite. Tallmadge was an almost-perfect choice to lead the Culper Ring. He was a respected merchant in New York, carrying on a thriving trade in flax, sugar, rum, iron goods, and dry goods, and had a second office in Oyster Bay, Long Island. He was so circumspect that the British thought he was a Loyalist.

Austin Roe, the ring's Long Island courier, brought Townsend's goods into the city, along

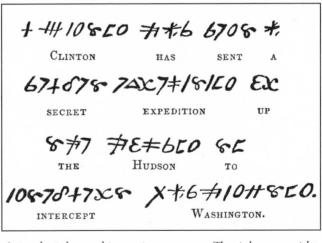

A simple cipher and its use in a sentence. The cipher was said to have been devised by Loyalists to communicate with family, friends and non-Patriots. More complex ciphers were developed as the skills of the users increased.

with coded questions, and carried answers back to Oyster Bay. These special "orders" were delivered to a pre-arranged drop box on the edge of a field Woodhull rented in Setauket. Roe knew the recipient only as number 722 — actually "Samuel Culper Sr.," the code name for Woodhull.

Woodhull sent messages to Washington via boatman Caleb Brewster (725), who anchored his whaleboats in any one of six Long Island Sound coves. The contact depended on a female spy's clothesline. A black petticoat on the line meant Brewster was ready to row. Beside the undergarment would be from one to six white handkerchiefs, each number representing a cove where Brewster would be that night.

James Rivington's New York newspaper, The Royal Gazette, *fervently promoted the British and Loyalist cause during the war. Cautiously friendly with members of Washington's spy ring, Rivington was not revealed as a double agent until 1959.*

After dark, Brewster received the messages, hoisted sail and sneaked his boat through English patrols in Long Island Sound as he headed for Fairfield, Connecticut. There, a courier sped the messages to Tallmadge, who would get them to Washington in Morristown, or wherever he might be. The system was never breached.

Another highly effective and, for the participants, highly risky, American spy ring was established on Staten Island. Its proprietors were multi-generations of the Mersereau family.

The Mersereaus became involved in spying in late November 1776, when Washington asked the family patriarch, Joshua Mersereau, to suggest someone who could stay behind as a spy in New Brunswick as American forces fled out of town to escape an onrushing British force. Joshua recommended his young son, John, who had a withered arm and could not be an active warrior.

John's youthful appearance and fine manners convinced the British that he was a Tory. They let him return to Staten Island, where his family lived. He smuggled messages to the

Americans through a courier who worked as an apprentice in his father's shipyard. When the apprentice was captured by the British, John added the risky job of courier to his spying duties.

Paddling a raft to New Jersey to meet contacts was extremely trying for handicapped John. He eased his burden by devising a simple but ingenious device for protecting himself. He put messages in a weighted bottle and dragged it behind the raft with a stout cord. If apprehended, John could sever the cord, the bottle would sink, and Mersereau would become nothing more than a fisherman out for his daily catch.

The Mersereau trio, John, the younger; Joshua, his father; and John the elder, his uncle, crossed the channel between the island and New Jersey untold times. None was ever caught.

Spies sought anonymity, of course, but no one ever pursued the role more zealously than Lieutenant Lewis J. Costigan of the First New Jersey Brigade. When Washington wanted information on the British position in New Brunswick in late December 1776, he asked Colonel Matthias Ogden, First New Jersey commander, to name someone familiar with the town. Ogden chose Costigan because he had lived there previously.

Instructed personally by Washington, Costigan was asked to ascertain the strength of the British in New Brunswick and the size of their baggage train. Knowing what the general wanted, Costigan slipped into New Brunswick and secured the information. He was stopped and arrested by a British patrol as he left the town on January 1, 1777. Since he was in full uniform, he was not charged with spying or any other serious crime.

The British sent Costigan to New York as a prisoner on parole. Nearly nine months later he was exchanged, but instead of leaving New York and returning to his regular Army outfit as was customary, he stayed in the city and became a freelance agent without portfolio. He somehow learned the network of spy connections and began sending Washington secret messages on information he gained by walking about New York and chatting with British officers.

Costigan signed his communications "Z" and they were forwarded to Washington at Middlebrook with that one-letter signature. Washington never knew the identity of this underground agent, although that was not unusual in the secret service's passion for security. However, the general acknowledged receipt of a "Z-mail" as late as January 2, 1779.

On March 15, 1779, two months after Costigan had returned to active duty, Washington asked what had happened to "Z." He did not learn until 1782 the identity of the spy who never officially came in from the cold. Costigan wrote the general that year, asking for reimbursement for £113 to cover expenses he had paid out of his own pocket while spying in New York. He was paid — in his real name.

Washington returned in the summer of 1780 to the masterful double cross that had worked so well in fooling Howe in the winter of 1777. To start, British agents learned in the late spring of 1780 — probably almost as soon as Washington was told — that a French fleet was on the way with several thousand well-equipped, well-conditioned soldiers. With his main army in New York drained by the campaign in the south, Clinton asked London to have the British Navy intercept the incoming flotilla and destroy or weaken it before the vessels docked in Newport, Rhode Island.

British spies had reached into Washington's Morristown headquarters and into the very halls of Congress in Philadelphia for knowledge of the approaching French. But spy rings run in both directions: American spies brought Washington news that Clinton was working on a plan to intercept the French.

The Culper Ring went into action, and soon the British offices in New York were flooded with misleading information that the Americans planned to attack New York with 10,000 or 12,000 troops as soon as the British sailed for Rhode Island. That killed thoughts of intercepting the fleet. The actuality, which the British should have known, or at least suspected, was that Washington would have been lucky to get 4,000 physically fit troops into action.

The British and the Americans both used the printed word to deceive or to delude. Late in May 1780, only two days after a mutiny of the Connecticut Regiment, when spirits were sinking in the American ranks, a handbill, titled *Address to the Soldiers of the Continental Army*, was clandestinely distributed throughout the Jockey Hollow camp. It began with a blunt message:

> *The time is at length arrived, when all of the artifice and falsehoods of the Congress and your commanders can no longer conceal from you the misery of your situation; you are neither Clothed, Fed, nor Paid. Your numbers are wasting away by Sickness, Famine, Nakedness, and rapidly so by the period of your stipulated services, being in general expired.*

It was impossible to deny these facts. The survival of America was on the brink. The solution was simple, the British writer said:

> *You must quit your leaders and join your real friends who scorn to impose on you, and who will receive you with open arms, kindly forgiving all your errors.*

More regularly, if less bluntly, newspapers in both New York and New Jersey scorned the enemy's course of the war. New York's leading paper, The *Royal Gazette*, edited by the strident — and capable — James Rivington, kept up a non-stop campaign of boosting Loyalist support and damning the American cause. Fast-moving Rebel spies transmitted copies to Morristown. The newspaper was, in effect, another eye on New York, however slanted, for American spies.

Long after the war ended, it became known that Robert Townsend, leader of the Culper spy ring, and Rivington actually were good friends, business associates, and co-conspirators. Townsend was a silent partner in a tavern owned by Rivington and frequented by British officers who talked freely of strategies as rum loosened their tongues. What Townsend did not hear personally, Rivington, the quintessential double agent (known as "Number 726"), was willing to supply.

Rivington continued to write his bitter, acidic attacks on the Americans, and Townsend even contributed unsigned articles from time to time to the *Gazette*. What either said in the New York newspaper was nowhere near the truths they scribbled to send off to Washington via the Culper Ring.

Neither side knew of it, but a double-dealing that would dwarf all spy action in the war was on the horizon. A Mr. Anderson, for the British, and a Mr. Monk (or Mr. Moore), for the Americans, were engaged in secret talks that, if successful, could stun the Americans into surrender.

Page one of the first New Jersey Journal, *printed on February16, 1779, featured the war as seen from Granada. Most issues of the* Journal *featured "news' fom far-off places, usually a month or more old.*

Managed News

Shepard Kollock, a journeyman printer who had become a lieutenant in the artillery corps, was permitted to resign from the army under peculiar circumstances on January 3, 1779. General Henry Knox approved the resignation on the promise Kollock would "establish a paper in the State of New Jersey, in defense of freedom."

Kollock had followed a long journalistic trail. Born in Delaware, he had his first journalistic experience on Philadelphia's *Pennsylvania Journal*, owned by his uncle. He then journeyed to St. Christopher in the West Indies, to serve as a journeyman on an island newspaper. When his brother became an officer in the British army, Kollock decided to seek a commission in the Continental army.

After long artillery service in the field, Kollock willingly undertook establishment of a pro-army newspaper through which information and misinformation could be funneled into the British spy pipeline. Two centuries later, the United States armed forces would call this "managed news."

Kollock set up shop in a tavern on the main street in Chatham and acquired a printing press and type, both scarcities at the time. The greater problem was paper. The army helped by sending old tents from Morristown to be converted into newsprint. Kollock set up a paper mill on the Passaic River in Chatham. One of his earliest advertisements was for "clean linen rags" for his mill.

The first issue of Kollock's weekly *New Jersey Journal* appeared on February

16, 1779. It cost "three shillings in produce or three shillings, nine pence in hard money" for each quarter of the year. There was no startling army misinformation — or much other news in a paper dominated by local advertisers. The weekly ads supplied information and cause for gossip in a busy crossroads village.

The *Journal* was, for its day and its purpose, a reasonably good newspaper, with straightforward accounts of local happenings as well as details of the numerous skirmishes on the plains east of the Watchung Mountains. But it stuck by its founding credo to mislead the enemy whenever possible. The "news" must at times also have astonished the soldiers in Jockey Hollow, particularly the long, pleasant article in midwinter 1780 that told of the comforts and well being of the troops hutting amidst the oaks

Shepard Kollock

south of Morristown. It was an attempt to delude the British into thinking that all was well in Jockey Hollow. Enemy spies must have laughed as heartily as soldiers in the Jockey Hollow huts.

Early in July 1780, when enemy forces moved out of Elizabeth toward Springfield, Kollock moved his entire operation — press, type, paper and work tables — to nearby Bottle Hill (Madison) for a few weeks.

Kollock welcomed submissions from his readers as long as they were not "too personal," "too poignant" or were "without rhime (sic) nor (sic) poetical beauty." He once rejected an essay on "The Pleasures of Celibacy" because "we profess ourselves advocates for the connubial state." In short, he accepted nearly everything with which he agreed.

The *Journal* improved slowly, both in its mission to present Washington, the army and the nation in a good light and in coverage of local news. After the war, it continued publication and became the *Elizabeth Daily Journal*.

In 1783, Kollock expressed his objectives for his little country newspaper, perhaps not objectivity:

> The editor, while a publisher of the New Jersey Journal, exerted every faculty to stimulate his countrymen to oppose the galling yoke we were threatened with, and to maintain the cause of freedom and the rights of mankind even at the risk of his personal safety.

Chapter Fifteen

The TRIAL *of* BENEDICT ARNOLD

An elegant carriage drawn by four fine horses raced into snowy Morristown a few days before Christmas in 1779, circled the town green and stopped at one of the taverns. Out stepped a medium height, sturdy two-star general, the very image of military success in his spotless, tailored uniform and his intensely polished black boots. He limped noticeably, evidence that his rank and prestige had been hard won.

He had what would today be called charisma, in his ease with the group of officers who welcomed him, and his ruggedly handsome, dark face, somewhat marred by a very large nose. The dark skin and prominent nose allegedly had caused Indians to call him the "Black Eagle." His eyes, ice-gray and piercing, were remembered forever by anyone who looked into them. On the December day of his arrival, flakes from the light snow that sifted across the frozen streets highlighted his thick black hair.

He was Major General Benedict Arnold, hero of Ticonderoga, Quebec, Lake Champlain, Danbury, and Saratoga, a soldier esteemed by some in both Congress and the army as superior to George Washington in military skills. Washington valued Arnold's abilities and his bravery, and several times came to his aid in difficult personal situations off the battlefields.

Arnold needed any help he could get. His long record of success in battle had been perpetually tainted by an odor of rascality and even implications of downright thievery. He had been accused of, but never prosecuted for, mismanaging his army accounts. His sudden rise to fortune in 1778-79 as the American commander in Philadelphia provoked the question: how could he live so regally on the meager pay of an American major general?

Arnold was not in Morristown to consult with Washington or even to be received by him. He had come to face a court martial for a string of minor incidents that allegedly had occurred in Philadelphia. Few believed the charges. Washington had urged Arnold to ask for the trial, believing that a certain verdict of innocent would end the gossip and speculation regarding Arnold's activities in Philadelphia.

How could a group of his peers find guilty a man who had served his country so well since he left his Connecticut home, his wife, and three sons to take his militia unit to Boston after the battles of Lexington and Concord in 1775? Nearly everyone knew, in 1779, of his vaunted military record and his reputation as a daring officer who led his men into battle rather than

One of the most recognized names in American history is that of Benedict Arnold, the highly respected American officer who sought to sell out to the British even as he faced a court martial in Morristown in December 1779.

ordering them to close with the enemy while he coached from the rear.

Nearly any officer or enlisted man with long service could recite Arnold's exploits and tell of his twice-wounded leg. They could recount the skills he first demonstrated, in May 1775, at the English-held Fort Ticonderoga on Lake Champlain. His men and Ethan Allen's Green Mountain Boys had jointly overcome British defenders and had entered the fort together as a symbol of shared conquest.

Arnold returned home from Fort Ticonderoga to find his wife had died, his three sons were adrift, and that his superiors had charged him with mishandling funds allocated for the Ticonderoga affair. Most gallingly to Arnold, Allen was hailed as the sole conqueror of Ticonderoga. Most popular accounts of the capture of the fort credited Ethan Allen and his Green Mountain Boys as the heroes, with little mention of Arnold or his troops.

Dickerson's Tavern, where Benedict Arnold was tried in 1779, stood at the corner of Spring and Water streets. The tavern was badly damaged by fire early in the twentieth century and was rebuilt as "The Yellow House." That structure was later demolished.

Arnold was absolved of the money mismanagement, but his life had begun to spin in a series of cycles that had led toward his upcoming court martial — brilliant in battle, ignored in acclaim, and shadowed in assorted charges that would demean his character and tarnish his luster off the battlefields.

Forever in the memory of his soldiers was Arnold's almost-legendary attempt to subdue the British at Quebec in the autumn and early winter of 1777. The journey to Quebec was in itself an intense saga of fording the rapids of Maine's Kennebec River and the portage of boats through swamps and forests to avoid waterfalls. He held his army together to survive a hurricane of historic proportions that swelled the Dead River — the approach to the St. Lawrence River — from its normal width of sixty yards to 200 yards.

Four days after the hurricane, Roger Enos, a Continental brigade commander, quit camp on October 21 and headed back home with 300 Connecticut men and assorted stragglers. Arnold had sufficient reason to call it desertion, but a court martial tried Enos only on charges of "quitting without leave." He was acquitted.

On New Year's Eve in 1775, Arnold was badly wounded in the right knee in an unsuccessful attack on Quebec. The Canadian expedition was a lost cause, but Arnold became the last member of the doomed campaign to leave the scene.

Another fury of suspicion swept over Arnold when he returned after the Canadian struggle, once more tainting his "whirlwind hero" image. One charge accused him of pilfering the baggage of officers captured in Canada. Another urged Congress to investigate his questionable spending of $55,000 of the $67,000 that had been allotted him for the expedition. Perhaps most tellingly (and most prophetically) was the later declaration by Major John Brown of Massachusetts, who said of Arnold, "Money is this man's god, and to get enough of it he would sacrifice his country." No charges were pressed against Arnold, but Brown's bitter words were burned into many memories.

Arnold joined the main army in Morristown early in 1777. His enemies in Congress dealt him an especially cruel blow in February by promoting five brigadier generals to major generals, in order of seniority, Lord Stirling (William Alexander), Thomas Mifflin, Arthur St. Clair, Adam Stephen and Benjamin Lincoln. None matched Arnold's length of service, much less his battlefield conquests.

Arnold promptly submitted his resignation. Washington begged him to reconsider, vowing that he had not been consulted in the promotions and was not responsible for the blatant, unprofessional slap at his best officer. Arnold agreed to remain in the army.

Although Arnold was described as "sulking in his tent like some rustic Achilles," he reconsidered when asked on April 23 to hasten to Danbury, Connecticut. There, a strong British force had burned much of the important rebel depot and torched nineteen dwellings and twenty-two barns and storehouses. Arnold, aided by General David Wooster, punished the British as much as possible, sending them in headlong retreat to their boats on Long Island Sound.

The invaders lost 154 killed and wounded, against twenty Americans killed and eighty wounded. Wooster was mortally wounded and Arnold had one horse shot from under him and had another wounded, but he escaped unscathed. Three weeks later, Congress gave the brigadier general a new horse, completely outfitted.

Arnold's finest performance, however controversial, came in the second Battle of Saratoga that began on October 7, 1777. He had contributed little to the first battle on September 19, often called the Battle of Freeman's Farm. Arnold had been in the thick of the fighting, but when he returned to the rear to get more troops, General Horatio Gates, in command, astonishingly ordered him to stay off the battlefield, charging him with disobeying orders. Arnold's men returned to fight without their redoubtable leader.

If Gates had prevailed, Arnold also would have sat out the second battle in a tent as far away from the action as possible, since Gates had ordered him out of action. Arnold defied his superior's order to remain beyond the field of action and galloped into the fray when General Ebenezer Learned's brigade became locked in a stalemate with Hessian troops. Learned, a Gates' pet, had contributed little to the first battle, but Gates cited him for his "valiant behavior."

Arnold spurred to the front of Learned's brigade, with neither an invitation nor an order to join the action. In response, Gates added unintentional comic relief by sending a major clattering after Arnold, ridiculously waving orders for him to desist and return to the rear.

Arnold became an inspiring, whirling dervish, spurring his steed back and forth between the armies, urging the Americans to follow him. Learned's regiment rallied to capture a stronghold, and four other regiments followed Arnold in a bloody, successful raid that captured the redoubt held by General Heinrich von Breyman and his Hessian troops, a key to the British defense. Arnold was injured during the assault, being hit again in what was called "his Quebec leg." He was incapacitated for many months.

The British heaped praise on Arnold for his "true military instinct" at Saratoga and respected his front line fury. His American detractors claimed that Arnold's heroics were unnecessary and that he added American casualties to a cause that had been won before his reckless exhibition before the troops. However, Congress officially thanked him, along with Generals Gates and Lincoln, for the defeat of British General John Burgoyne at Saratoga.

Most importantly for Arnold's pride, Washington received orders from Congress to promote him to the rank of major general and to correct his length of service so that he would be the highest ranked major general in the American army. Arnold had been vindicated, especially in his own mind, although his days of aggressive battlefield action were ended because of the injury sustained at Saratoga.

Thus, as the American army prepared to break camp at Valley Forge to chase General Clinton across New Jersey for the Battle of Monmouth, the injuries that kept Arnold chair-bound made him a natural candidate to command Philadelphia when the British left. He entered the city on June 19 and immediately set up imposing headquarters in one of the finest houses in America, the large, handsome Penn mansion where British General William Howe had enjoyed the high life of the Quaker city. If money were "this man's god," as John Brown had declared after the Canada expedition, the opportunity to display it had come.

In controlling Philadelphia, the capital of both the United States and Pennsylvania, Arnold served two civilian masters. Several factions in the town — patriots who had returned; Loyalists and collaborators who had remained; and neutrals, including a large Quaker population, complicated the task of running the city.

Arnold's power and imposing life style commanded awe and envy; his huge expen-

Benedict Arnold, the central figure in this drawing, is shown just after leading a successful charge against a strong Hessian redoubt. Despite being barred from the field by General Gates, Arnold dashed into action, galvanized his troops, and became the hero of Saratoga, his last battlefield action.

ditures evoked suspicion. His mansion required a housekeeper, groom, coachman, and a half-dozen other servants. His lavish parties enthralled the wealthy and enabled him to cut a wide swath through society. He sped through Philadelphia in his elaborate coach drawn by his matched team of four horses. All of this supposedly was accomplished on a major general's monthly income [pay and expenses] of $332 in Continental currency with its greatly depreciated value.

This royal lifestyle, on Continental pennies, invited speculation that he was involved in illegal personal deals that muddied his exalted reputation. Joseph Reed, president of the Pennsylvania Council, quickly became his foremost enemy. However, Reed bided his time until he felt the moment was right to attack the commander.

If Arnold's lifestyle made no economic sense, his association with known Philadelphia Tories certainly was not sound political judgment. The thirty-eight-year-old Arnold met, wooed, and eventually wed a nineteen-year-old beauty named Peggy Shippen, daughter of

As Arnold's troops struggled northward in the autumn of 1775, he led his soldiers through unexplored terrain and aided them as they dragged their boats between numerous and increasingly icy streams.

one of the city's most prominent Loyalists.

During the British occupation, Peggy and her Tory social set had thoroughly enjoyed the young, eager and high-stepping redcoat officers in the city. Among Peggy's special British friends was Major John André, described as "ambitious, industrious, capable and engaging." Evidence of André's attachment to Peggy was his sketch of her (see page 214). André put aside his social and artistic talents and marched away with Clinton when the British headed for New York, but he soon would reenter the lives of the newlywed Arnolds.

Whatever caution and restraint Arnold might have retained disappeared after he married Peggy on April 8, 1779. As a wedding gift, Benedict gave her Mt. Pleasant, a handsome, expensive mansion fronting the Schuylkill River. Peggy was used to wealth, and the demands that reflected her social upbringing escalated after the marriage. It is not true, however, that she drove Arnold to his ruin. He was well on to road to deceit and treachery before they were wed.

Joseph Reed moved against the city commander in February 1779, when he presented Congress with eight charges of misconduct against Arnold, who issued an angry denial and demanded an immediate investigation. Congress found Arnold innocent of all charges.

Unconvinced, Reed induced Congress to refer the charges to an army court-martial. Arnold's known arrogance and scorn for fellow officers insured that the army would be all too willing to take on the cocky major general. It seemed that after years of suspicion and allegations, the hour had come to nail Arnold to his Philadelphia wall.

Arnold agreed to the court-martial only after Washington suggested it would serve to clear his name. A place and date were set: the Middlebrook encampment, on May 1. This was postponed to June 1, when a fourteen-man court assembled, and almost immediately adjourned because the British had started what seemed to be a long-awaited expedition up the Hudson River.

Four days after the May postponement, Arnold sent Washington a near-hysterical letter that began, "If your Excellency thinks me criminal, for heaven's sake let me be immediately tried, and if found guilty, executed. I want no favor; I ask only justice."

The summer drifted into fall, with no acceleration of the trial. Finally a new date was reached — December 23 in Morristown. Between the aborted trial when the Watchung hills were aglow with flowering dogwood trees, and December, when a brutal winter gripped Morristown, Arnold and Peggy had been busy weaving, with André, a web of astounding treason that had nothing to do with Reed's rather parochial charges.

A few days after Arnold's springtime emotional plea for a trial and execution if guilty, he began initial contacts with the British to see what kind of important intelligence from a major general they could reward handsomely. There would have to be a substantial benefit for the Arnolds, of course; Benedict Arnold was not an inexperienced negotiator.

Joseph Stansbury, a mild Tory who liked to think of himself as neutral, would be the go-between, an easy task because he was a well-known and well-liked proprietor of a china shop in Philadelphia. On May 10, Stansbury met with John André to discuss details. Neither doubted that Arnold, who used the code name "Mr. Moore," would become their secret conspirator. Channels were established to permit "Mr. Moore" to send information to André through Stansbury. Peggy was a partner from the beginning, carrying messages and exchanging instructions.

Some time in June 1779, Arnold proposed to the British that he return to active military duty, seek an important post (such as West Point), lose it in an orchestrated attack, and surrender the post and whatever soldiers were present. In a touch of calculated meanness by Arnold, each American captured in the surrender would net him two guineas in hard specie.

However, recompense for captured soldiers alone would not endow sufficient security and peace of mind for the Arnolds. Benedict asked Clinton for $10,000 to compensate him for any "losses" he might suffer if the Americans suspected his double-dealing. Arnold demanded the fee even if he could not deliver a major command to his former enemy. Clinton reneged and broke off negotiations.

Not even a hint of Arnold's bold duplicity existed in American minds when the court martial opened on December 23 in Dickerson's Tavern (also known as Norris' Tavern) in Morristown, at the corner of Spring and Water streets in "The Hollow." Arnold had to face only the minor charges stemming from the Philadelphia allegations but he took no chances. He prepared carefully, donning his best uniform, wearing his shined black boots, and making sure that he was well coiffed. He had to play to perfection the role of a deeply offended, severely crippled American hero. He knew that only one man in the courtroom — himself — was aware of his greater treachery. It must have no part in this hearing.

Just before he entered the spacious barroom where the trial would take place, Arnold removed a two-inch lift from the boot on his injured leg. He limped into court as a wounded victim of the war and was greeted with respect, awe, and even admiration. The young general had defined for himself his role in the courtroom drama about to begin — a brave soldier wounded in body and spirit, outwardly without a deceitful thought in his mind. He was ready for what he would proclaim was an injustice of the highest order.

The fourteen officers of the court, including Generals Howe, Maxwell, Stark, Smallwood, and Knox, were all familiar to him. Arnold had fought with them on distant fields, talked with them between battles, and had, at Valley Forge, sworn fealty to the American cause as a major general, on a Bible held by Henry Knox.

Arnold opened his case with proper regret, tinged with indignation that he was being accused of any crimes. On the other hand, he assured the panel of officers, it was a consolation to be tried by officers possessed of "delicate and refined sensations of honor."

He continued his eloquence in what listeners would long remember as a *tour de force*. He modestly proclaimed his feats on battlefields, the wounds he had suffered gladly, and his obedience to "the present and necessary war against Great Britain." Mixing Latin phrases with soaring oratory, he lifted his voice to conclude he was being "charged with practices which his soul abhors."

Eventually, the court martial took up the first charge — that Arnold had issued an illegal pass to the Tory captain of the brig *Charming Nancy*, permitting him to sail the ship to Egg Harbor, New Jersey.

Arnold cheerfully admitted issuing the protection [pass] but declared he was merely trying to "prevent the soldiery from plundering the vessel." He did not, of course, reveal that he was secret part owner of the *Charming Nancy*.

What about the second charge, the court asked, that he had on his arrival in Philadelphia as the city's commander closed all the shops to prevent anyone — even army officers — from purchasing goods, while he "privately made considerable purchases for his own benefit"?

This brought an angry response from Arnold. He said he was following orders from Congress and threw those orders on the panel's desk. As for purchasing goods for his own

As depicted in this drawing from his self-portrait, Major John André was a handsome British adjutant general and personal aide to General Henry Clinton.

profit, he was almost weeping as he whispered: "if this is true, I stand disgraced as the vilest of men; I stand stigmatized with indelible disgrace." He paused, then added, "The blood I have spent in defense of my country will be insufficient to obliterate the stain."

The third count, evidence of the Pennsylvania Council's eagerness to get him, charged that he had ordered a sergeant to do menial chores. It was no coincidence that the sergeant was the son of William Matlack, secretary of the Council and a sworn enemy of the general. Arnold replied in stiff military dogma: "When a citizen assumes the character of a soldier, the former [is] entirely lost in the latter." In other words, a soldier has no recourse but to obey an order.

The final question had the sternest implication: why had Arnold commandeered a dozen army wagons and drivers and sent them across New Jersey to bring back the *Charming Nancy*'s cargo when word came that a British foraging party was alleged to be loose along the New Jersey shore?

The embattled general insisted he had used the wagons "to remove property which was in imminent danger of falling into the hands of the enemy." Arnold added that the deputy Quartermaster had approved the action. For the first time during the trial he sensed that the board was skeptical.

After several adjournments, the board reconvened on January 20 for summations. Arnold rose, seething with anger. Most of his oratory was directed at the Pennsylvanians, who, he said, were responsible for "the torrent of aspersion which has been poured forth against me." He accused them of an "artful appearance of tenderness" toward him during the trial.

"Did they mean by this," he asked venomously, "to pour balsam or to pour poison into my wounds?"

The panel adjourned. Speculation was rife throughout the camp. On January 22, Colonel Ebenezer Huntington wrote his friend Samuel Blachley Webb: "General Arnold's trial will be over in two days... good defense and a very spirited one... expect that he will be acquitted with Honour."

Arnold was not acquitted. Four days after Huntington's prediction, the court-martial board found the general guilty of the first and fourth charges — the issuance of the permit for the *Charming Nancy* to be moved and the commandeering of wagons to bring the ship's goods back to Philadelphia. The court asked Washington to issue a reprimand to Arnold.

Washington waited until Congress approved the court martial decision and had printed fifty copies of the proceedings. Arnold waited impatiently for Washington to invite him to headquarters for the reprimand; to his astonishment and chagrin, the reprimand was issued in a taut, impersonal paragraph of a General Order on April 6, 1780:

> *The commander in chief would have been much happier in an occasion of bestowing honors on an officer who has rendered such distinguished services to his country as Major General Arnold; but in the present case a sense of duty and a regard to candor oblige him to declare that he considers his conduct in the issuance of the permit as peculiarly reprehensible, both in a civil and military view, and in the affair of the wagons as imprudent and improper.*

Arnold was stunned, although the reprimand was mild and had not harmed his army career or affected his lavish standard of living in Philadelphia. Clinton and André were still in Charleston. Arnold had no way of knowing how they would react when they returned to New York. He still had ample time to become a traitor — if that was the way he chose to go. If he decided to continue as a highly respected American general, that course was still open. Washington held him in high trust.

Arnold was in limbo. The chastened, angry general could only bide his time.

The Yankee's
RETURN FROM CAMP.

FATHER and I went down to camp,
　　Along with captain Gooding
There we see the men and boys,
　　As thick as hasty-pudding,
　　　　　Yankee doodle keep it up,
　　Yankee doodle dandy;
CHO.—*Mind the Music and the step,*
　　　　　And with the girls be handy.

And there we see a thousand men,
　　As rich as 'Squire David;
And what they wasted every day,
　　I wish it could be saved.
　　　　　Yankee doodle, &c.

The 'lasses they eat every day,
　　Would keep an house a winter,
They have as much that I'll be bound,
　　They eat it when they're amind to.
　　　　　Yankee doodle, &c.

And there we see a swamping gun,
　　Large as a log of maple,
Upon a duced little cart,
　　A load for father's cattle.
　　　　　Yankee doodle, &c.

And every time they shoot it off,
　　It takes a horn of powder;
It makes a noise like father's gun,
　　Only a nation louder.
　　　　　Yankee doodle, &c.

I went as nigh to one myself,
　　As 'Siah's under-pinning;
And father went as nigh again,
　　I thought the duce was in him.
　　　　　Yankee doodle, &c.

Cousin Simon grew so bold,
　　I thought he would have cock'd it;
It scar'd me so I streak'd it off,
　　And hung by father's pocket.
　　　　　Yankee doodle, &c.

But Captain Davis has a gun,
　　He kind of clap'd his hand on't,
And stuck a crooked stabbing iron,
　　Upon the little end on't.
　　　　　Yankee doodle, &c.

And there I see a pumpkin shell,
　　As big as mother's bason,
And every time they touch'd it off,
　　They scamper'd like the nation.
　　　　　Yankee doodle, &c.

I see a little barrel too,
　　The heads were made of leather,
They knock'd upon it with little clubs,
　　And call'd the folks together,
　　　　　Yankee doodle, &c.

And there was Captain Washington,
　　And gentlefolks about him,
They say he's grown so tarnal proud,
　　He will not ride without 'em.
　　　　　Yankee doodle, &c.

He got him on his meeting clothes,
　　Upon a slapping stallion,
He set the world along in rows,
　　In hundreds and in millions.
　　　　　Yankee doodle &c.

The flaming ribbons in their hats,
　　They look'd so tearing fine, ah,
I wanted plagueily to get,
　　To give to my Jemima.
　　　　　Yankee doodle &c.

I see another snarl of men,
　　A digging graves, they told me,
So tarnal long, so tarnal deep,
　　They 'tended they should hold me.
　　　　　Yankee doodle, &c.

It scar'd me so, I hook'd it off,
　　Nor stopp'd as I remember,
Nor turn'd about till I got home,
　　Lock'd up in mother's chamber.
　　　　　Yankee doodle, &c.

Sold, wholesale and retail, at 132, Ann Street, Boston.

An early version of the familiar "Yankee Doodle" song, a favorite marching tune.

Margaret Arnold, Traitor's Wife

She became Margaret Arnold, wife of Benedict, but when British Major John André made this sketch of her, she was Peggy Shippen, the teenage daughter of a noted Philadephia Tory and one of the city's most popular belles.

Few people would recognize the name Margaret Arnold, an important, if infamous, name in the American Revolution. But even casual readers of Revolutionary War history know the name Peggy Shippen, the nineteen-year-old socially-connected and beautiful Philadelphia miss, who stole Benedict Arnold's heart and might have hastened the blackening of his soul.

The death of Arnold's wife in June 1775 made him a highly eligible bachelor. His first new love interest was Betsy DuBois in Boston. Arnold wrote her at least two letters in the spring of 1778, both of which have survived. One sentence in an especially long letter asked, "Will you doom a heart so true, so faithful, to languish in despair?" Miss DuBois didn't care what happened to Arnold's heart.

Benedict met Peggy Shippen in early September 1778, shortly after he had taken command of Philadelphia. The general had saved copies of his letters to Miss DuBois and recycled them to send to Peggy.

As one of three daughters of William Shippen, a wealthy, Tory-leaning Philadelphia leader, Peggy had been popular with British officers who occupied the city during the winter of 1778. A very special friend was Captain John André, a young British officer described as "ambitious, industrious, capable and engaging." Among evidences of André's attachment to Peggy was his sketch of her (see opposite page).

Peggy was barely eighteen when she met the thirty-eight year old Arnold. She liked his high style of living and the generous expenditures that sustained it. Her affection for the ruggedly handsome commander grew, although there is no evidence she responded in writing to the ardor of Arnold's second-hand letters.

Peggy and Benedict were married on April 8, 1778, at Judge Shippen's house. Arnold was supported by a soldier during the ceremony and sat during the reception with his injured leg propped up by a campstool. Before the honeymoon ended, Arnold had made up his mind to conspire with the enemy.

Peggy is often suspected of being Arnold's link to André and her participation in her husband's role as a spy for the British is well known. She undoubtedly took part in the exchange of messages between Arnold and the British; however, the extent of her complicity in Arnold's final dealings is unknown.

The new Mrs. Arnold was a large factor in Arnold's desperate need for money. Whatever caution and restraint Arnold might have retained disappeared.

Arnold visited Peggy in their bedroom just before he fled from West Point to join the British. He undoubtedly told her that he had made plans to flee to the British. However, when he slammed the bedroom door shut and hastened down the stairs and out of the house, there were no sounds of grief or outrage on Peggy's part.

When Washington and his staff returned to Arnold's headquarters, Peggy suddenly erupted, screaming that her baby's life had been threatened. Her hysterics impressed not only Washington but whole generations of historians as well who were not aware of her perfidy. Washington believed Mrs. Arnold was stunned by the sudden turn of events. and offered her safe passage to her Philadelphia home — which she accepted.

Chapter Sixteen

CONGRESS DEMANDS
Some ANSWERS

C ongress grew increasingly weary of George Washington's gloom-and-doom letters from Morristown during the winter of 1780. Day after day, the commander's
complaints and predictions of total collapse poured into Philadelphia. He needed
money, arms, food, clothing, and everything else an army requires to maintain parity with
its enemy.

Washington's negative messages were nothing new; he had begun writing them almost from the day he had taken command of the army in Cambridge on July 3, 1775.
Week after week, year after year, he had properly laid the onus on Congress. His theme
in 1779-80 could be boiled down to a single question: where is the money to keep your
nation's army in the field?

Recruiting, paying, supplying and transporting soldiers required a well-defined national treasury and a national system of paper money solidly backed by gold and silver.
The revolutionary Congress had neither. Continental dollars had become fantasy money
without a hard dollar in a national treasury. Worse, there had never been a tax plan to build
up such a treasury.

As early as September 1775, Washington sent Congress a letter that could have been
a prototype for most of the letters of complaint and dismay that he would write again and
again through the years:

*The military chest is totally exhausted. The Paymaster has not a single dollar in hand.
The Commissary General assures me he has strained his credit to the utmost for the*

The bright spot in Morristown's crippling encampment of 1779-80 was the arrival on May 10 of the Marquis de Lafayette with the joyous news that France was about to dispatch a major fleet and more than 5,000 well-equipped, well-trained soldiers. This diorama depicts the moment Washington welcomed his young French friend and ally.

---

subsistence of the Army. The Quartermaster General is precisely in the same situation, and the greater part of the Army is in a state not far from mutiny.

He concluded on a note that was both cautious and startling: "I do not know to whom to impute this failure, but I am of the opinion, if the evil is not immediately remedied and more punctuality observed in the future, the army must absolutely break up."

So it had been in 1775, when the complaints detailed the massive task of creating an army out of nothing, and so it was as 1779 merged into 1780, when the army seemed to be dissolving into nothing. The young nation was on its knees. It was futile to seek more financial help from Congress. That cupboard was bare, but where else could the general direct his pleading?

By the spring of 1780, Washington's pleas for help had come to be akin to the fabled boy who cried wolf once too often. Congress grew complacent about the commander's unending predictions of total collapse. If that view were right, why hadn't the collapses ever come about?

As spring followed the winter of 1780, it was time, if not well past the time, for Congress to get a handle on the army quartered in the New Jersey hills. The truth was that British commanders in New York probably were far better informed than Congress on the state of the army at Morristown. Their spies had filtered back the encouraging news — from a British standpoint — that the enemy Army was rapidly melting away through desertions and the ending of enlistment terms.

The British did not have to send a delegation to Jockey Hollow to know that at least half of the 10,000 soldiers who had marched into Morristown the previous December were gone from camp. Those enemy spies knew — as Congress seemingly did not – that if the rate of attrition continued, Washington would have difficulty rounding up enough regulars fit for a rigorous summer campaign.

Congress voted in the early spring of 1780 to send a three-man investigative committee to Morristown to get a close-up view of the allegedly distraught American Army. The visit was not to shower praise on the troops and buck up their leader but to see what truths, if any, lay behind the constant negative reports and the forceful demands streaming from headquarters.

Congress spent weeks wrangling over who should go to Morristown and what they should seek. By mid-April, they chose three delegates: Philip Schuyler of New York State, John Mathews of South Carolina, and Nathaniel Peabody of New Hampshire.

Schuyler, a former general in the Continental Army, was a surprise choice for what he called the "triumvirate." On April 8, he wrote Colonel Alexander Hamilton, his future son-in-law, that "I shall not be on the committee," citing the impropriety of appointing a member of Congress who had been in the army and "will probably have a bias in its favor." He also warned that certain members of Congress would frustrate every effort to relieve "my amiable chief [Washington] from his well grounded anxiety."

Schuyler, Mathews, and Peabody set off on horseback from Philadelphia about two weeks after the investigation had been ordered and called on Washington at the Ford Mansion on April 28. The instructions they carried proved Congress was not seeking to better the lives of the troops. The committee had instructions to consult with the commander in chief on matters that had earned the scorn of Congress — then see where it could cut the numbers of troops and slash funds.

First, they were to ask Washington "about the propriety of reducing the number of regiments." The committee had the power — after conferring with the general — to "reduce, incorporate, or unite components of the Army." The just-ended harsh winter in Morristown had very well taken care of the question of troop reduction; it would not be a problem for the Committee at Headquarters.

Secondly, the committee (and Washington) were to "limit the number of horses to be kept by the officers," a reform meant to reduce the amount of costly and difficult to obtain

Mrs. Washington in Morristown

Martha Washington paid long visits to Morristown during both winters the general spent in town — the first winter in The Arnold Tavern, the second in the Ford Mansion. It was her custom to make the long, arduous trip north during every winter of the war.

She came somewhat late for the 1777 winter, not surprising since her husband did not arrive in Morristown until January 6. She stopped in Richmond, Baltimore and Philadelphia on that March trip north, staying in the latter town with Benjamin Randolph.

Major Caleb Gibbs of Washington's Life Guard rode to Philadelphia to bring Mrs. Washington to Morristown in December 1779. They returned in a borrowed or rented sleigh, since Mrs. Washington's "chariot" [carriage], four horses and two servants were left in Philadelphia until the end of January, when Gibbs returned to bring the carriage, horses and servants to Morristown.

The General's lady arrived in Morristown on New Year's Eve. There apparently was no special party to celebrate the coming of a new year, nor was there much celebrating all winter. Mrs. Washington wrote sparingly during the winter but in a letter written after she returned home, she said "the poor General was so unhappy that it distressed me exceedingly."

Martha departed for Virginia "about the middle of June," as she wrote in a letter dated July 14, when she reached Mount Vernon. She said she found herself "so much fatigued with my ride." The trip home took about one month. She vowed to never again leave for camp so late: "I suffered so much last year by going late that I have determined to go early in the fall before the frost sets in."

forage needed to feed the animals. Equally, soldiers who had been used solely as servants were ordered returned to regular duty, "as far as is consistent with the convenience of the officers they serve." Such "convenience" overlooked army regulations that said soldiers were to be used as fighting men, not servants.

Thirdly, the committee was ordered to suggest to Washington "such plans for the convenience of the officers and soldiers with respect to clothing and commissary supplies as will tend to remove all just ground for complaint." In this grudging admission that there might be room for dismay in the camp, Congress said it "sincerely laments that there should be any room" for such aberrations.

Thinly-veiled charges in the form of "suggestions" also ordered a searching study of General Greene's quartermaster department, of the commissary department, the hospital and medical departments, the hide department (where the making of desperately needed shoes began), and the departments of ordnance and military stores. Economy was the watchword.

The Committee at Headquarters had broad, even dictatorial, powers. It could "discharge unnecessary officers," "retrench expenses," and "reform or abolish departments." One paragraph summed up the basic burden of the committee as Congress saw it from distant Philadelphia:

> You are to abolish unnecessary posts, to erect others, to discharge useless officers, to stop rations improperly issued; and are hereby further authorized to exercise every power which may be necessary to effect a reformation of abuses and the general arrangement of those departments which are in any wise connected with the matters committed to your charge.

The instructions imposed an aura of guilt without trial in such frequently used terms as "unnecessary posts," "useless officers," "rations improperly issued," and "a reformation of abuses." If that litany of suspicions were proved, Washington and Greene would stand exposed as charlatans who had let the army slide into a shambles despite the heroic efforts of Congress and the nation. Washington welcomed the investigation, however, believing that it was a chance to convince Congress of the genuine distress in Jockey Hollow.

Schuyler, Mathews, and Peabody first paid their respects to Washington, presented their orders, listened to his side for several days, and then set out vigorously to see matters for themselves. A less able committee might have accepted most, or all, of the charges at face value and brought in the proverbial new broom to sweep clean an alleged situation. This trio had come to work, to see, to judge.

It was far from the most propitious time to investigate the camp. The Chevalier de la Luzerne, the French minister to Congress, had arrived in town in April with the good news that both Lafayette and French ships and soldiers were on the way.

A potential new ally also seemed possible with the simultaneous arrival at headquarters of Don Juan de Miralles, "a gentleman of distinction from Spain" who was recognized as that nation's unofficial representative to America. Mirales was very ill and was immediately assigned a bed in the Ford Mansion, where he was diagnosed as suffering from "pulmonic fever," likely a form of pneumonia. Ten days after his arrival, he died in the mansion on April 28.

There had to be ceremonies to welcome the French and Spanish delegations, of course. Baron von Steuben marched his four best–clad and best-drilled battalions before Luzerne and Continental officers on April 24. That portion of the gala day ended with a thirteen-gun salute.

In the evening, the Chevalier was feted in high style at a ball, probably staged in the military storehouse near the Morristown Green. A "numerous collection of ladies and gentlemen of distinguished character" gathered for fine food, rare wines, and an evening of dancing. If anyone cared to estimate how much food such a costly affair might have bought for hungry soldiers, that discordant populist note was not recorded. An army purportedly on the edge of ruin might not have been expected to spend so lavishly on entertainment limited to officers.

On May 10, exactly two weeks after it knocked on Washington's door, the committee hastily finished its first report and immediately sent Mathews galloping toward Philadelphia with a ticking bomb for Congress. The preliminary study's stinging viewpoint could shatter Congressional complacency. The goal of pillorying Washington and his complaints had backfired wildly.

Congress heard, for example, that the supply situation was at least as critical as Washington had said, chiefly because of "a want of money," but also because of the need to transport state supplies over long distances. "The impracticability of conveying forage from states remotely situated," said the committee, "is too evident to require any comments on our part."

Deeper into the report, the committee bared its soul and stunned Congress:

> Before we had an opportunity closely to view and examine into the real state of things, we had no conception of the almost inextricable difficulties in which we found them involved.

Indeed, said the report, the army had so many "distresses" and "repetition of want" that "it has had a very pernicious influence on the soldiers." The committee warned: "Their patience is exhausted." There should have been no misunderstanding the alarming summary:

A Funeral to Remember

Don Juan de Miralles, "a gentleman of high rank in Spain," created a stir when he arrived in Morristown late in May 1780, bringing hope that Spain might enter the war on the side of America. His quick departure created a far greater stir.

Miralles died on May 29 after a short illness. His funeral, described in full detail by Dr. James Thacher, set a standard unlikely ever to be matched in Morristown:

> *The corpse was dressed in rich state and was exposed to public view, as is customary in Europe. The coffin was most splendid and stately, lined throughout with fine cambric, and covered on the outside with rich black velvet, and ornamented in a superb manner.*
>
> *The body was decorated in splendid full dress, consisting of a scarlet suit, embroidered with rich gold lace, a three-cornered gold-laced hat and a genteel cued wig, white silk stockings, large diamond shoe and knee buckles, a profusion of diamond rings decorated the finger, and from a superb gold watch set with diamonds, several rich seals were suspended.*
>
> *On the way to the graveyard, generals and members of Congress led a mile-long procession. Six field officers were pallbearers and the coffin was borne on the shoulders of four artillery officers in full uniform.*
>
> *A Spanish priest performed the service at the grave, in the Roman Catholic form. The coffin was enclosed in a box of planks, and all the profusion of pomp and grandeur were deposited in the silent grave in the common burying grounds near the church in Morristown. A guard was placed at the grave lest our soldiers should be tempted to dig for buried treasure. It was understood that the corpse was to be removed to Philadelphia.*

Actually, the last resting place of Miralles is not known, although it most definitely is not in Morristown.

Their starving condition, their want of pay, and the variety of hardships that they have been driven to sustain, has soured their tempers, and produced a spirit of discontent which begins to display itself under a complexion of the most alarming hue.

If this spirit should fully establish itself, it must be productive of some violent convulsion, infinitely to our prejudice, at home and abroad, as it would evince a lack of means, or a want of wisdom to employ them, either of which must bring our cause into discredit and draw in its train consequences of a nature too serious to be contemplated without the deepest anxiety.

A formal portrait of Marie Joseph Paul Yves Roch Gilbert du Motier, the very young Marquis de Lafayette. His handsome appearance, family ties and an eager determination to fight in the American cause endeared him to Washington, who met the eager and wealthy French nobleman in 1777, when Lafayette was only nineteen years old.

The committee's stunning, blunt message to Congress was clear: Pay the troops, feed them, clothe them, and arm them properly NOW. If not, the nation must be prepared to face a serious consequence: mutiny.

Mathews dropped the shocking report on Congressional desks and raced back to rejoin Schuyler and Peabody in Morristown. The reconvened committee returned furiously to work; this was no two- or three-week junket out of Philadelphia. If they were to buttress their initial angry message to Congress, they needed more evidence. The committee would remain in Morristown until fall.

The Congressmen talked to committees of officers and went out to Jockey Hollow to see the many vacant huts and the sorry-looking, surly soldiers. They visited outlying posts to talk with soldiers even less secure than those at Jockey Hollow. Some kinds of quick fixes had to be applied to the camp lest the entire cause collapse into the spring mud of Jockey Hollow.

In the minds of some, if not many, members of Congress, the visit would be an opportunity to rein in outspoken, often impolitic Quartermaster General Nathanael Greene. He had forcefully echoed the commander in chief's pleas for help. From a Congressional standpoint, he certainly was an easier target to bring down than Washington.

The committee tried desperately to get the truculent Quartermaster General to the table. Everything pointed to the likelihood that he would mean trouble and delay for the visiting Congressmen. Greene flatly refused to cooperate with the Congressional trio unless the committee in turn agreed to conduct a full-scale investigation of his department to determine "whether it has been conducted properly or not." If that were done, he promised on May 3 to "most cheerfully give every assistance." The impasse was never resolved. Greene's weeks as quartermaster general were numbered.

Greene's department was the army's biggest spender. By the spring of 1780, Greene's quartermaster department was spending an average of $407, 393 a month and had hired more than 3,000 men. The department supervised wagons, boats, supply depots, and purchasing agents. It employed twenty-eight deputy quartermasters general, and 109 assistant deputy quartermasters general. It was, for its time, a huge, expensive — and very necessary — war machine.

Staff members, including Greene, were paid commissions on their purchases, ranging from one to five percent. Theodore Thayer, in his biography of Greene, *Strategist of the American Revolution*, wrote "he earned approximately $170,000 in specie from his commissions." Greene shared his commissions with officers on his staff. Other sources doubt the size of his commissions, since a hostile Congress had to confirm such payments. Greene also was suspect as a part-time owner of a shipping company and an iron furnace in Batsto, New Jersey. The army traded with both of them.

If there was considerable cause for raised eyebrows, there also was no questioning the quartermaster general's dedication to his nearly impossible job. Neither was there doubt that Greene simmered at whispered charges that his department was corrupt.

When Washington first sent Greene to Philadelphia to confer with Congress after the winter of 1777 at Morristown, the quartermaster's confident, brusque manner prompted several congressmen to complain that he was dominating the thoughts of Washington.

Greene had proved his bravery and skills as a military tactician on several battlefields and only very reluctantly took on the nearly impossible role

General Philip Schuyler, wealthy and prominent scion of a distinguished colonial Dutch family, father of Betsy Schuyler, and a leading member of the Committee of Congress sent to investigate the army at Morristown.

of quartermaster general. He wanted to be in combat, very frankly declaring that valor could be proved, and glory earned, only in battle. Washington persuaded him to take on the thankless quartermaster role.

Greene accepted, protesting, "while I am drudging in an office from which I shall receive no honor and very few thanks, I am losing an opportunity to do justice to my military character."

By May 13, after about two weeks spent studying the condition of the army, Schuyler believed the deplorable situation was virtually beyond control unless Congress lodged "dictatorial powers" in General Washington. If that seemed too power-centered, Schuyler

Betsy Schuyler of Albany spent the winter of 1780 in this house, which her uncle ad aunt, Dr. and Mrs. John Cochran, rented from Dr. Jabez Campfield at 5 Olyphant Way in Morristown. There, Betsy was courted by Colonel Alexander Hamilton.

believed that, at the very least, a "small committee, composed of men of ability," must be named and housed in Morristown, or wherever Washington was lodged. Washington agreed on the "absolute necessity that a small committee should immediately be appointed to reside near headquarters."

He felt Schuyler would be perfect on such a permanent committee, believed Mathews had "understanding and integrity," and declared that he would trust Peabody, "had I not some doubts about his discretion."

A powerful, small group could, in Washington's judgment, "act with dispatch and energy," and could provide for exigencies as they arose. Plans could be opened to them "with more freedom and confidence than to a numerous body."

General Clinton soon would be on his way home from his smashing victory at Charleston. The American army had not been improved, enlarged, or made more capable by the trio from Congress. No additional funds were available; Congress was truly flat broke. Even if the committee's report boded well for a future army, the recommendations might be far too late if the British unleashed the might of their army on New Jersey in the summer of 1780.

The Courtship of Betsy

If there had been a nomination for the "Couple of the Year" in 1780, the award would have gone, without question, to Colonel Alexander Hamilton and Miss Elizabeth (Betsy) Schuyler. The twenty-three-year-old colonel met Miss Schuyler, twenty-two, in Morristown in February, and married her in December at the home of her wealthy father, General Philip Schuyler, in Albany, New York.

They were social and economic opposites. Born in the West Indies, Hamilton was orphaned at age eleven. Largely self-taught, he came to New Jersey in 1772, and was admitted to King's College (now Columbia University) and earned a law degree. He enlisted in the New York Artillery in May 1775 and served with distinction at Trenton and Princeton before becoming a brilliant aide-de-camp to Washington in March 1777.

Elizabeth was born to great wealth and social prestige as the daughter of General Philip Schuyler, a member of one of New York's oldest, most honorable and wealthiest Dutch families.

The Hamilton-Schuyler romance began in the winter of 1779-80, when Betsy was living in Morristown with her aunt, Gertrude Schuyler Cochran and her uncle, Dr. John Cochran, Washington's personal physician. The Cochrans rented Jabez Campfield's house, a short distance from the Ford Mansion.

Hamilton told a friend that he sought a woman who was "young, handsome, I lay emphasis upon a good shape; sensible, a little learning will do; chaste and tender." As much as anything, he was interested in a prospective bride's "fortune, the larger stock of that the better."

Betsy met all of Hamilton's qualifications. Another Washington aide, Tench Tilghman, described her as "a brunette with the most good natured, lively eyes I ever saw, which threw a beam of good temper and benevolence over her whole countenance."

Tilghman said that when Hamilton met Betsy he was "a gone man." Soon after the two met, Hamilton began visiting her nearly every evening, under the careful eye of Mrs. Cochran. The two became engaged by springtime. Philip Schuyler gave Hamilton a hearty welcome: "You cannot, my dear Sir, be more happy at the connection than I am…. I shall therefore only entreat you to consider me as one who wishes in every way to promote your happiness, and I shall."

Hamilton's marriage to Elizabeth Schuyler brought him the wealth he needed and the social standing that he coveted, as well as the love of a beautiful woman. During their twenty-three-year marriage, Betsy bore him eight children.

Chapter Seventeen

The POT BOILS OVER

MUTINY!

If one word could shake the American army to its foundations, it was mutiny. Words of action, such as "the British are attacking" could inspire solidarity and promise action against a common enemy. Mutiny could mean dissolution and hatred beyond understanding — and perhaps beyond reconciliation.

An uprising of soldiers during the deadly winter of 1780 should have been expected from the freezing, hungry, disillusioned men trapped in the huts at Jockey Hollow. Time lay idle on their hands; they could lie in their crude bunks and be overwhelmed by the endless injustices heaped on them. However, morale should have been on the rebound in Log House City by mid-May of 1780. Spring had come to the Watchung Mountains and to Morristown. Native dogwood trees were in full white, showy dress. Wildflowers abounded in the meadows and along the streams; robins, goldfinches and bluebirds joined in a spring symphony. Overhead, flocks of ducks and geese were on the wing, pausing in the Great Swamp before resuming their northward flight.

But there was no joy in Jockey Hollow. Bountiful weather did not ease unending hunger pangs. Emaciated soldiers, hungry to the point of illness, grumbled and fumed on the parade ground as they spent their days in what to them were meaningless drills.

Congressmen Philip Schuyler, John Mathews, and Nathaniel Peabody, had lingered in camp far longer than anyone, including they themselves, had intended. The Congressmen recognized, more pointedly than even the men themselves, that Jockey Hollow was a roiling pot of anger and mistrust, spiced by awareness of injustice from their countrymen.

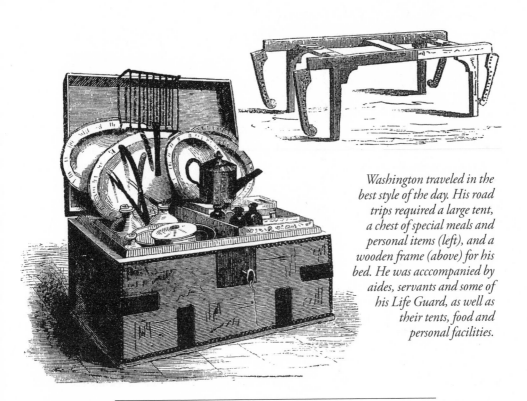

Washington traveled in the best style of the day. His road trips required a large tent, a chest of special meals and personal items (left), and a wooden frame (above) for his bed. He was acccompanied by aides, servants and some of his Life Guard, as well as their tents, food and personal facilities.

The pot rapidly approached the point of boiling rebellion.

Near-mutiny was nothing new or unexpected in an army that had grown from scratch. Its independent militiamen from small New England towns and forests, Virginia plantations and Blue Ridge hills rebelled at Washington's insistence on discipline and order when he assumed command of the Continental army in 1775. In the long years of war that followed, nearly every state's troops exploded in anger at some point.

Washington knew the ugly threat of defiance as early as September 10, 1775, when 500 of Pennsylvania's vaunted, but undisciplined riflemen threatened to free by force one of their number who had been jailed in the main guardhouse at Cambridge, Massachusetts. Dr. Thacher described the jaunty riflemen as "dressed in white frocks, or rifle- shirts, and round hats."

They also displayed an arrogance that astounded even the poorly trained militia already assembled in or near Boston. Numerous minor infractions by the self-centered riflemen in succeeding months were treated lightly. In September, when a Pennsylvania sergeant was confined to the main guardhouse in Cambridge, his fellow riflemen refused to countenance such an indignity.

"Shirtmen" turned out in force, threatening to carry out their unwritten code that they must forcibly release a jailed comrade. More than 500 other soldiers, not riflemen, were ordered to post themselves around the jail. Several other regiments were turned out under arms.

That uprising on September 10 is known in history as "The Mutiny on Prospect Hill." Officers, including Charles Lee and Nathanael Greene, and possibly Washington himself, persuaded the angry men to drop their arms and face punishment. A Pennsylvania regiment surrounded the mutinous riflemen and escorted them back to camp.

Thirty-three of them were court-martialed. Each was convicted of disobedient and mutinous behavior. The ringleader, John Seaman, received a mere six days behind bars. He also had to pay the fine of twenty shillings inflicted on all the convicted men, who were released and allowed to rejoin their units. The army was new at handling free spirits; twenty shillings scarcely hurt even a low-paid private.

As the war dragged on, dissatisfied soldiers often protested vigorously against what they considered to be injustice and unfairness, only to be pacified or quickly punished before the troubles escalated into mutiny. But nothing had prepared the American soldiers or their officers, much less the earnest, concerned Committee at Headquarters, still in town, for the May night in 1780 when the pot boiled over.

Fear became reality on the evening of May 25, when the seething aggravation exploded into mutiny by two regiments of the Connecticut Line quartered in Jockey Hollow. It should not have been a surprise: Connecticut soldiers had been wrangling with officers since November and December of 1775, when Washington was reorganizing the army.

As November 1775 had neared its end, disgruntled Connecticut men refused to perform their duties, claiming their terms of enlistment were up. On December 1, 1775, some started for home without leave. Washington rode after the men, brought most of them back and sternly warned them not to leave until they received written discharges. There was no mutiny per se that December day, but the bold attitude of the Connecticut soldiers verged on an incipient uprising.

In those early days of shaping an army, Washington wrote of his anguish in dealing with men who were "under no kind of government themselves" and who could destroy what little control he had as their commanding general: "Could I have foreseen what I have, and am likely to experience, no consideration upon earth should have induced me to accept this command."

Connecticut troops were of course far from the only rebellious Continentals, but there was a thread of independence bordering on impudence that linked them with rebellion throughout most of the war. Two important disorders, or perhaps they were near mutinies, were related by one of them, Joseph Plumb Martin. Since he was one of the very few foot soldiers who wrote at length of their service, it leads one to wonder whether mutinous incidents in other regiments have gone forever unnoticed because no one reported them or even mentioned them in passing. At any rate, what follows concerning strong-willed Connecticut men are Martin's depictions of the atmosphere, in his words or paraphrased.

In January 1779, Martin and his Connecticut regiment were involved in a serious disorder that was at first masked in nighttime comedy devised by the Connecticut Line. As Martin related the incident, the New Englanders had been starving and freezing, as usual, but now encamped in their home state, they were "determined that if our officers would not see some of our grievances redressed, the state should."

At first, the men simply paraded in front of their tents after evening roll call, carefully leaving their arms in their tents. Almost immediately, officers appeared, led by their colonel, and "expressed a deal of sorrow for the hardships we were compelled to undergo." That might well have ended the affair, except that one intemperate officer rashly scolded the men for " mutinous conduct." Other, more sensitive, officers sensed the anger those words had provoked; they talked softly to "soothe the Yankee temper they had excited."

The soldiers returned to their huts but sleep eluded them. They decided that if they couldn't sleep, neither should any officer have the privilege. They loaded an old musket with powder, fixed a long fuse to ignite the powder, and were in their tents when the old weapon roared its outrage. Officers rushed out, peeped into tents, saw only soldiers feigning sleep, and left. As soon as the officers were presumed to be asleep, the ancient weapon was fired again. More attention, more frustration; both lasted through the night. Each interruption of sleep eased the tension, but the joy of bothering their leaders did not quell tempers or end plotting to get even.

A few nights later, in a second episode, the regiment again lined up on the parade ground, this time fully armed and ready to march through Connecticut. After demonstrating when roll call ended, they planned to "disperse to our homes." During parade ground talk of this plan, a belligerent major strode into sight, telling the men they might better be sleeping in their warm huts than standing on a cold parade ground.

"Yes sir," responded the leader of the angry troops. "Solomon says that 'the abundance of the rich will not suffer him to sleep.' And we find that the abundance of poverty will not let us sleep." A colonel stepped up and "the old mode of flattery and promising was resorted to and produced the usual effect. We all once more returned to our huts and there spent the remainder of the night, muttering over our plight."

The heated threat of mutiny ebbed into calmness that January night, but the embers of resentment and frustration continued to burn in the minds of the Connecticut men. In time, these embers would flare into open flames.

Surgeon James Thacher, one of the young officers close to the men in Jockey Hollow, knew well of the "repeated disappointment of our hopes and expectations" and warned

WASHINGTON'S DESK, WASHINGTON HEADQUARTERS, MORRISTOWN N J.

From this desk, Washington originated hundreds of letters to Congress, officers, friends, and others, seeking supplies desperately needed in Morristown. His aides actually wrote the finished letters.

that "the confidence of the army in public justice and public promises is greatly diminished and we are reduced almost to despair for many soldiers,"

Dr. Thacher also noted that "our poor soldiers are reduced to the very verge of famine; their patience is exhausted by complicated sufferings, and their spirits are almost broken." He observed that soldiers had a "diminution of that enthusiastic patriotism and that ardent attachment to our cause, by which they were formerly distinguished."

Among the soldiers, too, the young surgeon recognized a bitterness regarding pay, which Thacher grandly called "pecuniary compensation." Soldiers who had formerly reenlisted for a small bounty or none at all, now found in the ranks with themselves others who had enlisted for a bounty of more than ten times the nominal value.

The young surgeon sensed that the camp was teeming with dissent, "creating a considerable degree of relaxation in discipline and an unusual number of desertions from our ranks." As May dwindled away, Martin's Connecticut regiment became increasingly morose. The mood passed beyond mere despair on May 25.

Some of the men from a Connecticut regiment had spent the morning of that day with detachments of other state regiments, helping to dig graves for eleven men scheduled to be executed for various crimes the next day. Eight were to be hanged; three would face firing squads composed of their fellow soldiers. The sight of eleven freshly dug graves close to the scaffold lingered in their minds.

That evening, after the disgruntled Connecticut men wandered across the parade ground, "growling like sore headed dogs," they began snapping at officers and disobeying orders. A pompous adjutant lost his composure and called a soldier a "mutinous dog." The spark had been struck, but instead of directing his anger at the officer, the soldier unexpectedly shouted to his fellow soldiers, "Who will parade with me?" The entire regiment fell in. They chose no leader, lest he face hanging when, or if, the spreading defiance went unchecked.

A drummer beat out signals. On the first drum roll, the men shouldered their arms. On the second, they faced to the front, and on the third the regiment moved out "with music playing" toward two other Connecticut regiments, "forty or fifty rods ahead of us." Officers lost their heads, running alongside the columns, scolding the men as if they were naughty schoolboys.

Martin recalled that when one soldier called a halt, several officers "seized upon him like wolves on a sheep and dragged him out of the ranks, intending to make an example of him." They changed their minds when several soldiers pointed their bayonets, "thick as hatched teeth," at them and compelled a quick release of the prisoner.

The officers tried to quell the mutineers, first with the soft lure of food, then with the big stick of threats. When one of the officers said cattle had just been driven into the compound for the men, a private yelled, "Go butcher them, then." Sardonic laughter swept across the parade ground.

Lieutenant Colonel John Sumner strode onto the parade ground to try the rough approach. He brusquely ordered the men to shoulder arms. They looked through him as if he did not exist. He then denounced them with "a whole quiver of the arrows of his rhetoric." That was no more effective than the cattle ruse. The colonel "walked off to his quarters, chewing the cud of resentment all the way."

Officers quickly assembled the Pennsylvania regiment and, without telling them of the mutiny fomenting nearby, spread them through the forest to block the Connecticut troops if they paraded off the grounds. One of the Pennsylvanians, learning of their mission to thwart fellow soldiers, called out, "Let us join the Yankees."

The Pennsylvanians at that point were quickly sent back to their quarters, a major turning point in the situation. If they had joined the Connecticut insurgents, the war might well have come nearly to an end in Jockey Hollow on that balmy evening in May. Instead, the incensed men milled about on the parade grounds, filled with anger for "ungrateful people" who did not know or care "while we are keeping a cruel enemy from them."

Colonel Walter Stewart of the Pennsylvania Line saved the night — and perhaps the war effort — by walking gently through the ranks, asking why the men had not gone to their officers? After bursts of scornful laughter, a spokesman for the rebellious men said that they had talked with their officers, without satisfaction.

Stewart patiently told the slowly relaxing men " your officers suffer as much as you do." He said officers had no money: "I had not a sixpence to buy a partridge that was offered to me the other day." Far more important than that, Stewart asked if the men knew "how much you injure your own characters by such conduct?" He then clinched his argument:

> You Connecticut troops have won immortal honor to yourselves the winter past, by your perseverance, patience and bravery, and now you are shaking it off at your heels.

It made sense to the proud, angry men. The mutinous fury ebbed. The men slowly become less tense, gave up the fight, became less agitated, and wound up with "just bitterness and despair." That is exactly where they had begun the day. Nothing had been lost. Neither had anything been gained.

Washington seized the moment. The day after the mutiny, he wrote Congress, telling them of the tempest and letting them know once more that "constant instances of want are too much for the soldiers." He told Congress that "we have everything to dread; indeed, I have almost ceased to hope." He sent a separate letter to Joseph Reed, resident of Pennsylvania, declaring that Pennsylvania must assume the burden of feeding the troops. "The matter is reduced to a point," Washington said. "Either Pennsylvania must give us all the aid we ask of her, or we can undertake nothing."

The commander exploited the fact that Lafayette had brought news that France was sending a fleet and thousands of soldiers. He rammed home the point of potential international embarrassment:

> The Court of France has made a glorious effort for our deliverance, and if we disappoint its intentions by our supineness, we must become contemptible in the eyes of the world.

Out in the Jockey Hollow woodland the day after the mutiny, only one of the graves dug for the eleven men scheduled to be executed held a body; the other ten men had been spared death. The grave held Private Samuel Crawford, who on May 26 became the last man to be hanged at Jockey Hollow (See Chapter 8.)

But the severe discontent and deep feelings of injustice were not buried that day. They would return. The men of Jockey Hollow were not automatons without feelings. Instead, they nurtured a deep sense they had been abandoned by their nation.

A Mini-Second Parting

The long years of the Revolution frazzled the tempers of officers as well as the men in huts. Alexander Hamilton, George Washington's most trusted and intelligent aide, came to an abrupt parting with his chief on February 16, 1781. Nearly six years of mutual admiration and respect exploded in a moment of petulance and temper.

Hamilton gave his version of the incident in a letter written to Philip Schuyler, his father-in-law, on February 18, 1781, two days after the damaging split. According to Hamilton, the parting came at the top of the stairs at headquarters in New York.

"He [Washington] told me he wanted to speak to me in his office," wrote Hamilton. "I answered that I would wait on him immediately." Hamilton paused to speak briefly (in his remembrance) to another officer, and upon reaching the second floor, found Washington at the head of the stairs, fuming:

"Colonel Hamilton, you have kept me waiting at the head of the stairs these ten minutes [and] I must tell you, Sir, you treat me with disrespect."

Hamilton said he replied "... I am not conscious of it Sir; but since you thought it necessary to tell me, so we part."

"Very well Sir," said Washington, "if it be your choice."

Hamilton certainly seemed too ready to resign and Washington only too eager to accept the resignation. It must be presumed the two had been storing animosity for quite a while.

Soon after, Washington tried to close the gap but the mercurial Hamilton wanted none of that. Weeks dragged by with no apparent change in Hamilton's attitude, but with no impassioned need to leave immediately, either. Hamilton left his office on April 30. He had found the duty he desired — a return to the artillery.

Hamilton led a column at Yorktown with courage and skill, and was brevetted Colonel on September 30, 1783. He left service in December. As the United States was being formed, he played an important role in drafting a report that led to the Constitutional Convention in 1787.

When Washington became President of the United States, he chose Hamilton to be his Secretary of the Treasury. Hamilton proved himself worthy of his President's trust.

Chapter Eighteen

The SOLDIERS WASHINGTON
HAD to TRUST

olonel Elias Dayton, commander of the Third New Jersey Regiment in Elizabeth, wasted no time on May 26, 1780, when he took one look at the front page of a special edition of the *Royal Gazette,* the New York newspaper edited by British propagandist James Rivington. The page gushed forth the news: *Clinton had captured Charleston!*

Dayton wrapped the paper, hailed an express rider, and ordered him to get the package to Washington without delay. He scribbled a note, saying that he suspected the news was a lie, based on Rivington's reputation for twisting the news to mislead the Americans.

Washington rejected Dayton's effort to suggest a bright side. After reading the details in Rivington's article, including a list of the captured American regiments and generals known to be in Charleston, he recognized that this was not mere propaganda.

Three days later, the frigate *Iris* sailed into New York with distressing proof. Charleston had surrendered on May 12, with a loss of 5,500 prisoners, 391 guns, and huge store of ammunition. It seemed only a matter of weeks before England's hero of the moment, General Henry Clinton, would return to unleash his tough, experienced, and jubilant army on New Jersey.

Washington knew there was no time to lose. He asked the messenger to wait while he wrote a short answer to Dayton:

> *I most sincerely wish that your suspicions of the truth of Rivington's publication may prove well grounded, but I confess it bears too many marks of authenticity.*

The fastest communication during the Revolution were the hard-riding express riders who carried messages from Washington and other officers to distant points, and helped round up troops in case of an attack.

He then ordered Dayton to make arrangements for defense of the Elizabethtown area — *without loss of time* — "in case the enemy should make an attempt upon you." Washington did not specifically say so, but since no men could be dispatched permanently from the weakened, distressed Continental Army at Jockey Hollow, Dayton had only one recourse: the New Jersey militia.

The militia! Washington had openly mistrusted all militia units for most of the war, too often with good cause. The most cited and most understandable early reason for the commander's mistrust came at the battle for Long Island in August 1776, when 8,000 Connecticut militiamen were pressed into action. Only 2,000 of them remained on the field when that battle ended. Seventy-five percent of them had fled. Writing of this defection, Washington told Congress on September 24, 1776:

> *If I were called upon to declare under oath, whether the militia had been most service-able or most hurtful upon the whole, I should subscribe to the latter.*

Slightly more than two months later, as the meager American army was retreating across northern New Jersey, Washington bitterly declared that he had "small encouragement to hope for much assistance from the militia of this state."

That rebuke swelled into a stinging indictment in late November as the American army was leaving New Brunswick in its headlong flight toward the Delaware River. In a letter to his brother, John Augustine Washington, the general fumed that "the conduct of the Jerseys has been most infamous." He expanded the denunciation:

> *Instead of turning out to defend their country and affording aid to our Army, they are making their submissions [to the British] as fast as they can. If they, the Jerseys, had given us any support, we might have made a stand at Hackensack and after that at New Brunswick, but the few Militia that were in Arms, disbanded themselves.*

Washington likely included in that catch-all denunciation the "Flying Camp" he had organized in New Jersey in July 1776, ordering Brigadier General Hugh Mercer to have 3,000 troops ready to speed wherever they might be needed. Mercer believed in early July that he could count on 1,200 New Jersey men, but by the end of the month most of them were back in their fields harvesting hay.

Mercer's mobile strike force was never more than a token idea, undermanned, poorly armed and ill supplied. Morale was low and thievery was high. Flying Camp soldiers pillaged the countryside, prompting Abraham Clark of Elizabethtown (one of New Jersey's signers of the Declaration of Independence) to write in October: "We have not had the enemy among us, but Staten Island hath not suffered from the British troops scarcely the tenth part of the damage this town hath from the militia."

Despite Washington's almost constant scorn for the militia as all but worthless, New Jersey's citizen soldiers became active and useful almost immediately after the Americans had crossed the Delaware River to the comparative safety of Pennsylvania.

The willingness of the New Jersey militia to engage a substantial British contingent was severely tried on December 17, 1776, in a little-noted early militia test. That day, General Alexander Leslie, seasoned commander of the British rear guard, launched a probe toward the Watchung Mountains to see what rebel militia might be on the British flanks. He sent 800 of his regulars toward the Gap in the Watchung Mountains near Springfield to accomplish part of the mission.

Upon hearing that the British were approaching, Major Oliver Spencer, commanding an Essex County militia unit, sent a rider racing toward Chatham to alert Colonel Jacob Ford, Jr., and his Morris County Militia, and Colonel John Cleves Symmes, whose Sussex County Militia was also in Chatham. The colonels led their units eastward and surged into the gap at the Short Hills.

Just as the sun began to set over the Watchung Mountains, the militiamen met the British in a short skirmish that might be called the First Battle of Springfield. The New Jersey militiamen stymied Leslie and the British before darkness set in.

Both sides retired for the night. The militiamen rose at first light, ready for a renewed enemy attack. Dawn revealed that the British had departed. Leslie had found what he sought: there *were* militiamen on the flanks, ready and willing to fight. It was by no means an American victory but neither was it a demonstration of craven Americans cowering in the hills. The untested militia *had* responded, despite the possibility of annihilation.

With Washington apparently set for winter across the Delaware and the British and Hessians settling down for a season of inaction in Trenton and New Brunswick, the countryside between the towns and the Watchung Mountains erupted in spontaneous, uncoordinated guerrilla warfare, a version of militia action. It kept enemy soldiers pinned within their New Brunswick and Trenton compounds after dark as December 1776 wore down.

Seemingly overnight and with no central plan, the New Jersey countryside became a place of horror for the enemy after dark. New Jersey civilians, angered by the depredations and plundering of Hessian and British soldiers, began counter-attacking. Every bush, every copse, every tree, became possible harbingers of death for enemy soldiers.

Dread of this largely unseen force made the enemy wary as it foraged through the Middlesex countryside in December. Hessians in Trenton complained that "we have not slept one night in peace since we came to this place." By December 18, British forces were forbidden to move anywhere outside of New Brunswick without an escort.

Then, after the critical successes at Trenton and Princeton, as Washington's army moved into its Morristown winter quarters on January 6, 1777, the militia erupted in its most concerted performance of the war. Time after time militiamen engaged the enemy, without high level strategy meetings or even much interchange among the commanders — almost as if the militia had suddenly been blessed with super powers and omniscient understanding of the best way to confound the enemy.

The New Jersey Militia had another chance to show its abilities in June 1778, when Brigadier General Philemon Dickinson's New Jersey Militia harassed and hindered British General Henry Clinton after he moved his army and its ponderous baggage train across the Delaware River from Philadelphia on June 18, ready to begin its march across New Jersey to New York City. The march, as has already been shown, ended in a draw on the plains of Monmouth.

Numerous other such instances of success should have encouraged Washington. He wrote Governor William Livingston on December 21, 1779, pleading that militia officers have a cogent plan ready — "without loss of time" in the likelihood of a British invasion.

First, he sought assurance that "conventional signals" — the alarm guns and the beacons on the Watchung crests — would be in working order to spread the alarm if an invasion came to New Jersey. Second, the general wanted certainty that each militia unit had an exact rendezvous point after answering an alarm.

"That Damned Old Rascal"

William Livingston, first governor of New Jersey (as a state rather than a royal colony), garnered more hatred from the British than anyone other than George Washington. He earned it with a sharp pen rather than a swift sword.

Although he was considered a liberal, his major passions did not include separation from England. He was replaced in the Continental Congress in the spring of 1775 for fear that he might oppose a declaration of independence. He promptly answered a call to command the New Jersey Militia.

When independence was declared and he was named governor, Livingston embraced the cause of revolution: "Whoever draws his sword against his prince must throw away the scabbard. We have passed the Rubicon. We cannot recede nor should I wish we could."

British officials were infuriated by his many brilliant essays. When it was rumored the English General Henry Clinton would be recalled, he wrote:

I should be very sorry to have Clinton recalled through any national resentment of him, because as fertile as that country is in the production of blockheads, I think they cannot easily send us a greater blunderbuss, unless… it should please His Majesty himself to do us the honor of a visit.

The British often dispatched raiding parties to capture him, always unsuccessfully. In 1779 the Crown offered "two thousand guineas and a life pension for that damned old rascal, Governor Livingston, delivered dead or alive."

Livingston responded in typically taunting fashion, calling the British "blockheads" for taking "so much pain and running such a risk to assassinate an old fellow whose place might instantly be supplied by a successor of greater ability and greater energy."

Livingston survived British threats and offers on his head. As governor, he was re-elected each year throughout the war, and until his death in 1790.

The General was practical, insisting that each man must have his own weapons and carry "ten days or a fortnight's provision, to be paid for by the public [New Jersey citizens]." If that were not assured, he told Livingston, considering the paucity of the army's supplies, the militia would be "an encumbrance rather than an assistance."

Livingston assured Washington on December 26 that the New Jersey Militia would build or reconstruct the huge wooden beacons strung atop the Watchung Mountains and on other hilltops, to be burned as vivid alarms if the British invaded New Jersey. The ignition of one beacon would alert other beacon tenders; blazing beacons would light all the peaks within minutes.

However, the governor warned he could not promise how quickly the beacons could be completely rebuilt: "Whether the people will come as cheerfully as heretofore, considering the general depreciation of patriotism, I cannot determine."

Whether the people will come as cheerfully as heretofore. That said it all. If "the people" — the New Jersey Militia — would not respond diligently merely to build or maintain beacons, how would they respond if ever the beacons flamed in warning that the British were coming?

Hit-and-run militia action, gradually growing more skilled and more organized, continued throughout the winter of 1780. Small detachments of British or Hessian troops — often accompanied by Loyalists in British uniforms — would cross the Hudson River and enter the so-called "neutral zone"— the land between the Watchung Mountains and the Hudson River — to seek provisions such as cattle, or wood needed for fuel. New Jersey militiamen would strike fiercely from the shadows. Soon, enemy foraging parties dared not enter the neutral ground without strong-armed support.

After a set-to with the American militia, Hessian Captain Johann Ewald expressed the bewilderment and respect that the citizen soldiers engendered among the enemy and gave a clear view of American militia tactics:

> *What can you not achieve with such small bands who have learned to fight dispersed, who know how to use every molehill for their defense, and who retreat as quickly when attacked as they advance again, and who will always find space to hide? Never have I seen these maneuvers performed better than by the American Militia, and especially that of the Province of New Jersey. If you were forced to retreat against these people you could certainly count on constantly having them around you.*

Washington continued to hold his dim view of the local troops. For one thing, they were beyond the discipline and training that he demanded from his Continental troops. A militiaman could come and go as he pleased; punishments were slight. The key element seemed to be whether a citizen soldier was fighting to defend his own part of the nation.

Militiamen could be aggravating to a commander, but it was evident that the loose structure and uncertain behavior of the part-time soldiers was the product of bewildering state government regulations rather than a lack of courage or compliance by the militiamen.

In New Jersey, where the militia would be most sorely tested because the state lay adjacent to the British headquarters in New York, regulations changed constantly and reached a depth of absurdity. One of the last New Jersey laws passed in 1777 was "A supplementary Act to an Act to explain and amend an Act for the better regulating the militia and the Supplement Act thereto."

Washington wrote Livingston in disgust over the New Jersey Legislature's incredible, endless tampering with its militia regulations. He asked how "an assembly of gentlemen, eyewitnesses to the distresses and inconveniences that have their principal source in the want of a well-regulated militia, hesitate to adopt the only remedy that can remove them?"

The General urged Livingston to plead with the state's lawmakers: "For Heaven's sake entreat them to lay aside their present opinions [about the state's militia] and waiving every other consideration let the public good be singularly attended to." If the legislature did not heed the advice, and the British suddenly attacked, Washington concluded, "your Assembly may perhaps wish that their militia were in the field."

Militia units in Essex and Morris counties by the spring of 1780 already were extensively on guard in the neutral ground, alternating units on a monthly basis — one month on duty, one month at home. They knew the terrain well and surely remembered good defensive locations as they traveled back and forth in their rotations. Behind the Watchung Mountains, other militiamen had been performing routine guard duty for years at bridges and other possibly critical locations. They ranged in age from boys in their early teens to men in very late middle age.

Boys just entering puberty were anxious for action. David Bogert joined the Bergen County militia at age thirteen and served in the company for two years before he was admitted to militia status. He was taken prisoner in a neutral ground skirmish, was exchanged, and returned to action. He served throughout the war, receiving only eight dollars in pay for his several years in uniform. Most militiamen fared little better.

Tim Ford, son of former militia colonel Jacob Ford, Jr., deceased in 1777, also itched for action. His turn would soon come, as it would for hundreds of other very young volunteers.

Teen-aged Ashbel Green, son of virulently patriotic Presbyterian minister Jacob Green of East Hanover, was teaching school in Bottle Hill (now Madison) soon after the war began. His early militia career included guarding bridges over the wide Passaic River at East

Hanover and Chatham. (Green later attended the College of New Jersey in Princeton and became its president in 1812.)

Jacob Arnold, the well-to-do proprietor of The Arnold Tavern at the Morristown Green, where Washington spent the winter of 1777, was a militia activist. Arnold had a volunteer horse troop that rendered yeoman service on the battlefields and was a constant carrier of messages that had to be delivered rapidly between commands or between units on a battlefield.

The most colorful New Jersey Militia personality was hard-fighting, scantily-educated, loud talking General William Winds, who wasted no time getting into uniform after the war started. His zeal was unmatched: he always wore his uniform and carried his loaded musket even to church. He endlessly rebuked faint-hearted militiamen who were less than ready for war. His stentorian voice echoed across battlegrounds and parade grounds with the intensity of a bullhorn.

Meanwhile, Loyalists in New York increasingly fretted about Knyphausen's unwillingness to attack the severely diminished American forces. One of the New York leaders was former New Jersey Governor William Franklin.

The city's vigorous, hawkish Loyalist cabal fretted that no action was planned against the Continental Army west of the Hudson River. Franklin joined forces with William Smith, scion of one of New York's leading families; Governor (and Major General) James Robertson, newly-commissioned Royal Governor of New York; and Major General William Tryon, the ruthless officer who had burned and pillaged his way along the Connecticut coast in July 1779.

The quartet swept into the leadership vacuum created when Clinton departed for Charleston, leaving no orders or even any of his characteristically strange "hints" about how officers, including General Knyphausen, should conduct a campaign against Washington. The unofficial situation for the Hessian was thus "do nothing until I return."

As weeks of inaction stretched into months, the impatient Loyalists intensified their criticisms of Knyphausen's *laissez faire* conduct of military matters. By late May of 1780, their criticisms had become rancorous demands for an assault on what they believed was an almost defenseless New Jersey. Franklin knew, via British spies, that the American army had lost huge numbers of men, that few had reenlisted, and that mutinous thoughts stirred in Jockey Hollow. The ex-governor scoffed at fears that New Jersey militiamen might total as many as 16, 000 soldiers.

A crucial time for decision for the schemers came on May 28, when a frigate brought the brief message that Charleston had surrendered. Clinton offered no clue as to when he would be back in New York or what Knyphausen should do in the meantime. Time was running out for the German commander. His critics insisted that Washington's defenses

A New Jersey militiaman leaving his home and family is memorialized in this magnificent statue in the Morristown Green.

would crumble easily if Knyphausen invaded the state. They believed New Jersey Loyalists and neutralists tired of the long, futile war would receive a British/Hessian army eagerly.

Knyphausen had to make a decision: should he launch an attack, which, if unsuccessful, would at the very least arouse Clinton's anger? On the other hand, if successful, it would earn the Hessian the plaudits that had never been his in the British army.

Franklin pushed for what he believed would be an easy victory. Such success could well clear the way to his returning to New Jersey as a hero and as the first deposed Royal governor to resume his seat in British America.

Only the unknown strength of the New Jersey Militia gave reason for pause. If aroused, and if they fought as well as they might, they could make a tremendous difference. Knyphausen's advisers felt there was not much chance of such an aroused militia.

That opinion was not restricted to the New Yorkers. On May 16, 1780, Congressmen Philip Schuyler and Nathaniel Peabody, who had been studying the situation in

Morristown for several weeks, warned fellow Congressmen "it would be hazarding too much to rely altogether on aid from the militia." Experience, they wrote, showed that militia brigades frequently retire from the field "in such critical conjectures & when their continuance would be of the highest importance."

The first days of June ticked away. No word leaked from New York about any kind of troop mobilization. Clinton soon would be back at his home base. The time had come for Knyphausen to make the decision that could change the course of the war, perhaps even end it.

The British were about to move in some fashion. Behind the Watchung Mountains, thousands of militiamen gathered about their fireplaces or talked as they visited during lulls in spring plowing.

The twilight of the American Revolution had come. Militiamen had to decide whether they would prevent the sun from setting on the American cause.

An Early Warning System

Sentries atop the Watchung Mountains kept a constant watch on the broad plains in the valley to the east, looking for indications that a British force might be crossing the Arthur Kill near Elizabethtown and preparing to strike westward toward Morristown. Detecting the enemy was easy enough; the problem lay in alerting the thousands of militiamen spread over a huge area behind the mountains.

As early as 1777, early detection system may have begun near the Short Hills Gap with an eighteen-pound cannon nicknamed "Old Sow." It is said that a tar barrel was placed atop a twenty-foot pole nearby to light if a night alarm became necessary. It is more likely that a carefully planned alarm system was not begun until late 1778. General William Alexander (Lord Stirling), one of Washington's most trusted officers, drew the basic plan (shown on the opposite page) to strengthen defense of the winter encampment in Middlebrook. The order was written in Alexander's hand: "The figure of the Beacons will appear thus."

Alexander planned wooden structures "about sixteen feet square" at the base, "to diminish as they rise like a pyramid & should be eighteen or twenty feet high." The spaces inside and between the logs would be filled with dry brush to insure rapid flaming. The outside logs would also be dry enough to catch fire almost instantly. The first of eight beacons erected to Stirling's specifications was described as "a large fire on the Mountain in the Rear of Pluckemin." Five others quickly rose on the Watchung slopes that sheltered the American army in 1778-79. Another beacon was built on a hill overlooking an approach to Princeton. The eighth was on "the hill in the front of Martin's Tavern" east of the Middlebrook camp.

Fifteen other beacons were built at locations as far away as the Atlantic Highlands in Monmouth County and at several locations in Somerset and Hunterdon counties. The northernmost beacon was on "Pigeon Hill, about four miles northwest of Morristown." A beacon was also scheduled to be erected on the high hill a few hundred feet west of the Morristown Green, probably on the site now known as Fort Nonsense. The lighting of any one beacon was the signal to fire all the others. Within minutes, a warning could be spread over hundreds of square miles, alerting militia forces deep into New Jersey.

The beacon sites quickly fell on hard times. General Arthur St. Clair wrote Washington from Springfield on January 31, 1780:

> *The signals for calling out the militia have been very much neglected, and are down in some places and I cannot find who has the care of them. I have requested Mr.*

General William Alexander (Lord Stirling) illustrated his order to erect beacons on the hills outward from Morristown. This rough sketch shows a 20-foor-high beacon that would be 20 feet square at the bottom and four feet sqare at the top.

Caldwell to have them re-established and proper persons appointed to give the alarm in case of necessity but I am not certain but this may interfere with some regulation of the state, which some time ago put that matter into the care of the militia generals, and it has gone into the hands of the subordinate officers in gradation until it is nobody's business.

This reinforced Washington's feeling that the alarm system was defective. He recognized the value of the beacons but sensed that soon they would be put to the test.

Brigadier Nathaniel Heard described the twenty-three sites in a list that appears in A.E. Vanderpoel's *History of Chatham*. The sites are also located on a topographic map published in 2005 by James T. Raleigh of the Philip Freneau Press.

Three of the beacon sites now are occupied by modern communication or relay towers. Other sites are now lookout spots in county or state parks. No physical evidence of the actual beacons exist, either because their dry wooden construction fostered quick rotting after the war ended, or because the joyous victors burned the structures in celebration after the victory at Yorktown.

Chapter Nineteen

The INVASION *of* NEW JERSEY: *Act One*

B ritish and Hessian troops slipped silently ashore at De Hart's Landing near Eliza-bethtown at about midnight on June 7, 1780, and marched inland for an hour without anyone knowing of their presence. Suddenly, at about 1 a.m., musket shots fired by a small American patrol blazed from the darkness. The suspense of when Great Britain would unleash its vaunted military power on New Jersey had ended. The long-anticipated battle for the crucial state — the final assault in the British view — had begun.

Screams of anguish among the invaders moving west on what is now New Point Road proved that the randomly fired bullets had found targets. The stunned invaders imme-diately returned the fire, aiming at the point where the muskets had flared. Their bullets brought equally agonized cries.

British hopes for a surprise landing, followed by a brisk, easy dash westward toward Springfield and perhaps on to Morristown, vanished with those first American shots. The surprise volley was an omen that the British might well have carefully considered: almost from the start, the mission had gone awry.

The small American unit that fired the opening salvo was there because Washington had become unnerved by reports of lax American security in and near Elizabethtown. He dispatched his personal Life Guard of about 150 men, led by Major Caleb Gibbs, to monitor the situation. Timothy Ford, seventeen-year-old son of the late Colonel and Mrs. Theodosia Ford, was in the detachment as a volunteer observer.

Gibbs and his men sighted the enemy at a most propitious time; the late night dark-

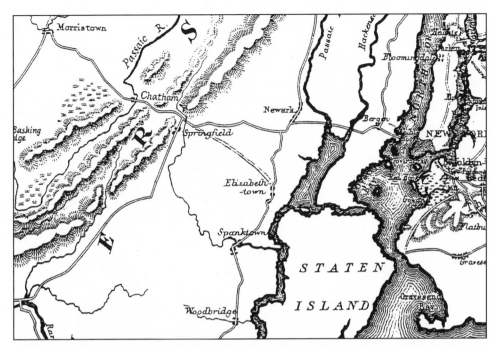

The setting for the June 1780 invasion of New Jersey is clear in this topographical map. Once across the Arthur Kill from Staten Island at Elizabethtown, the gap west of Springfield opened the way to Chatham and Morristown. The Great Swamp and the Passaic River were obstacles, but not nearly as daunting as the gap at The Short Hills.

ness was a plausible hour for surveillance. The Life Guard's volley ended all reason for British hope for surprise by throwing the secret invasion into complete disorder. Brigadier General Thomas Stirling, commanding the first invasion wave, had been assured there would be little or no American resistance.

Instead, one of the first randomly fired musket balls slammed into Stirling's hip. The injury caused a ninety-minute delay and gave the defenders ample time to spread word of the attack. Worse, Stirling's fighting had ended before the action was barely underway. Command fell to the next senior officer, Hessian Colonel Friedrich Wilhelm von Wurmb.

Tim Ford also had his short military career ended. Two bullets from the British response lodged in the youth's thigh. Ford was crudely bandaged at the scene before being placed on a litter for the long carry home to Morristown.

Stirling's injury gave the Americans a huge edge. A messenger galloped toward Morristown to rouse Washington, and another raced to alert soldiers at the gap in the Short Hills. By the time Stirling was bandaged and taken back to the Arthur Kill, the

Early on the morning of June 23, 1780, British and Hessan troops passed Governor William Livingston's mansion on the edge of Elizabethtown.

towering wooden beacons atop the gap were ablaze. Widely scattered tenders were lighting their beacons along the Watchung crest. Booming cannons also awakened sleeping militiamen in the valleys to the west.

The exhausted messenger reached the Ford Mansion at about four a.m., rousing the general, who dispatched a rider to Jockey Hollow with orders to get two Connecticut and two Pennsylvania regiments on the road to Springfield. The Continental regulars were at least a day away from the conflict. This first facet of the invasion, for better or for worse, would belong to the less than 1,000 Continental troops stationed near Elizabeth and the New Jersey Militia. The early morning delay near Elizabethtown had provided the critical time needed to alert the citizen soldiers.

Back in Elizabethtown, most of the first wave of invaders was fully ashore and moving inland. The early morning exchange of shots had to be dismissed as an unlucky happening for the invaders. Far worse, from a strategic standpoint, where were General Wilhelm von Knyphausen, his officers, and their thousands of British and Hessian soldiers?

Indecision and consternation had seriously impeded the Hessian general. As his fleet set sail from New York to carry Knyphausen and his army to Staten Island, a small boat signaled the flagship to come about. Major William Crosbie, Clinton's adjutant, boarded with the astounding news that his general and his large army were aboard ships somewhere near Chesapeake Bay, headed for New York City.

A hasty shipboard conference agreed the invasion of New Jersey would have been aborted if the message had come before the first wave of men had been unleashed near Elizabethtown. Now, with Stirling's First Division already crossing to New Jersey, it was too late to call off the expedition. Those advance troops had to be supported.

Knyphausen was beset with anguish. He had ordered the invasion of New Jersey without Clinton's knowledge, advice, or consent, a highly risky step for a man second in command — more so because it was being risked by a Hessian general, too often dismissed by snobbish British hierarchy as a high-ranking vassal hired to bring the German soldiers to America and to keep them under control.

Knyphausen pressed on. His reinforcements eventually landed on the northern end of Staten Island, many hours behind time. They had to be unloaded and sent racing to the rendezvous point opposite De Hart's Landing near Elizabethtown. His thousands of British and Hessian regulars and Loyalist troops did not reach New Jersey until well after dawn. With little more than a token pause, they set off at a brisk pace for Connecticut Farms to the northwest, about seven miles from Elizabethtown Point.

As the day began, the defending American force consisted of Maxwell's 741 men in the New Jersey Brigade, the 150 members of Washington's Life Guard who had followed Major Gibbs to Elizabethtown, and about 360 militiamen, totaling some 1,250 defenders. Coming at them would be at least 5,000 well-drilled, well-fed, well-armed attackers, with another 2,500 on the way as a backup.

The invaders' First Division rolled westward. Their orders called for the regiment to be in Connecticut Farms (founded in 1667 by Connecticut farmers and now called Union) before noon. The British hopes for an easy foray were fast being dashed; the roads to Connecticut Farms had come alive with angry, determined militiamen hastening in from the back country.

Brigadier General William Maxwell was the ranking American officer when the battle began. His First New Jersey Brigade carried the American cause throughout the morning, fighting for time and giving up land as grudgingly as possible.

Major General Philemon Dickinson, commander of the New Jersey militia, was not on hand in the early, defining stages of the battle. It made no difference to Scotch Willie Maxwell. The veteran warrior sensed that if his Continentals held the center, the emerging militia would smite the British flanks like vengeful bees in a disturbed honeycomb.

The British and Hessians marched toward Connecticut Farms confidently and, at first, with little opposition. Suddenly, the militia became a fierce force. Farmers, teachers, blacksmiths, storekeepers, hired hands, butchers, bakers, and candlestick makers, each with his own musket, ammunition, and food, streamed into the battle zone to join the fight.

Each of them found his own little fortress, behind boulders, walls, thickets, trees, buildings, or whatever offered even a little protection. They would shoot, stand boldly to reload their muskets, and then shoot again with a rapidity and courage that rattled the oncoming enemy. The militia presence grew with each passing minute, swelling the ranks of the soldiers in homespun.

The Hessians later reported that on that June day the Americans would fire one or two shots, then "run off as hard as they could…they ran much faster than we. They are a long-legged make, most of them without shoes and stockings and without coats."

Later, former general Philip Schuyler, who was with the Committee at Headquarters in Morristown and who earlier had openly doubted the militia's abilities, would report:

> I find the enemy were made to believe that if they came out in force, our army would not fight, the Country would submit and they would possess themselves of all our stores. They were surprised to find the militia so firm – some were heard to say the Americans fight like bulldogs.

It was difficult to differentiate among Maxwell's American regulars, militiamen, and local unattached citizens who appeared with their muskets and a contagious zeal. The thickly wooded, sparsely settled area was perfect for guerilla-style war. The Hessians knew this and had trained a regiment in the techniques of the "American style" of fighting. But the New Jersey militiamen had been prepared by honing their woodland guile and marksmanship to obtain food. Their technique could not be imitated on short notice.

Shortly before 8 a.m., Maxwell arrayed his men outside Connecticut Farms, on two peaks at the top of a ravine through which the west branch of the Elizabeth River flowed. The first Hessian attempt to cross the river brought a hail of bullets that ended all thoughts of a quick fording of the stream. Later, a penetration of Jaegers (hunters) armed with short-barreled rifles came so close to the Americans that they had to be repulsed by American bayonets dripping red blood. The unorthodox short Jaeger rifles were not fitted with bayonets.

Maxwell's force slowly retreated to the west of the village and the British and Hessians poured into Connecticut Farms as jubilantly as if they had stormed a heavily fortified Rhineland mountain castle. Gun smoke shrouded the river valley and the forests and orchards that surrounded it. Thousands of British bullets and hundreds of cannonballs

Much to the surprise of the British, Hessians, and other American soldiers, the New Jersey militia fought fiercely and effectively on the first day of the British invasion.

aimed too high had ripped twigs and branches from fruit trees, strewing white blossoms across the orchards. Among those blossoms lay the bodies of many British and Hessians, dead or too seriously wounded to crawl from the carnage.

The British had full control of Elizabethtown and the waterfront, prompting several large groups of refugees (Loyalists) to cross the Arthur Kill to help (or to plunder) wherever possible. They arrived in time to participate in the infamous, brutal destruction of Connecticut Farms.

Parson James Caldwell, the fiery Elizabethtown Presbyterian minister known as "The High Priest of Rebellion," had moved his family to Connecticut Farms after his Elizabethtown church and parsonage were burned. Caldwell was on the battlefield that morning, to bind up wounds and to comfort badly wounded soldiers.

As the British stormed into the town, an unknown assailant shot Mrs. Caldwell dead in her home. It might well have been a stray bullet that entered a window, but the shooter has been variously described as a British or Hessian soldier. A report written long after the Revolution by an aged veteran even attributed the murder to an American soldier's stray bullet.

The British left Connecticut Farms in ruins. Their torches fired fourteen houses, the meetinghouse, and dozens of barns, chicken coops, pigsties, and even fruit trees and flowering shrubs. In their wake they sowed the seeds of a fury that would never be forgotten. The senseless killing of Mrs. Caldwell galvanized a civilian population already appalled by the wanton destruction of the village.

Incensed militiamen had found their cause and were turning out in droves. All of the American fighting in the early hours had been performed by Maxwell's undermanned Continental troops and the huge militia support that had been generated.

Knyphausen learned that the four Continental regiments hastening toward Hobart Gap from Morristown had not arrived by early afternoon, but fearing their arrival, the Hessian called off the attack in mid-afternoon. By early evening his confused, shaken army was in full retreat toward Elizabethtown. On the way, the intense darkness fused into a spectacular storm that a British officer called "the darkest night I can remember in my life, with the most heavy rain, thunder, and lightning known in this country for many years."

The British settled into an unassailable position in Elizabethtown. Knyphausen sent his Jaegers across a hastily built, 238-yard-long pontoon bridge to Staten Island in quest of ammunition. An uneasy truce settled over the battle zone between Connecticut Farms and Knyphausen's headquarters. Both armies knew that further action awaited Clinton's return to New York.

Washington moved his headquarters to Bryant's Tavern in Springfield and asked Major General Benedict Arnold, out of active duty for a long time, to command the troops that inevitably must again face the British. Arnold refused because of his war injuries, suggesting he would prefer a less active command, such as West Point. General Nathanael Greene got his wish for battlefield duty, assuming command of the wing near Springfield that Arnold had rejected. General Friedrich von Steuben, master of discipline and tactics, assumed command of the forward troops close to Elizabethtown.

Most of the militiamen returned to their homes and their fields, as was expected once Knyphausen settled down in Elizabethtown. The citizen soldiers had performed brilliantly, but their orchards were in full flower, their corn was as high as a donkey's knee, and they were about to harvest their first crops of radishes and lettuce. Fields were abloom in The Garden State, as it was known then. And a British army, firmly settled in Elizabethtown, signaled that the curtain had gone down only on "act one" of the invasion of New Jersey.

Speculation returned. Would the New Jersey militia, rightfully pleased with its strong performance in the opening battle, return when the British resumed the assault?

This imaginative scene from a panel of the Vail mansion bronze door shows the Washingtons watching the Springfield battle from a nearby hilltop.

Hessian Hirelings

Throughout the war, Hessian soldiers fought in America — not because they had a passion for the principles of King George III or an animus against Americans; rather, they were rented to the king as a result of a series of English treaties signed with German princes in 1776.

Although the German soldiers in America were all called Hessians, only about half of them from came from the province of Hesse-Cassell. The rest came from several of Germany's nearly 300 territorial divisions.

England turned to Germany in 1776 because there were only about 20,000 soldiers in the British Army, an army about to invade a continent nearly 3,000 miles to the west. There were many reasons for not joining the King's army. The pay was poor; a miserable eight pence a day, with most of this being eaten away by expenses levied by the army. Only those desperately poor could put up with the infamous brutality from non-commissioned officers, compounded by miserable living conditions, the near-impossibility of rising in rank, and the horrors of a long ocean voyage.

The German princes were paid as if their men were domestic animals. The British agreed to give Hessian men the same pay as the British soldiers, which was low by any standard. For each Hessian soldier killed, a German prince received a fine sum in payment as if he had lost a valuable animal, but the soldier's family or relatives received nothing. The prince also received payment for wounded men: two wounded equaled one killed. If an entire German unit perished at sea, the British paid in full and provided a replacement.

On the American retreat across New Jersey in 1776, Hessians were blamed for most of the looting, plundering, raping and killing, although British soldiers were also cited as running wild. If the Hessians behaved badly, it should have been no surprise: a British officer later testified that the German recruits were told that they were headed for a country that was "rich in plunder" — theirs for the taking.

Thousands of Hessians were forced into service — about 30,000 eventually served in America and Canada, under their own officers. Their three commanders in chief in America during the war were, in order of command, Generals Leopold Philip von Heister, Friedrich Wilhelm von Lossberg and Baron Wilhelm von Knyphausen. All of them were from Hesse.

The Germans fought in every major campaign during the war, but never won a decisive battle when Hessians were pitted exclusively against American forces. Their two worst performances were at Trenton on December 26, 1776, and in the second phase of the Battle of Saratoga in October 1778.

The best known of the Hessian commanders, Baron von Knyphausen, was fifty years old when he arrived in Boston in October 1776, bringing with him nearly 5,000 mercenaries. He led troops on Howe's advancement into Philadelphia in 1777, at Monmouth, and at Springfield in 1780. Knyphausen was acting commander in chief (in name only) of British troops when Clinton was on his successful mission at Charleston.

Only sixty percent of the Hessian soldiers returned home. About 5,000 deserted, or met young American women, married and settled down to raise families as immigrants in a nation that, for the most part, accepted them willingly. Another 7,754 were buried in America after deaths from disease or battlefield injuries.

A fanciful and overly brutal drawing of Hessian soldiers (identifiable by distinctive helmets) shooting or clubbing civilians at Connecticut Farms. The drawing undoubtedly was inspired by the shooting of Mrs. Hannah Caldwell during the battle.

Chapter Twenty

The INVASION of NEW JERSEY:
Act Two

G eneral Henry Clinton had every reason to expect a hero's welcome when he docked in New York after a leisurely return to the city aboard a slow-moving British Navy ship. His triumphs in America had been minimal until his stunning victory at Charleston, but he sensed that his Charleston success would erase memories of past blunders.

Clinton spent considerable time on the long voyage home drawing plans for his notion of a brilliant surprise strike at New Jersey. A new Clinton, daring and innovative, emerged in his carefully coordinated plan. His trusted, highly capable young adjutant general, Major John André, would take the plan on ahead via a speedy packet boat so General Knyphausen could prepare for his assigned role in Clinton's conquest of New Jersey.

No one in New York knew the exact whereabouts of Henry Clinton, but his return grew ever more compelling, and for General Wilhelm Knyphausen, ever more ominous. Clinton knew nothing of the Hessian general's unauthorized and futile invasion of New Jersey on June 7.

Four days after the first assault on Springfield, the British commander in chief's battle plan for a New Jersey invasion was in Knyphausen's hands. It stressed that the Hessian must wait "further orders as I [Clinton] judge requisite for conducting *my* designs with the proper secrecy and expedition." Secrecy and expedition: two words certain to intensify Knyphausen's angst.

Clinton's broad objective was not visionary: "a sudden unexpected move to seize upon their grand depot of military stores at Morristown and capture or disperse the forces that covered them." That was essentially what Knyphausen had desired, had tried, and had failed to accomplish. It was also the kind of move Loyalists had begged Clinton to make before he sailed for Charleston

However, the genius of Clinton's plan was in the details. The general envisioned a bold, two-pronged pincer movement. His troops from the Charleston campaign would debark at Perth Amboy, march hastily westward to Middlebrook, head north through Mordecai's Gap on the southern end of the Watchung Mountains, and sweep toward Morristown over lightly guarded roads. The mountaintop beacons would flame and the cannons would roar atop the Watchungs, but if all went as Clinton anticipated, most of the New Jersey Militia would already be committed to the gap at the Short Hills.

Knyphausen was to be ready to cross from Staten Island to Elizabethtown Point "the instant the fleet from

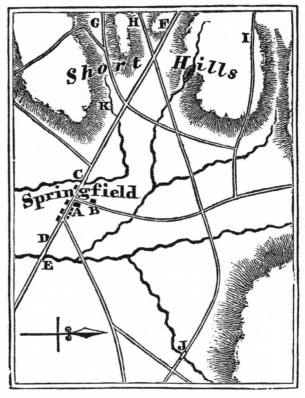

An 1844 map of Springfield and the Short Hills Gap shows: A. Springfield Church; B. The parsonage; C. Bridge on the main road, west of Springfield; D. High rise, west of the Rahway River; E. Bridge over the Rahway River; F. Principal road through the gap; G., H., and I, Lesser passes; K. High ground near Bram's Tavern. Washington briefly made his headquarters in this area.

Charleston arrives at Sandy Hook." He was to hasten westward toward Morristown. Clinton envisioned a Washington so distraught by the coordinated, fast-moving two-front war that surrender would be inevitable.

Poor Knyphausen! He had, without knowing it, utilized a major part of Clinton's plan and had failed miserably. As Clinton neared New York, he wrote in a fury "I had the mortification to hear by a frigate that joined us that General Knyphausen…had already entered the Jerseys with a considerable part of the New York force."

The general claimed that this "ill-timed, malapropos move" had seriously damaged his chance to surprise Washington: "The whole country was now in arms and every preparation made for opposing me with vigour." André, Clinton's chief of intelligence, declared that Knyphausen had on June 7 "exposed the troops in the march of a day to a loss of more than Carolina cost us." There is little question that André was parroting his general's opinion.

Immediately upon arriving at Staten Island, with his soldiers already debarked and on the way to Middlebrook, Clinton developed a new strategy as the result of three envelopes awaiting him upon landing. One contained Knyphausen's attempt to justify his failed venture into New Jersey. The other two, both in code, were from "Mr. Moore," and addressed to André. The two Moore letters offered Clinton a completely new, far-reaching strategy for ending the war. He seized it as if he had never devised his plan to conquer New Jersey.

Moore, code name for the highly-esteemed American Major General Benedict Arnold, told André that a French fleet and 6,000 troops would be landing in Rhode Island in "two or three weeks." Washington supposedly had told Arnold, a trusted general, this top-secret news at a dinner party in the Ford Mansion in Morristown.

Arnold's second letter brashly advised Clinton that "it would be a good stroke to get between General Washington and West Point" before the French arrived. Suddenly, the carefully planned two-pronged attack on Morristown was out. Moore, the French fleet, West Point, and a strategy for thwarting Washington on the Hudson River were in.

Clinton canceled the planned pincer movement, recalling the troops he had set in motion toward Perth Amboy to begin the circuitous back door approach to Morristown. Approximately 3,800 men reboarded the ships, ready to sail up the Hudson River toward West Point. Only the mounted, fast-riding Queen's Rangers were dispatched by Clinton to aid the hapless Knyphausen.

The Hessian general and the New Jersey invasion had been consigned to a sideshow, a diversion to aid Clinton's plan to proceed northward on the Hudson River. If the Knyphausen venture were successful, Clinton could take the credit. If not, the Hessian would be doubly punished for his impetuous move earlier in June.

Washington realigned his forces near Elizabethtown for the Knyphausen assault he knew must come. He placed General Friedrich von Steuben in charge of a Continental division and an expected 1,168 militiamen stationed near Elizabethtown.

Most of the June 7 volunteer militia valiants had disappeared into the spring air. To the Baron's anger and despair, about 600 of the militia assigned to him vanished, probably temporarily due to a one-month-on, one-month-off rotation policy that had also handicapped Maxwell a fortnight before.

Supporting Steuben's force, well to the rear near the gap in the Short Hills, were Continental regiments commanded by General Nathanael Greene. Washington arrived in Springfield on June 19 to inspect defensive positions and to tell Greene he believed what spies were telling him: Clinton would sail northward in force to attack West Point.

The commander in chief planned to weaken the Springfield defense by moving two Connecticut and two Pennsylvania regiments northward to offset the expected Clinton move on the Hudson River. General von Steuben had been sent north the previous day to prepare for the arrival of the Connecticut and Pennsylvania regiments. Steuben's departure elevated Greene into command of the seriously depleted American forces.

Major General Arthur St. Clair commanded the 2,556 officers and men who left Springfield early on June 22 and headed toward New

While Baron Von Steuben, who served at Springfield, often is depicted as stout and severe, in this drawing he is shown elegantly riding his horse.

Jersey's northern boundary with New York. Washington tarried in Springfield to write several letters on June 22. One praised "the conduct and bravery of the officers and men of Maxwell's New Jersey Brigade in annoying the enemy" on June 7.

A second letter declared "the behavior of the militia has been such as to do them signal credit and entitled them to the warmest approbation." Significantly, he wrote of the militia: "there has never since the commencement of the contest been a more general ardor."

That ardor was rooted in the fact that New Jersey militiamen finally were doing what they were expected to do — protect their farms, their towns, and their homes — just as the storied Massachusetts Minutemen had done when they befuddled the British at Concord

The substantial home of Colonel Theunis Dey in Preakness became the nerve center of the American army following the Battle of Springfield. Washington moved in on July 1 and remained there, on and off, until November 27. During this period Washington was firming relationships with the French army commanders and Benedict Arnold was revealed as a traitor.

and Lexington on April 19, 1775.

Knyphausen's attackers, numbering about 5,000 men, moved out of Elizabethtown in two columns at 3 a.m. on June 23. They were traveling light, leaving their supply wagons in town. This was expected to be a day of swift movement, a storming into Springfield, a run through the gap at Short Hills, and, if all went well, a sprint into Morristown before nightfall.

The way from Elizabethtown to Connecticut Farms was essentially a replay in fast action of June 7, except that Continental regulars already were in position near the gap in the Short Hills and the militia was fully prepared. About an hour after the enemy had moved out of Elizabethtown, pickets of the Essex County militia made the first contact with Knyphausen's men, firing several quick bursts at the invaders before skillfully moving back toward Connecticut Farms.

The seven miles to the outskirts of that burned-out village were *déjà vu:* a constant harassing by the militia from sheltered positions and severe disruptions of the advancing British columns. The familiar hit-and-run pattern of the militia, and the relentless muskets of the Continental infantry, kept the advancing British and Hessians off guard.

The Elizabeth River's deep ravine in front of Connecticut Farms, so troublesome for the British on June 7, prompted a long halt before British Lieutenant Colonel John Graves Simcoe, a daring battler, made a move. His hard-riding Queen's Rangers entered the ravine at a gallop, crossed the river at high speed, and headed their steeds upward into the orchard atop the ravine. There, General Maxwell's men were waiting, as they had been slightly more than two weeks before. This time, the speed and daring of Simcoe's cavalrymen forced Maxwell to withdraw hastily toward Springfield. His role atop the ravine was to delay, not stop, the resolute Queen's Rangers.

Westward, the beacons had flared atop the Watchung Mountains and alarm guns had blasted a warning at 6 a.m. to call regulars and militiamen to action. Joy and relief seemed to infuse the troops. An officer in Stark's brigade, headed for Springfield, would write that "animation and composure seem to pervade every countenance [and] every arm is nerved for defense."

Nevertheless, the confident invaders pushed relentlessly toward the main bridge over the Rahway River, the last major obstacle to entry into Springfield. Colonel Israel Angell and his Rhode Island troops were posted on a small rise west of the bridge. Other defenses spread along the river, in the woods and behind stonewalls. Buildings on the west side of the river were manned by regulars and six militia regiments that had poured out of the hills.

Shortly after 11 a.m., eight hours out of Elizabethtown Point, Knyphausen finally launched his "very heavy column" of about 2,000 soldiers in a massive attack at the Rahway River bridge. Six cannon blasted away at American positions.

Across the river on a small rise, Angell and his men awaited the charge, a mere 160 "rank and file" musket-bearing infantry and a small group of artillery to man the Americans' single cannon. Knyphausen's troops swung toward the bridge in long marching columns, taking advantage of the long stretch of straight road until the one American cannon began to wreak havoc in their ranks.

The English and Hessians sought to cross the river in force, many of the Jaegers wading the stream, others walking on beams left when defenders ripped planks off the bridge to slow the advance. The way to Springfield and beyond seemed open, but in a show of incredible skill and gallantry, Angel's doughty defenders held fast, minute after vital minute.

With faces blackened and burnt by the gunpowder smoke and muscles aching from incessant action, Angell's 160 men held off 2,000 crack enemy troops for forty minutes.

They ran out of time, but before they retreated in orderly fashion, they had completely derailed British hopes for a swift dash toward Morristown.

There were more orchards filled with sharp-shooting militia, more confusion in the British ranks — and even an astoundingly long rest for lunch called by Knyphausen after his troops controlled Springfield. Yet it is probable that the invasion was doomed to ultimate failure by Angell's heroic stand at the bridge.

Dr. James Thacher, who was on or near the battlefield all day, witnessed "death and carnage." He wrote of Captain-Lieutenant Thompson, felled by a cannon ball that shattered both hips. The captain pleaded with Thacher to amputate both his legs at the hips. He was beyond help; he died the next day. When another wounded soldier begged for help, Thacher dismounted to help him. Within seconds a cannonball shattered a fence a few feet away.

As the enemy settled down for its incredibly long rest that more befitted English gentlemen paused for tea, smoke and flames rose from the village of Springfield, being burned to the ground in savage vengeance. Thacher reported that "the church and twenty or thirty other buildings" were torched. A later count said nineteen buildings were burned, with only two left standing. The British high command insisted that all of the arson was the work of "some refugees" who had followed the army from Elizabethtown.

The Springfield Presbyterian Church was a fair military target. It was filled with military supplies approved of and gathered by Pastor James Caldwell. By 1778, the congregation had forsaken the building crammed with public stores and held services in "the garret of the old parsonage as a temporary place of worship."

The assault had been ruined for the invaders, unless, as Thacher wrote, they were satisfied with "the honor of burning a village." Detachments briefly penetrated into the first rise of the Short Hills, but Continental troops and the aroused and inspired militia never lost control.

Victory for the Americans, by what amounted to default, was assured shortly after 2 p.m. when Knyphausen received a startling message from General Clinton, ordering him to cease fire and return to Elizabethtown. There, by Clinton's order, the entire attack force would prepare to quit New Jersey the following morning.

Clinton had written the decision well before he left Staten Island in the morning. He had no idea where the British and Hessians might be when Knyphausen received the order. For all he knew, they might have been pounding through the gap and on the way to Morristown when the order reached the general, or their dead and wounded bodies might have been scattered from Elizabethtown to Springfield. Clinton seemingly had seen the surge to Springfield as nothing more that a sideshow for his own strategy.

Unaware of plans for the forced withdrawal, a few of the British pressed on. Colonel

Cosmo Gordon and his Cold Stream Guards, augmented by a few Jaegers, pressed deep into the gap, reaching a position directly beneath the alarm gun atop the stronghold. Gordon realized the slaughter that would ensue if he continued to thrust his men against the steep cliffs. His Cold Stream Guards beat a retreat and rejoined the main army at Springfield, as it slowly began its return to Elizabethtown.

The drive into the gap earned the attention of General Greene. As the short battle for the pass ensued, he took time to apprise Washington of the battle to that point. The outcome was still in doubt, in Greene's mind, but he assured his chief that although the invaders were "directing their force against this pass," he was "determined to dispute [it] so far as I am capable."

Knyphausen started back to Elizabethtown at about 3 p.m., followed for most of the way by intense fire from the militia and Continental troops. At one point the American pressure was so great that the retreating army broke into "a full trot." The entire British force was back in Elizabethtown by 7 p.m.

The fleeing force had lost all desire to stay in New Jersey, as Knyphausen had done on June 8. This time, under the brightness of a full moon, baggage began to flow across the floating bridge even as the last stragglers were approaching the town. Then, in their most precise operation of the day, the artillery marched across the bridge to Staten Island, followed by the cavalry, the infantry, the pickets, and the Queen's Rangers. They never returned to the state.

The moon disappeared under heavy clouds at about 1 a.m. as a German regiment completed its destruction of the floating bridge and was ferried to the island on flatboats. With the enemy fully on Staten Island, a heavy thunderstorm broke across the Arthur Kill, drenching the glum enemy and making sleep impossible.

Clinton's hope to control the Hudson River also was played out to a quick, unfruitful end. The British commander had planned to debark his soldiers at Tarrytown, about twenty miles north of New York City. From there, the goal was to ferry them across the river to secure a firm position between the Americans and West Point — as Arnold had suggested.

It was yet another Clinton blunder: advance regiments of Americans already had seized the strategic ground. The disconsolate British reboarded their vessels and sailed back to the city. Clinton resumed his morose, ineffective game of watching to see what his enemy would try next.

The seventeen-day Battle of Springfield, and the thwarting of Clinton's quick sail up the Hudson, ended any pretense by the British that they could ever occupy New Jersey or control the Hudson River. The British high command in London had decided that the best course of action would be to concentrate on conquering the South, although its headquarters (and Clinton) would remain in New York.

For the Americans, the seventeen successful days in repulsing the British and Hessians provided proof of two important strengths that long had been mere conjecture: the strength of the position at the gap in the Watchung Mountains and the capabilities of the once-despised militia. Even though a few English troops got well into the gap, they found it impregnable to a full passage through. As for the militia, it is certain that Knyphausen's powerful invaders could not have been thwarted at Connecticut Farms and Springfield without the thousands of eager, capable, and resolute New Jersey militiamen who twice streamed from the hills to defend their home soil.

Despite the many thousands of words exchanged on the seventeen days by American and British leaders, participants, and a multitude of historians, casualty records for the prolonged battle are hazy. The British had an estimated 500 killed, wounded, and captured. American casualties have been estimated at about one third of the British total.

There will always be doubts and questions about the British objectives in invading New Jersey. Dr. Thacher, on-the-scene observer and active participant, pondered that subject. "The particular object of the expedition [the battle of June 23] is not ascertained," he wrote. "If it was to force their way to Morristown, to destroy our magazines and stores, they were disappointed; if to burn the village of Springfield, they are welcome to the honor of the exploit."

But no better summation of the battle could be given than sixteen-year-old militiaman Ashbel Green's vision on the morning after the fighting as he looked over the still-smoldering embers of Springfield:

> *The whole scene was one of gloomy horror — a dead form, a broken carriage of a field piece, a town laid in ashes, the former inhabitants standing over the ruins of their dwellings, and the unburied dead, covered with blood and with the flies that were devouring them, filled me with melancholy feelings, till I was ready to say — is the contest worth all that?*

There is an ironic footnote: Arnold's two letters received by Clinton on his return to Staten Island had a major bearing on both the Battle of Springfield and the course of the war.

His faulty information about the French help on the way had spurred Clinton to act lest he be trapped in the Hudson River with no chance to sail. Unfortunately for both Arnold and Clinton, the timetable for the sailing was far too early.

And, without Arnold's alert, the British forces already on their way would have continued on the swing around the Watchungs to enter Morristown from the south. It is highly likely that Clinton's two-pronged pincer would have been successful. It is unthinkable that Washington's meager, impoverished Continentals, even with stout militia aid, could have withstood the impact of a powerful one-two punch from the British.

The traitor Arnold thus had unwittingly helped to save the country he was eager to sell out.

Parson James Caldwell on the steps of the church, his arms filled with hymnals.

High Priest of Rebellion

Parson James Caldwell of Virginia studied to become a Presbyterian minister at the College of New Jersey in Newark. Two years after his graduation in 1759, the twenty-seven-year-old clergyman became pastor of the First Presbyterian Church in Elizabethtown. In 1763, he married Hannah Ogden of Newark, whose ancestors on both her mother's and her father's side, had been among the founders of Elizabethtown.

Hannah Caldwell bore Caldwell nine children in the next seventeen years. His fervent sermons about sin and redemption took on an increasingly rebellious tone as America's attitude toward King George grew bitter. Elizabethtown's Episcopal minister called him "The Dissenting Teacher."

Caldwell's congregation at the start of the war included William Livingston, the first non-Royal governor of New Jersey Elias Boudinot, who later would become President of the Continental Congress, and Abraham Clark, one of New Jersey's five signers of the Declaration of Independence.

When Colonel Elias Dayton's Regiment of the First New Jersey Brigade left

Elizabethtown in April 1776, officers and men asked Caldwell to be their chaplain. He received permission from the Presbytery to do so and walked to Albany, New York, to join the regiment.

Caldwell was a chaplain but also a soldier. Six days a week he carried a musket; on the seventh day he preached — twice each Sunday if he felt the soldiers needed it. Anxious for the safety of his family, Caldwell returned home in the early fall of 1777 and removed them to Turkey (now New Providence). He continued his army service as a chaplain ad served two years as Deputy Quartermaster with an office in Morristown.

The Caldwell family soon returned to Elizabethtown but when British troops burned the parsonage in February 1779, Caldwell immediately took his wife and children to what he thought was safety in Connecticut Farms (now Union). He still preached on Sundays in Elizabethtown.

British soldiers ravaged Elizabethtown on January 25, 1780, burning as they went, destroying several houses and the church. Elder Cornelius Hatfield offered his red barn as a temporary place of worship. Caldwell entered the church with an armed guard. He walked to the makeshift pulpit, placed two loaded pistol on either side of the Bible and calmly declared, "Let us bow our heads in silent prayer."

On June 7, 1780, the British invaded New Jersey. Civilians fled Elizabethtown, taking with them moveable belongings, piled high on wagons or carried on their backs. As they streamed toward Connecticut Farms, residents urged Hannah Caldwell and her nine children to leave.

Mrs. Caldwell refused, believing that the invaders would not harm a woman with a child in her arms. However, Caldwell persuaded Mrs. Caldwell's housekeeper and maid to stay with his wife and their three-year-old son. Mrs. Caldwell was shot and killed, either by a stray bullet or by a deliberate enemy soldier.

The invaders retreated, and then returned to attack Springfield on June 23, 1780. When American artillerymen ran out of wadding for their cannons, tradition says, Caldwell broke open the doors of the Springfield Presbyterian Church, entered, and came out with an arm load of hymn books compiled by a hymnist named Watts.

"Give 'em Watts boys!" yelled Caldwell. The soldiers tore apart the hymnals and stuffed Watts' pages into their cannons. The British were turned back, but in their retreat burned much of Springfield, including the church where the Watts Hymnals had been stored.

Parson Caldwell was killed on November 24, 1781, at Elizabethtown Point by an American soldier on sentry duty. Witnesses differed as to whether the shot was deliberate or accidental, but a jury found the killer guilty. He was hanged on Gallows Hill in Westfield.

Chapter Twenty-One

BENEDICT ARNOLD REVEALED

George Washington's respect and admiration for Major General Benedict Arnold prompted the commander in chief to ask him to accept command of the beleaguered American forces at Springfield. The court martial decision that found Arnold guilty of minor infractions while in command of Philadelphia had been forgotten.

Arnold's medical excuse for refusing a battlefield command was backed by his persistent, outspoken insistence that he could be far more valuable as commander of West Point. Completely unknown to Washington, or any one else except a few of the enemy, was that the value — for Arnold — already had been committed to British General Henry Clinton if he would pay enough for it. Arnold was willing to sell out his country; the major imponderable for him was how much the sale was worth.

On June 15, 1780, midway between the critical two battles for Springfield, an increasingly eager, and ever more greedy, Arnold assured Clinton (via intermediaries) that he expected to command West Point soon. Two weeks later, he set the price for his honor: $20,000 "if I point out a plan of cooperation by which Sir Henry shall possess himself of West Point, the garrison, etc, etc, etc."

As Clinton pondered the offer, Washington extended to Arnold another high honor on August 1. As plans were being shaped with the French for the eventual move south by the allied armies, Washington offered Arnold the command of a wing in the combined forces. Again citing his war wounds, Arnold begged off. Two days later, the bargaining general had his blue chip: command of West point. He waited another two days then dispatched a gleeful letter to Clinton, along with news that his garrison was "in want of tents, provisions, and almost everything."

The West Point command included far more than the imposing stone fortress set high above the Hudson River. It stretched ten miles south to Stony Point, ten miles north to Fishkill, and ten miles east of Stony Point to North Castle. Control of these positions offered dominance of the Hudson River, from New York to Albany. This had been Clinton's enduring strategic priority, even in his tumultuous days as second in command to General William Howe.

Arnold established his headquarters across the river from West Point, in the home of Colonel Beverly Robinson, a Tory who had fled to protection in New York City. He then sent to Philadelphia for his wife, Peggy, and their infant and set out to earn his tainted gold. Peggy was not an innocent bystander; she had been part of the plot since its inception.

The conniving general also established a strong relationship with Joshua Hett Smith, brother of another noted Tory who had taken refuge in New York. Arnold's two aides, Colonel Robert Varick and Major David Franks, strongly disapproved of Smith, although they felt Arnold merely was engaged in some kind of dishonest profiteering scheme. Based on his reputation in Philadelphia, this could be expected of the Point's new commander.

Arnold stepped up his communcations to young Major John André, head of Clinton's intelligence service and the British commander's most trusted officer. André's popularity as an artist and performer matched his quick mind. During his tenure in Philadelphia with Clinton, André had become a special favorite among the city's belles, in particular Peggy Shippen, who saw a great deal of André while he was in town. After she became Peggy Shippen Arnold, she was often a courier in Arnold's link to André and Clinton.

By mid-September, Arnold's plan was in full motion. He had widely scattered his West Point men to outposts, leaving the installation nearly defenseless. Clinton had his forces ready to sail up the Hudson River as soon as he heard that Arnold had prepared a capitulating reception.

André was to get the operation underway by proceeding up the Hudson River on the British sloop *Vulture* to receive full details of West Point, including detailed maps, from Arnold. The major would travel as "Mr. Anderson," the pseudonym he long had been using in undercover dealings with Arnold. Clinton dispatched André on September 21, with a stern warning that he must wear his British uniform at all times so that, if captured, he would not be considered a spy.

Colonel Robinson, owner of the house occupied by Arnold, sailed with André to give the voyage the plausible excuse that he wanted to check his property. The *Vulture* would stand by to take both of them back to New York the next day. Shortly before midnight, André went ashore to confer with Arnold in a lantern-lit woodland cabin near Haverstraw, about fifteen miles south of West Point.

This map defines the Hudson River area where Arnold and André conspired to sell out West Point (top). Also marked is André's landing near Haverstraw, about a third of the way up the river. Immediately across the river is Teller's Point, whose cannons forced the ship Vulture to drop downriver. The artwork is suggestive of traitorous evil, and the snake's head points to where André was captured, just north of Tarrytown.

Treason of the Blackest Dye

The frantic beating of drums at 3 a.m at the main American camp near Tappan, just over the border from New Jersey, routed soldiers out of bed on September 26, 1780. Two regiments from the Pennsylvania Line were ordered to be ready for a quick move to West Point. All other regiments were ordered to be ready to march.

The troops were not kept in the dark. An order from General Nathanael Greene summarized a dire emergency that had originated at West Point. Greene put it this way:

> *Treason, of the blackest dye, was yesterday discovered. General Arnold, who commanded at West Point, lost to every sentiment of honor, of private and public obligation, was about to deliver up that important post into the hands of the enemy. Such an event must have given the American cause a dangerous, if not fatal wound. Happily the treason has been timely discovered, to prevent the fatal misfortune.*
>
> *The providential train of circumstances which led to it, affords the most convincing proofs that the liberties of America are the object of Divine protection. At the same time that the treason is to be regretted, the general cannot help congratulating the army on the happy discovery. Our enemy, despairing of carrying their point by force, are practicing every base art to effect by bribery and corruption what they cannot accomplish in a manly way.*
>
> *Great honor is due to the American army, that this is the first instance of treason of the kind where many were to be expected from the nature of our dispute. The brightest ornament in the character of the American soldiers is their having been proof against all the arts and seductions of an insidious enemy. Arnold has made his way to the enemy, but Major André, the adjutant general in the British army, who came out as a spy to negotiate the business, is our prisoner.*

Arnold gave his co-conspirator considerable written information and precise maps on West Point and its satellite installations. The conference ended much too late for André to return to the *Vulture*. He would rest during the day and be rowed out to the ship as evening settled in. The operation to that point was almost routine. Suddenly, in a series of uncanny early morning coincidences, the secret lives of Arnold and André began quickly to unravel.

At dawn, in full view of the stunned Arnold and André, Colonel James Livingston,

Benedict Arnold gave "John Anderson" this pass when they met to plan the takeover of West Point. Anderson (John André), allegedly was "on public business by my direction." The document was designed to get André to "White Plains or below."

commander of a shore battery at Teller's Point, on the east shore of the river "acting on his own" began firing two shore-based cannon at the *Vulture*, which had drifted too far north. The badly damaged ship weighed anchor and escaped downstream, leaving André literally high, dry, and needing another escape route.

Arnold insisted that André put the secret papers and maps beneath the soles of his feet and inside his stockings before he rode off on a horse on September 22, following the river-bank toward New York. André's traveling companion and guide, Tory Joshua Hett Smith, offered him a civilian shirt and coat before he left. When André demurred, Arnold warned him that in a British uniform he would be a certain target for ruffians who frequented the paths along the river. André agreed reluctantly, and, as it turned out, mistakenly.

André and Smith both had passes signed by Arnold. They traveled together until the next morning, September 23, when Smith left André and returned home. The fleeing

Riding serenely through woodlands (above), out of uniform, only a short distance from the British lines, Major John André (traveling as John Anderson) was about to meet the renegade American "Skinners." They called themselves "Volunteer Militia," but they were prepared to rob anyone. When the Skinners searched André (right), they found so many hidden West Point documents that they decided to turn him in at a nearby army outpost, hoping for a reward.

Briton had only a few miles to ride before he reached British outposts near White Plains. The road led through open territory where both Loyalists and so-called American "Skinners" (or " Volunteer Militiaman") hid beside the roads, waiting for strangers. André was well aware that he would be tried as a spy if he were caught in civilian clothing, carrying hidden West Point documents. He now had only one hope: the pass made out to "Mr. Anderson," signed by Arnold.

Sometime between 9 and 10 a.m., three men stopped André's horse near a bridge about a mile north of Tarrytown. One of them was wearing a redcoat, suggesting to André that his captors were Tories. Instead of immediately showing Arnold's pass, which might well have freed him, André naively blurted out that he was a fellow Loyalist. His assumption was wrong; they were renegade Americans. As such, they could keep the property of a captured enemy they brought to the nearest American post.

The "volunteers" asked for cash. When André could not produce any, they ordered him to remove his boots and socks, hoping to find hidden money. Instead they found the easily identifiable West Point documents. Reasoning that the documents surely would be worth some kind of special reward, the trio took André — continuing to insist he was Anderson — to an American outpost at nearby North Castle. While there was no immediate reward, the captors were later given André's watch, horse, saddle and bridle as their prize.

At North Castle, Lt. Colonel John Jameson examined the pass signed by Arnold. It was authentic enough. Jameson was initially inclined to send the suspect on his way, possibly with an escort. But he began to ponder the situation carefully: he had previously received orders from Benedict Arnold to admit a "Mr. John Anderson," traveling *into* the lines *from* New York City. That puzzled Jameson: this John Anderson was *behind* the lines, heading out, *toward* New York City.

The young Englishman foolishly blurted out that he really was Major John André, a British officer in the area to "meet a person who was to give intelligence." Jameson, still not certain of the proper next move, decided to send André, under guard, to Arnold at West Point. However, Jameson protected himself. He packaged the materials found on the prisoner and sent a messenger to carry them to Washington, believed to be on his way to meet the newly arrived French officers and soldiers in Newport, Rhode Island.

Later in the early evening, the case against André came full cycle. Major John Tallmadge returned to the North Castle post and heard the details about "Mr. Anderson" from Colonel Jameson. As the secret chief of Washington's intelligence service, Tallmadge knew something had gone seriously wrong. Despite the fact that Jameson outranked him, Tallmadge sent soldiers galloping off to bring André back.

The next day was Sunday; when Washington could not be located, the messenger returned to North Castle. Jameson added André's statement to the packet intended for Ar-

John André, receiving the warrant for his death after being found guilty of spying. He asked to be shot as a soldier rather than hanged as a spy, but his request was refused.

nold and redirected the entire mission to the West Point headquarters. Earlier in the day, Jameson had also sent a second messenger to advise Arnold of the British officer's arrest.

Neither messenger arrived at Arnold's headquarters on Sunday. The race to West Point was on — and none of the participants knew that the war teetered on the edge of a momentous crisis.

Meanwhile, Washington by mere chance had decided to inspect West Point on his way home from Newport. Alexander Hamilton and another aide arrived at Arnold's headquarters at about 9 a.m. on Monday morning and informed him that the commander was delayed but would come later. Hamilton said Washington wanted them to start eating breakfast without him.

Just before entering the dining room, Arnold stopped to see Richard Varick, one of his top assistants. Varick handed him a letter from Major Tallmadge. It was an older communication, reassuring Arnold that "Mr. Anderson" would be "taken care of" (accorded all amenities) when he arrived. Tallmadge had since taken care of "Anderson" but not in the pleasant, cooperative manner Arnold had requested.

Midway through the meal, however, both letters dispatched by Jameson were handed to Arnold. He read them slowly and without emotion. He then excused himself, stood up, pulled the messenger to one side, and ordered him not to speak of this to anyone. The general coolly sat down and finished his breakfast before excusing himself again. He went upstairs, told Peggy that he had been exposed and had to flee.

As the Arnolds talked, another aide, David Franks, answered a knock on his door. Washington's servant told Franks that "his Excellency was nigh at hand." The aide mounted the stairs, knocked on the bedroom door and informed Arnold. The general hastened down the stairs, telling Franks as he passed him "to inform his Excellency that he was gone over to West Point and would return in about an hour."

Arnold never returned. Only Peggy knew that he was hurrying down a rough pathway to his barge at the landing. He persuaded the bargeman to take him downstream to the *Vulture*.

Washington, Hamilton, Henry Knox, and the Marquis de Lafayette were not disturbed by Arnold's quick dash to check on something at the fort. They had a leisurely breakfast, and crossed the river to inspect the fort. Arnold's absence, while troubling, still had no dark overtones. If asked, all would have agreed that Arnold was an exceptional officer and a loyal patriot.

The inspection of the fort at the time was disturbing enough. It had been severely neglected; the few men manning the installation troubled Washington. Arnold had begun his promised task of disabling the fort.

Franks and Varick hastily discussed what they had seen and heard. Franks recalled that he whispered the unthinkable: that Arnold might have been engaged in some kind of treachery with Anderson (as they still knew him). Varick indignantly replied that such a thought injured "a gentleman and friend of high reputation."

Peggy Shippen sat quietly in her bedroom while Washington and his officers dined and left for their inspection tour. But when the group returned to the Robinson house at about 4 p.m., she began to scream wildly as a cover-up for Arnold's absence. Officers, including Washington, found her in her bedroom, "her hair disheveled" and "too scantily dressed to be seen even by the gentlemen of her family." She was screaming that Varick was trying to kill her baby. Peggy was buying time for Benedict.

Filled with compassion for Mrs. Arnold, Washington offered her safe passage to refuge with her family in Philadelphia. The wily Peggy, not knowing how Arnold would fare at the hands of the British, accepted.

Midway through Peggy's histrionics, Hamilton brought Washington an astounding letter from Arnold, written on the *Vulture* and delivered under a flag of truce. He asked no favors for himself but pleaded that Washington not blame Peggy for anything: "she is as good and as innocent as an angel." He insisted that his action, however it might appear, was actuated by "a principle of love for my country."

The major sacrifice to Arnold's treachery and his "principle of love" would be André. He was first brought to West Point after Arnold's flight and placed under a strong house arrest in Robinson's home, where the Arnolds had lived. He was taken across the Hudson River to the fortress on September 28, taken down river to Stony Point, then was led overland to imprisonment in Mabie's Tavern in Tappan, New York.

The handsome young André became an overnight object of sympathy for the citizens and soldiers of Tappan. He did not deny or excuse any of his actions, and his open honesty won the respect and support of those who would judge him.

Washington appointed a blue ribbon panel the next day, with Major General Nathanael Greene as president. Other major generals on the panel were William Alexander (Lord Stirling), Lafayette, Baron von Steuben, Arthur St. Clair, and Robert Howe. The panel convened on Friday, September 29.

The trial was quite brief. André testified frankly, offering full details, with no effort to spare himself or to plead not guilty. He told of his talks with Arnold, his receiving the documents and map, his flight in civilian dress and his capture by the three American militia, bogus or not. He denied nothing. He had all but signed his death warrant.

Every member of the board signed the verdict "that Major Arnold, adjutant general to the British army, ought to be considered a spy from the enemy; and that, agreeable to the law and usage of nations, it is their opinion he ought to suffer death."

Washington's order of execution by hanging was set for October 1 at 5 p.m., eight days after André's

John André, the tragic victim of Arnold's treachery, drew this self-portrait the night before his execution.

arrest. Clinton and his staff made a furious effort to save their officer, although Clinton rejected outright the suggestion by Alexander Hamilton that Arnold be exchanged for André. Washington postponed the execution for twenty-four hours to give the British further chance to submit any extenuating facts they might have.

There was not the slightest chance that Clinton would return Arnold, consigning him to certain death. From the British viewpoint, Arnold's defection was not a crime but a rightful act. His crime, in their opinion, was his service with the revolutionists; Arnold was thus, in Clinton's view, returning honorably to his lawful duty.

André knew he was guilty, but he could not see himself as an ordinary spy, however much the chain of circumstances made him look like one. He saw himself as an officer and a gentleman seeking to serve his country. If he had failed, he

This portrayal of André's hanging shows the moment the cart would be pulled out from under him.

wanted the concession that he had failed as a soldier, not a spy. He asked that he be accorded the honor of being shot as an honored officer rather than hanged as a spy. He likely knew even that simple appeal was useless; spies by tradition must face the noose.

Major Tallmadge, the first to realize "Mr. Anderson" was serving the British, grew increasingly fond of André. He walked with him to the place of execution and parted with him under the gallows, "entirely overwhelmed with grief that so gallant an officer and so accomplished a gentleman should come to so ignominious an end."

Tappan's streets were lined with sorrowful spectators on execution day. André walked down the main street, head held high, keeping step with the dirge played by the fifes and drums. When the hangman stepped forward, André jumped unaided onto the wagon beneath the rope. The hangman adjusted the noose on his neck.

Asked if he had anything to declare, André replied, "I have nothing more to say, gentlemen, but this: you all bear witness that I meet my fate as a brave man." The executioner cracked his whip. The horses lunged forward, pulled the wagon from under André's feet, and left him swinging in the crisp October air.

Hamilton wrote, a few days later, "among the extraordinary circumstances that attended him, in the midst of his enemies, he died universally esteemed and universally regretted."

Arnold reached New York, where the British awarded him £6,315. Thirteen days after Clinton learned of André's death and was seeking to overcome his grief over the loss of an officer he considered a son, Arnold wrote him a letter asking for the full £10,000 he had requested, an appalling lack of sensitivity, even for Arnold. He hoped Clinton "will not think my claim unreasonable when you consider the sacrifices I have made." He chose to forget that André was dead and he was alive.

Spy John André became a British hero and King George III ordered this sarcophagus to be erected in Westminster Abbey. André's remains were brought from Tappan to the Abbey and buried on November 28, 1821. The British lion and a figure of Brittania are atop the monument; a depiction of André's hanging is just below that. Next is a dedication to André, while the bottom panel describes the transference of his remains to the Abbey.

Clinton ignored the request, but did make Arnold a brigadier general in the English army and dispatched him and his troops to Virginia on December 3, 1780. Four hundred of his men perished on the voyage, but Arnold led his army up the James River to take Richmond, which his troops set to the torch.

Arnold led an attack on New London, Connecticut, on September 6, 1781, intended as a diversionary move to draw attention from the American and French armies headed for Yorktown. Nearly eighty Americans were killed — all but three of them after they surrendered.

Arnold showed no mercy. Although he denied any complicity in the burning of New London, a witness accused him of viewing the scene "with the apparent satisfaction of a Nero."

The sacking of Richmond and New London added to Arnold's infamy. The traitor, despised by British officers from the time he arrived in New York, became even more scorned. General Clinton rebuked him for his seemingly wanton taking of civilian lives. Not incidentally, the New London raid was the last major Revolutionary War happening in the North.

Peggy Arnold and her sons joined Benedict in New York. She too was treated with scorn and lived in constant fear that a thug might assassinate her husband. The pair moved to England in 1781. Arnold was received by the King and became a consultant on American affairs to the King and his Court.

Arnold died in 1801; Peggy died three years later. Their four sons all had careers in the British army and a great-grandson, Theodore Stephenson, was a major general in World War I.

The remains of Benedict and Peggy Arnold lie in unmarked graves beneath a church in an undistinguished part of London.

John André, the ultimate victim of their schemes, is remembered with a monument that stands among the gallery of heroes in Westminster Abbey.

Bring Arnold Back — Alive

Rudely awakened after midnight on October 21, 1780, John Champe, a twenty-eight-year-old Sergeant Major in Light Horse Harry Lee's regiment, stumbled sleepily to headquarters. There, Lee asked Champe to "volunteer" for a dangerous mission personally requested by George Washington: kidnap Benedict Arnold in New York — and bring him back alive.

Champe was to steal a horse, race to the Hudson River, cross as best he could and get close to Arnold. Somehow, he was to kidnap Arnold and bring him back across the river to face trial and probable execution in New Jersey.

The mission seemed impossible. American guards could seek to shoot him as an apparent deserter. The British would hang him as a spy if he were exposed.

Champe agreed to take the risks. He stole his company's orderly book to add authenticity to his flight, took a horse without requisition, galloped toward the Hudson River, and jumped in. By mere chance he was picked up by British sailors, who rowed him to New York. Champe enlisted in a Loyalist Legion Arnold was recruiting. A few legionnaires, including Champe, were assigned quarters adjacent to Arnold's residence, separated only by narrow alley.

Champe decided to kidnap Arnold shortly after midnight in the garden where he strolled each night. The traitor would be sedated, tied up, and rowed across the river. He set the kidnapping date for December 11.

Lee waited at the river but neither Arnold nor Champe appeared that night. The night before, the Loyalist Legion had boarded a ship bound for Virginia, where Arnold planned to "conquer rebel territory." If Champe were detected escaping, he would be executed. The Loyalist Legion sailed for Virginia on December 21.

Champe eventually escaped from Arnold's army near Richmond, but was still in great danger. If he were caught in British uniform, his fellow Virginians would vent their rage on a deserter-turned-Loyalist soldier. He fled with his wife and four children to what is now West Virginia.

After the war, General and Mrs. Washington received Champe at Mt. Vernon, and Lee recounted the kidnapping escapade at considerable length in his memoirs published in 1811. Champe died in Kentucky in 1798.

If the abduction had been successful, Champe would be a celebrated American hero. Instead, he is merely a sidebar in history.

Chapter Twenty-two

MUTINY *in* JANUARY

B rigadier General Anthony Wayne led about 2,500 "bad clothed men of Pennsylvania" into and through Morristown in the late afternoon of November 29, 1780. They were headed for Jockey Hollow, where an advance guard had refurbished enough huts to house the ten regiments of foot soldiers and the one artillery regiment that would be arriving.

That winter, troops were stretched in a long thin line from West Point to Morristown, the better to help in acquiring food from local sources. Washington's winter headquarters would be in New Windsor, New York, described by Washington as a "dreary station." Substantial numbers of troops, all members of veteran Pennsylvania regiments — as many as 2,500 if all were on hand — would be back in the Watchung hills for the fourth of the five major winters of the war.

"Bad clothed men" was Washington's description of the Pennsylvania regiments. Whether he intended it as a grim witticism or as an exact depiction, "bad clothed" aptly described the Pennsylvanians.

Wayne had despaired about his command's inadequate clothing since October, when he wrote his men were cutting the tails off their tattered long coats to provide patches for the short coats that resulted from the cuttings. These would "answer much better for the spring than the fall," Wayne acknowledged, but without the immediate drastic alterations, "we shall be naked in the course of the next two or three weeks."

Some of the Pennsylvania brigade huts from the previous winter had been razed to

This diorama shows Captain Adam Bettin about to be dragged from his horse and killed during the mutiny in Jockey Hollow on January 1, 1781. The depiction, while dramatic, is in error; Bettin apparently was fatally wounded as he chased a soldier on foot.

create a military hospital. The army thus would occupy the existing buildings of Hand's Brigade and part of the Connecticut Line huts. Gaps in the rows, created largely by local farmers helping themselves to wood, were filled in by huts the soldiers moved from the old Maryland area.

Some of the accommodations were presentable enough for immediate use, but many had to be refurbished to provide decent shelter for the soldiers and the wives who came to spend the winter with them, unattached women of the camp, and children expected to be in camp with their parents. Hoping to maintain a rapport with their troops, some officers worked beside the "poor naked fellows" to get all the huts ready for winter.

Many of the bedraggled Pennsylvanians easily remembered enlistment time in 1777, when they were promised an annual suit of new clothes that ranged through a long top coat to three pairs of breeches, two shirts, two pairs of shoes, a hunting shirt and many other warm pieces of clothing — plus a fresh new blanket. Many never even received the initial wardrobe; none had ever known the full annual replacement.

These "bad clothed" veterans were intensely bitter men, well aware that the approaching winter would find them once more on the short food rations that often verged on nothing. They had grown used to the failure of the army to feed them properly, much less to supply the occasional gill of rum that also had been a pre-enlistment promise. Most rankling, nearly all of them had not received in months their promised six and two-thirds dollars monthly pay.

Discontent had begun to swell in August, when the Pennsylvania troops were still at West Point. They had been rushed there in case of a major British assault after Benedict Arnold's attempt at to sell out the installation. Increasing soldier anger concerning the absence of pay prompted a response that became a fiasco.

In August the Council from Philadelphia dispatched a Lieutenant John Bigham of the Fifth Pennsylvania to bring $14,068 in Continental currency to pay bounties due recruits in the Line. Neither Bigham nor the money ever reached West Point. Later, when the lieutenant was cashiered, he frivolously claimed necessary expenses on his trip from Philadelphia to the campsite had used up all the money. Fortunately for the already low morale in camp, the penniless Pennsylvanians knew nothing of this.

Then, in an attempt to cover up Bigham's crass thievery, the Council established a subscription fund to raise money for the Pennsylvanians in Jockey Hollow. The subscription of miscellaneous coins netted £484 and two shillings. The Council dispatched Brigadier General James Porter of the Pennsylvania militia to carry the small treasure to Morristown. He reached camp on December 29.

How the money was divided is difficult to fathom. The kitty included eighty and a half English guineas, three French guineas (Louis d'or), five and a quarter gold Portuguese moidores, five Spanish pistoles, four ducats, one half-caroline, ninety-nine half johannesses, forty-three and a half Spanish dollars, and four English half shillings.

If it could have been divided equally, each Pennsylvanian might have received a dollar or two in hard specie, about what his Continental paper dollars would be worth for several months of service. But it was an impossible miscellany of coins to divide equally. Time had run out on many hoping for the pay due them.

As usual, food grew increasingly scarce in Jockey Hollow. On December 10, Washington wrote to Gouverneur Morris, a former Congressman and wealthy supporter of the rebellion, "it would be well for the troops if, like chameleons, they could live upon air, or, like the bear, suck their paws for sustenance during the rigor of the approaching season."

A week later, Wayne wrote Joseph Reed, President of the Supreme Executive Council a letter describing the desperation of his Regiments:

> We are reduced to dry bread and beef for our food, and to cold water for our drink.... This, together with the old worn-out coats and tattered linen overalls and what was

once a poor substitute for a blanket (now divided among three soldiers) is but a very wretched living and shelter against the winter's piercing cold, drifting snows, and chilling sleets.

"Believe me, my dear sir," Wayne warned Reed, "if something is not immediately done to give them a local attachment to this country, and to quiet their minds, we have not yet seen the worst side of the picture."

That same day the general set a time table for trouble in a letter to an old neighbor, Francis Johnson, colonel of the Fifth Regiment: "I wish the Ides of January were come and past. I am not superstitious, but I can't help cherishing disagreeable ideas about that period."

Ever fresh in mind was the Jockey Hollow mutiny of the Connecticut regiments the previous May, when Pennsylvania regiments were summoned to surround the mutinous New Englanders. What would happen on fast-approaching January 1, 1781, when enlistments would expire?

Rancor reigned in camp as the gloomy December neared an end. The Pennsylvanians flatly declared they would go home on January 1, when their three-year enlistments ended — even if many of them had no papers to prove when their terms of service began or ended. The determination to leave was no secret; the men had been declaring it since late summer.

Congress was helpless; warnings of mutiny had come from its own committee at Morristown the previous spring. Congress had neither money nor power — and certainly not the will or the mandate — to enact the taxes necessary to pay Wayne's men. The army had zero funds; Washington doubted that he could find enough money even to pay an express rider to carry a message to Hartford.

Most of the Pennsylvania men had signed on (or believed they had) with the standard option of three years or the duration. The government insisted that most of the enlistments had been for the duration of the war. Most of the men claimed they had chosen the three-year term. Neither side could readily prove its case with documents; negotiations based on a paper trail were at a stalemate.

The long-term enlistees had not been paid in a year. Foolishly, even callously, the Pennsylvania legislature paid new, six-month recruits a $25 bonus in hard specie on New Year's Day afternoon, a certain provocation for unrewarded soldiers already in camp. The word spread like wildfire; Jockey Hollow became a seething cauldron of hate and despair.

There is no complete on-the-scene account of the mutiny by either a soldier or an officer. The names of the mutinous leaders are not known for sure. Details of planning the affair have never been found, although there is no question the mutiny was carefully orchestrated and very well led. The story can be pieced together, however.

At about 10 p.m. on New Year's Day, leaders of the disgruntled Pennsylvanians sent a flaming rocket into the sky as a signal for the soldiers to gather on the parade ground. Anyone not aware of an impending mutiny – in surrounding communities as well as in camp — initially might have interpreted the rocket as a sign that the British were coming.

Soldiers ready to quit camp emerged from their huts, fully armed with loaded muskets. They raced through the compound, dashing into huts to make sure no one was hiding to escape the mutiny. The decision to leave camp was far from unanimous; ultimately about one-third of the men did not join the mutineers. Men in the second Pennsylvania Regiment were ordered at bayonet point to join the move from camp.

As a signal for men to assemble, the soldiers shot off several rounds from four cannons they had appropriated to take with them, along with ample ammunition. Fewer that half the men fell out initially, and not more than half of the Line eventually joined the mutiny.

Officers ordered the angry soldiers to return to their quarters. During an ensuing melee, two officers were shot and wounded and a third escaped from charging bayonet-wielders by running through the hutted area. Captain Adam Bettin, who ordered the infuriated mob to get back to quarters, was shot and mortally wounded by a mutineer after the captain allegedly chased him with an espontoon (a spear topped by an axe blade).

This was no easily controlled, spontaneous gathering of emotional grumblers. It was a well-planned mutiny, far and away the worst of the American Revolution and one of the worst in American military history. If these men decided join the British, the American cause would dangle by a very thin thread.

Wayne had wisely declined an invitation to a New Year's Day party at the home of Lucas Beverhoudt in Whippany, about ten miles from camp. The general was in his quarters close to the huts, quietly observing his thirty-sixth birthday, when he heard the cannon shots. He reached the wild scene while the mutiny was peaking and rode his horse through the angry army, urging the soldiers to desist. Shouted replies told him the mutiny was beyond his authority, declaring their business was not with the officers, but with Congress.

During the exchange of words, a soldier fired a shot over Wayne's head. The general opened his coat and roared in defiance: "If you mean to kill me, shoot me at once. Here's my heart." It was reported one soldier said he wanted to kill Wayne but was stopped by other men.

The mutineers-to-be raided the camp, taking food, wagons, and teams of horses. They hitched the horses to their cannons and loaded ammunition, food, and other supplies into wagons. Their leaders ordered a march out of camp toward Philadelphia at about 11 p.m. Wayne asked to lead the march but was told that if he wished, he could follow.

"I'll not leave you," Wayne responded. "If you won't allow me to march in your front,

I'll follow in your rear." The soldiers cheered him lustily — but firmly insisted he must ride behind their columns.

As the mutinous regiments left camp, the night-shrouded horizon to the east was likely ablaze. Militiamen may have fired the beacons in the belief that the roar of cannon they had heard echoing from Jockey Hollow signaled an enemy attack.

Fearful that the defiant soldiers might head toward New York to cast their lot with the British, Wayne and his officers lined up at the point where the road from the camp met the highway that led north to Morristown or south to Vealtown [Bernardsville]. They pledged themselves to sacrifice their lives if necessary to turn the men away from the direction [north] that eventually would lead toward the enemy.

There was no need for officer caution or bravado. The column of mutineers had no intention of joining the British. Most of them, as they proved in subsequent actions, would have expressed anger at even being suspected of possible desertion. As they reached the intersection where the officers were arrayed, they headed south.

Wayne decided he must follow them, to regain control if possible, but at the very least to be near if they wished to discuss their grievances. He chose Colonels Richard Butler and Walter Stewart, his brigade commanders, to join him on what loomed as a very dangerous mission. The rest of the officers returned to camp, where hundreds of non-mutinous men milled about in the darkness.

Stewart was a wise choice. He had been the cool voice of reason during the Connecticut mutiny in May 1780. Soldiers then had heeded his reasonable plea that they should not sacrifice in mutiny the "immortal honor" they had earned on battlefields of the past.

Fifers and drummers provided cadence for the calmer, but no less determined, mutineers as they headed through the darkness toward wherever would be necessary to discuss their plight with Pennsylvania state officials. The soldiers moved at a brisk, disciplined clip, and were in Vealtown long before dawn. They stopped to wait for small groups of men rounded up at camp and either convinced to join the marchers or forced to get in line. By the time the rebellious men resumed their march, they numbered more than 1,500 soldiers.

The column halted the second night at Middlebrook, site of the winter encampment in 1778-79. Sergeants convinced their fellow rebels that they should listen to Wayne's plan to champion their cause by seeking redress for the evils inflicted on them. Arrayed in a circle surrounding Wayne, Butler, and Stewart, the men listened respectfully to Wayne but insisted they must continue their march to Princeton.

Respect for Wayne as well as for themselves as soldiers dominated the marching men. Spectators along the way remarked on the military bearing of the men. They maintained a fast pace and strictly obeyed the orders of their leaders. Shabby and hungry they might be, but they demonstrated that their years in service had fashioned a disciplined, self-respecting unit.

The fast-moving mutineers marched into Princeton on January 3, coincidentally the fourth anniversary of the Battle of Princeton. There, foot soldiers pitched tents and encamped on a farm just south of the College of New Jersey campus. Sergeants bunked in Nassau Hall. Their officers likely found rooms in one of the taverns across the road from the campus.

The mutineers completely controlled Princeton. Guards were placed on every road leading into town to insure that only those approved by the leaders could enter the area.

Representatives of the mutinous troops disclosed their demands to Wayne on the afternoon of January 4, the first full day in Princeton. They insisted that all men enlisted in 1776 and 1777 were to be "without any delay discharged; and all arrears of pay and depreciation of pay be paid to the men, without any fraud, clothing included."

Men enlisted in 1778 or later would serve three full years, then be dismissed with the same terms of pay as the earlier enlisted men. Recent recruits would return to camp where they would receive all promised pay, bonuses, and clothing. The mutinous men wanted guarantees that "no aspersions" would be cast on them and that no punishment would be meted out to any of them.

Wayne correctly replied that he had no power over enlistments and payments but promised to convey the terms to Congress and the Pennsylvania Council. He promised to support all soldiers justly eligible for discharge. The mutineers told him that his assurance was much too vague.

It took two days for word of the uprising to reach Washington, who read Wayne's terse message at noon on January 3: "The most general and unhappy mutiny took place in the Pennsylvania line about 9 o'clock last night. It yet persists; a great proportion of the troops, with some artillery, are marching toward Philadelphia."

British spies carried word of the mutiny to Clinton, far faster than the news reached Washington at New Windsor. Rumors of a possible strike into New Jersey by Clinton's troops prompted the Pennsylvania men to assure Wayne they would "act with desperation" against any threatening British move.

President Reed of the Pennsylvania Council headed toward the mutineers on January 4. As he proceeded, he sent a message to representatives of the dissident soldiers asking them to send representatives to meet him in Trenton rather than in Princeton. The request was rejected out of hand.

Bolstered by Congressional instructions "to bring the matter to as speedy, safe, and honorable an issue as possible," Reed and his party entered Princeton on Sunday, January 7. The mutineers lined up in perfect military order to receive the visitors. Reed met almost immediately with the soldier leaders and began negotiations for a settlement of the demands.

Meanwhile, as anticipated, Clinton stepped up his efforts to get the mutinous Americans to desert to the British army, with generous terms for enlistments. On Friday, January 5, he dispatched John Mason and a guide named James Ogden with a list of promises to the Americans if they would march to join enemy regiments.

When the spies reached Princeton a day later, Mason was permitted to talk with the mutiny leaders. Mason and Ogden were then seized by the mutineers and kept as hostages while the American sergeants discussed capitulation terms with Reed.

The discussions continued for two days before a compromise was reached on January 8. No man would be held beyond the time for which he freely and voluntarily enlisted; a commission would decide disputed terms of enlistment; a soldier's oath would be accepted if his papers could not be found. Other matters, such as adjustments in pay for the depreciation of the Continental currency and clothing supplies, would be settled as soon as possible.

The emergency was over. About 1,250 infantrymen and sixty-seven artillerymen were discharged, leaving about 1,150 men on the rolls. Eligible men were discharged by January 21, many of them after having signed a false oath. A high percentage of the discharged soldiers later re-enlisted.

Mason and Ogden were tried as spies, found guilty, and hanged on January 11. The mutiny had not been about bowing to an enemy; it was about squaring off with a weak, penniless American government.

Mutiny burst into the open again, at Pompton, New Jersey, on January 20, when 300 rebellious New Jersey troops left camp and walked fifteen miles to brigade headquarters in Chatham to demand better conditions. They were ordered to return to their camp. Professing "a great affection for their officers," they returned quietly to Pompton after being promised a hearing on their complaints.

None of the niceties of Princeton befell the New Jerseyans. Three among the Pompton mutineers were selected to be shot. The executioners would be twelve of their comrades. Two were executed, but the third was pardoned. The first man to face his executioners did not die immediately. The squad reloaded and finished the cruel job. The harshness ended overt thoughts of mutiny in the rest of the army.

Despite the troubled atmosphere, there was still a war to be fought, particularly in the south, where the British were firmly in control. The three-year French Alliance would continue to be a major disappointment to the American public until more than half of the year 1781 had expired. Finally, in August, every element of the coalition came neatly together, with a strong sense of urgency. The road to Yorktown was about to open.

They Called Him "Mad" Anthony

Anthony Wayne, born on New Year's Day, 1745, knew early on that he wanted to be a soldier. In two years at his uncle Gilbert Wayne's school, Anthony seemed interested in little other than military lessons. His uncle was at a loss concerning the boy's future, but told the boy's father "he may perhaps make a soldier." The schoolmaster had a complaint: "He has already distracted the brains of two-thirds of the boys in my charge by rehearsals of battles, sieges, etc."

Eventually young Wayne became a surveyor and was sent to Nova Scotia by a Philadelphia firm to survey 200,000 acres of land the firm hoped to acquire. The firm lost interest and Wayne returned to Pennsylvania to become a noted tanner.

He was a well-liked community leader, despite a certain cockiness. As the war approached, he espoused the cause of independence and soon became a colonel in the Pennsylvania Line in January 1776. His dreams of becoming a soldier had come true.

Sent to Canada in June 1776, he managed to lead his 200 men out of a near-disaster. He wrote a self-serving note to Benjamin Franklin: "Col. William Allen and I have saved the Army in Canada."

Wayne assumed command of Fort Ticonderoga and inherited a band of angry soldiers. Amid signs of mutiny, Wayne placed a pistol in the chest of the ringleader and quelled the threat. This was not the glorious military career that Wayne had imagined.

He was finally promoted to brigadier general on February 21, 1777, and joined Washington's army in Morristown. He won some acclaim for his attacks on British forces as they entered New Jersey in the spring of 1777.

He later performed well at Chadd's Ford, Pennsylvania, as the British neared Philadelphia. Soon after he was shamed when British troops annihilated his soldiers on September 21 in what has been called the "Paoli Massacre," but he was redeemed when his troops performed well at Germantown. Then at Monmouth, his soldiers restored battlefield order when General Charles Lee shaped a debacle for the Americans.

When he was replaced as leader of the Pennsylvanians, he decided to leave the army. He changed his mind though, when he was put in command of a regiment of skilled veteran Pennsylvania men, who called him "Mad Anthony" in tribute to his daring battlefield performances. His greatest triumph may have been at Stony Point on July 16, 1779, when his planning and leadership won an incredible victory. Later, after Benedict Arnold's defection, he rushed troops to West Point once the treason had been revealed.

Then, on his thirty-sixth birthday on New Year's Day 1781, his world fell apart at Jockey Hollow. His beloved Pennsylvanians mutinied and marched southward

to Princeton to seek improved conditions and the discharges most felt they had earned. Wayne followed them and kept the mutiny from getting out of hand.

Douglass Southall Freeman, the Virginian famed for his erudite seven-volume biography of George Washington, wrote: "In Wayne, as Washington appraised him, the spark of daring might flame into rashness, but it was better to have such a leader and occasionally cool him than forever be amid the valor of men who feared they might singe their plumes in battle."

Chapter Twenty-three

The CLEAR ROAD *to* YORKTOWN

O n July 11, 1780, an express rider galloped into Preakness (about fifteen miles north of Morristown), where Washington had begun a sojourn of more than two months after the Battle of Springfield. He carried the news that the American commander had been anticipating since the first French promises of help: "Yesterday afternoon the long expected fleet of our illustrious ally appeared off Newport …the signals were all made and the fleet [was] standing in to the harbor."

A week later, the French commander, Jean Baptiste Donatien de Vimeur —the Comte de Rochambeau — wrote Washington from Newport that he had brought more than 5,000 soldiers with him. The French fleet, commanded by Admiral Charles Louis d'Arsac, the Chevalier de Ternay, anchored in the Rhode Island port. The admiral's fleet had eight ships of the line, two frigates, and two galliots (shallow draft boats).

The message could not have come at a better time. Washington had just written Congress that "in a little time we shall have no men; we have lived on expedients till we can live no longer."

As Washington wrote that, fewer than one thousand new American recruits had been enrolled after strenuous recruitment. The army strength that summer was said to be 9,000 men, exclusive of militia, but only 3,278 of them were fit for duty — and few of those were being paid, or fed and clothed as promised on enlistment.

And now, in one day, America had added 5,000 fresh French soldiers, professionally trained, well armed, well fed, well clothed — many more such precisely well prepared and well equipped men than Washington had led at any one time during the entire war. He had

Washington was America's hero on the long march from West Point to Yorktown. Crowds gathered along the roadsides and in every town, hoping to see him or possibly touch his boot or horse.

Washington and a few ranking generals, French and American, stopped at Mt. Vernon — the first time since the commander had left in 1775. He also stopped at his home on the triumphant trip back north from Yorktown.

assembled far greater numbers at times, and his men certainly had attained a commendable professionalism in camps and in battles, but they were always ill equipped, worn out, hungry and discouraged. The darkness without end had begun to brighten.

Almost immediately, however, a good news/bad news cycle recurred. Washington was told that twelve British ships blockaded Newport, nullifying hopes for quick naval reinforcements or even use of French ships already in the harbor. Expectations dimmed even more in early September, when another fleet of sixteen British vessels from the West Indies arrived in the northern waters. The French fleet was for the moment more than neutralized; it faced probable annihilation if the British dared move against them — which they never did.

Washington dispatched Lafayette in July to carry America's official greetings to the French in Newport but delayed his official meeting with the French commanders until September 20. He put General Greene in charge of the American army at Preakness, and left for Hartford, Connecticut, on September 17 with his staff officers and attendants to meet their French counterparts.

The cordial, bilingual Hartford meeting introduced Washington and his staff to Rochambeau, Ternay, and their staffs. A French officer, Claude Blanchard, wrote that

Jean Baptiste Donatien de Vimeur, Comte de Rochambeau, the French commander who brought a force of 5,500 well-equipped French soldiers to America on July 10, 1780.

the French were "enchanted" by Washington; they liked his "easy and noble bearing, extensive and correct views, and the art of making himself believed."

Washington presented three alternatives for Franco-American consideration: An assault on New York City by the combined forces if the French fleet could evade the British ships in the Newport harbor; sending the French ships to Boston and letting the allies strike strategically at Clinton to prevent further aid to the south; or, least desirable, sending a winter expedition into English-held Canada.

Of the three possibilities, the Americans most favored an attack on the British in New York, but the French did not have sufficient ships or additional soldiers to make that feasible. Rochambeau emphasized that although his orders placed him under Washington's command, he would not divide his land and naval components because he wanted all of his units led by the American commander — and no one else. No firm commitments were made for action that summer.

Nearly a year passed with no agreement between Washington and Rochambeau on how best to use their allied forces. Arnold's treason disrupted all plans deep into September. The focus shifted to the southern states, where the American cause had suffered badly under a series of inept generals, until Washington dispatched Nathanael Greene to restore order to the cause in Virginia and the Carolinas. Greene assumed command, in Virginia, on December 2 1780, of an army of fewer of than 2,500 men, not more than 800 of whom were ready for combat.

Greene successfully kept the British at bay in a series of battles, mostly best described as "strategic defeats." The details of Greene's campaign are beyond the scope of this book, but he succeeded in delaying major British successes in the area where the enemy felt the war could be won.

General Charles Cornwallis, the corpulent British officer better known as Lord Cornwallis, served in America almost from the start of the war and, despite his disastrous loss to Washington at Princeton, was a capable officer. He was second in command to Clinton and became the ultimate loser in the British capitulation at Yorktown.

Finally, on August 14, 1781, long-awaited favorable news reached Washington: De Grasse was on his way from the West Indies to the Chesapeake, with 29 warships and 3,000 troops, the powerful asset desperately needed by Washington and Rochambeau. The severe negative was that De Grasse was on a strict schedule; he must return to the West Indies not later than October 15. But he had opened a two-month window of opportunity — sixty days to win the war.

Almost simultaneously, on August 22, Lord Cornwallis, commander of the southern British forces, made his final move. He marched his 9,000 officers and men into Yorktown, and stationed a small supporting force across the York River at Gloucester. The position seemed strong, with access to the sea — a particular plus because his army could be protected and supplied by ships. Cornwallis neglected the obvious: any fleet, of any naval power, could sail into the river.

Cornwallis had a strong option: he would know of any allied American-French operations by land or by sea far enough in advance to leave Yorktown and return to the wide-open spaces along the Carolina seafront if he so chose. He never picked that course.

Washington was on the move within six days. He and his 2,500 troops, about half his army, and Rochambeau's 5,000 men began the 450-mile journey from near West Point to Yorktown on August 20, seeking to get as big a jump on Clinton's awareness as possible. The sudden movement puzzled Clinton more than it alerted him. His spy system had broken down, as confused as the command.

The relatively weak Continental forces left to guard the Highlands had to be Washington's major concern. The recent arrival in New York of a strong force of Hessians boosted Clinton's army to more than 15,000 rank and file. Washington gambled, leaving about 2,500 men, and the New Jersey militia, to protect the Highlands over the long stretch from West Point to Morristown.

Washington's gift of sly deceit came quickly to the fore. First, his army was hauling a large number of small flatboats, each capable of holding forty men, to give British spies the illusion that the allies intended to cross the Hudson River into the city, or perhaps to cross the Arthur Kill to Staten Island. Most ominously, the Franco-American alliance might combine the two assaults.

To lend further credence to a New York attack, Washington sent about fifteen skilled French bakers to Chatham to build stone and brick ovens large enough to bake 3,000 to 4,000 loaves of bread daily — sufficient to feed an army waiting to invade New York. The ovens were located under a shed about sixty-five feet long on the east side of the Passaic River. Another group of soldiers went through the area acquiring other supplies that would support a long stay in Chatham. Some special storehouses are said to have been built, but because of the time necessary, it is more likely that the stores were placed in neighboring houses and barns.

To give the hoax a solid base, a letter leaked to Clinton declared that the invasion of New York was a certainty. The *New York Mercury* reported on August 27 that at least 6,000 soldiers were in Chatham "and their greatest distance from Staten Island is no more than nine miles."

Clinton prepared for an invasion. He felt sure that his skilled army could smash the American and French invaders if New York were attacked either directly from the Hudson River or from Staten Island. Unfortunately for him, by the time he had his defense in order, the supposed invading armies had begun marching four columns southward through New Jersey, one American column apparently headed toward Staten Island, a second American force headed through Chatham, and two units of the French army marching inland toward Morristown and beyond.

The *New York Mercury* let its readers know on September 3 that the feared American attack on the city was a deception. By then, the American and French lines were crossing the Delaware River. The *Mercury's* editor, Hugh Gaines, imagined residents of Elizabethtown and Chatham pondering their fates: "In winter we were told we should be in New York in the spring, in the spring we believed we should certainly walk the streets of that place in September, and now instead of attacking that City, supported by a powerful French navy, our whole army is leaving us to the mercy of our enemies."

That was true enough. There was little to keep Clinton from pouring his army across the Hudson, perhaps in time to attack the rear guard of the Franco-American army on its way to Yorktown or perhaps sweeping into New Jersey to occupy the state.

Washington and Rochambeau rode into Philadelphia on August 30. Three days later the combined troops entered the city. The march to Philadelphia and southward was a huge inspirational and social success as well as a military coup de grace. At every overnight stop the French bands played in public squares, giving local people a chance not only to hear the polished music but also to observe the grace and charm of the visiting soldiers. The French wore handsome, colorful uniforms, which, day after day, seemingly looked new, well tailored and unblemished.

The French troops were hailed with awe and appreciation wherever they marched, but the unquestioned focus of the long march was George Washington, the most revered individual in America. People stood along the streets in villages, small towns, and cities to see and to cheer America's first national hero.

The allied forces marched on, through dust and summer heat, through rain and persistent drought. They averaged about twenty miles a day, with the front of the line often about a day ahead of the rear. They were up and on the way by 4 a.m., and marched until noon. After a pause for lunch, the men walked rapidly until nearly sunset. It was a grueling schedule.

Maryland offered relief for the marching men. They boarded French transports at Head of Elk, Baltimore, and Annapolis and sailed down Chesapeake Bay to the Virginia Peninsula west of Yorktown.

Cornwallis now knew the strong, growing force was near but could do nothing except wait in what had become a trap of his own making.

Washington, Rochambeau and their staffs rode inland, heading for a visit at Mount Vernon, reached on September 9. Washington had left his home more than six years be-

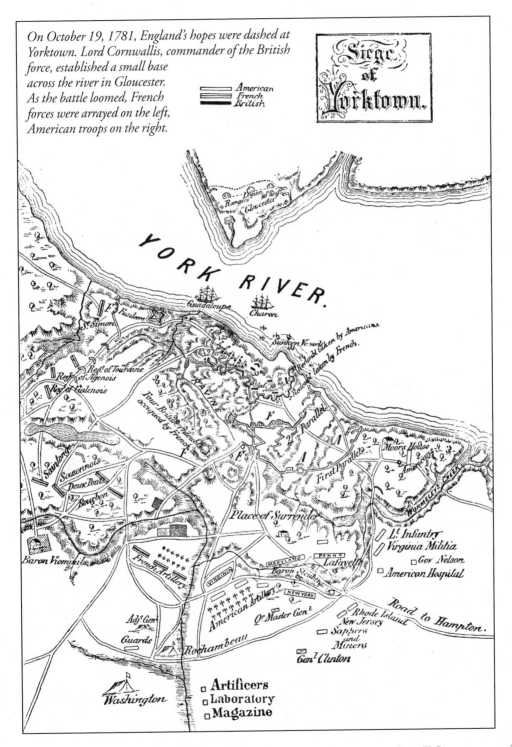

On October 19, 1781, England's hopes were dashed at Yorktown. Lord Cornwallis, commander of the British force, established a small base across the river in Gloucester. As the battle loomed, French forces were arrayed on the left, American troops on the right.

American
French
British

Siege of Yorktown.

fore and had not seen it since. The pause gave him a chance to entertain Rochambeau and his top officers, as well as some of his own staff. The diversion lasted three days before the push to Yorktown was resumed.

On August 29, an impressive armada began sailing into Chesapeake Bay. The British at first thought the fleet was part of the Royal Navy, but as ship after ship arrived, it became plain the ships were French. Five days later the British flotilla under Admiral Graves also came into the river, unaware that French ships were already there in force.

Graves turned tail and sailed outward into the open sea. The French followed suit and, on September 5, the two fleets clashed in the open Atlantic Ocean. The French mauled the English fleet so badly it had to return to New York for repairs. The waters of the Chesapeake belonged to the allies. Cornwallis should long before have recognized the only chance for escape was via the mainland, about to be occupied by the Franco-American army.

Cornwallis would not have admitted it, or perhaps not even known it, but time had begun to run out for him. The first allied soldiers reached the outskirts of Yorktown on September 28, just as darkness fell. With the addition of American regiments already in the South and an influx of militia, Washington eventually would command about 11,000 Americans and 8,800 French troops.

On Sunday morning, September 30, the advancing allies moved into three outposts abandoned by the British and by nightfall Washington's forces were within a mile of Yorktown's main defenses.

Ground for siege positions was broken after sunset on October 6. The next morning, astonished British troops saw a nearly finished trench 2,000 yards long and about 600 to 800 yards from their own positions in town. The first allied mortar shells and cannon balls began pouring into Yorktown on October 9, and, by the next morning, forty-six pieces of allied artillery were so effective that the British return fire was reduced to about six rounds an hour. British defenses had been weakened enough by October 14 to permit two daring assaults on redoubts within the outer British defenses, one led by French officers, the other by Americans.

On the night of October 16-17, Cornwallis tried to ferry some of his able-bodied soldiers out of Yorktown and across the York River to Gloucester, but a shortage of boats and an exceptionally severe storm thwarted the escape. The next morning the allies started the heaviest bombardment yet — as many as 100 pieces were said to be in constant action.

Sometime between 9 and 10 a.m. on October 17, a British drummer boy appeared on a parapet between the lines, beating the signal for a parley. A British officer appeared, waving a white handkerchief, and as the roar of cannons died down, carried a message of surrender from Cornwallis to Washington.

The British asked for twenty-four hours to submit surrender terms. Washington gave them two. Final terms were ironed out by the morning of October 18. Washington demanded that Cornwallis sign by 11 a.m. The defeated army was to march across a parade ground at 2 p.m. in surrender.

French and Americans lined both sides of Hampton Road, down which the British would march to the surrender point. The red-coated enemy appeared promptly at 2 p.m., marching to the slow, doleful beat of a military band.

Pleading illness, Cornwallis sent a deputy, General Charles O'Hara, to the field of surrender. In a breach of military etiquette, O'Hara presented himself to Rochambeau rather than to Washington. While Rochambeau pointed him toward the American com-

Comte Charles Hector Theodat d'Estaing, the French admiral whose strong fleet insured the victory at Yorktown.

mander, Washington was not about to be upstaged. He coolly told O'Hara that since the British had chosen to act through a deputy, O'Hara must deal with Washington's deputy, General Benjamin Lincoln. O'Hara complied.

Cornwallis surrendered 8,180 British and Hessian soldiers — about one-fourth of all British forces in America. An additional 830 naval personnel surrendered to DeGrasse. The British lost 596 men, killed and wounded. Despite the ferocity of the fighting, American and French losses were a mere 125 men. The British also surrendered huge amounts of materiel: 214 pieces of artillery, 7,320 small arms, twenty-four transports, many small craft, forty wagons and teams, 269 horses, and huge stores of ammunition and supplies. Very welcome was a military chest containing £2,113.

It took four days for details of the surrender to reach Congress in Philadelphia and

Washington is seen inspecting French troops in the Yorktown trenches in this 1881 illustration for Harper's Weekly, *commemorating the 100th anniversary of the British surrender. The successful storming of two British redoubts on October 14 ended all British hopes. Cornwallis asked for a ceasefire on October 17 to discuss surrender.*

about a week to be distributed to all Americans via the newspapers of the day. There was cautious belief that the war had all but ended at Yorktown.

News of the stunning loss reached England on Sunday, November 25. Lord North, the indefatigable British Prime Minister and close adviser to King George III throughout the war, is said to have greeted the overwhelming loss with an anguished cry, "Oh God! It is all over!"

The war had not ended, of course. The British still held Savannah and Charleston and were still strong elsewhere in the South. Most important, it had a powerful army in New York and Clinton was still the British commander.

A never-to-be-answered question is why Clinton did not take advantage of Washington's absence to make some kind of substantial move across the river into New Jersey for revenge, food, or both; up the Hudson River to divide New England from the south, as he had always claimed he desired; or even to move southward to engage the allies in another monumental showdown. His army of about 15,000, properly led, might have made a difference. Once more, Clinton did nothing.

BE IT REMEMBERED!

THAT on the 17th of October, 1781, Lieutenant-General Earl CORNWALLIS, with above Five thousand British Troops, surrendered themselves Prisoners of War to his Excellency Gen. GEORGE WASHINGTON, Commander in Chief of the allied Forces of France and America.

LAUS DEO!

A few days after the victory at Yorktown, Americans were asked to remember the virtual end of the war.

Washington never returned to Morristown or Jockey Hollow, except for short visits. Only one brigade was stationed in Jockey Hollow in 1781-82. The huts in Jockey Hollow were deserted. The Ford Mansion heard no more boots clicking across the floors. The beacons never flared again on the Watchung Mountains.

But neither Jockey Hollow nor the Ford Mansion ever faded completely away and the Watchung Mountains never completely succumbed to the invasion of nineteenth-century civilization.

The Magnificent Bakery Hoax

Washington's gift for trickery came to the fore during the early weeks of August 1781 when he began leaking word that a long-awaited attack on New York was about to begin.

First, secrets were whispered to patriots with the well-founded awareness that they would quickly be spread to loyalists and then transmitted to the British in New York. Next, a flurry of written dispatches fell into enemy hands, giving details of an impending attack on the city. The misleading dispatches were also leaked to the French and American forces, letting them in on "secret advance notice" that the combined forces were about to strike New York.

Later, the Comte de Rochambeau, commanding the French army, admitted being completely fooled. He wrote that "where the imposition (hoax) does not completely take place at home, it would never sufficiently succeed abroad." Simply put, anything that didn't fool the American and French armies was not likely to fool British General Henry Clinton in New York.

The inescapable truth was that the allies were about to move somewhere south. New England craftsmen had spent much of the summer building many flatboats, each capable of holding forty men. Where else but in a crossing of the Arthur Kill, between New Jersey and Staten Island, would such craft serve any purpose?

The boats solidified the growing illusion that the allies intended to cross the Hudson River into the city, or perhaps cross the Arthur Kill to Staten Island and attack the city from the south. More ominously, word spread that the Franco-American alliance might combine the two assaults. Any of these moves had to have frozen Clinton in his tracks.

The anticipated attack began to play out August 13, when fifteen neatly uniformed and exceedingly polite young Frenchmen marched into Chatham, led by the Chevalier De Villemanzy. They had orders to establish an army base, complete with a series of storehouses to hold supplies for the assault on New York. Most impressively, the Frenchmen began building a series of brick ovens beneath a sixty-five-foot-long shed along the eastern bank of the Passaic River.

Simultaneously a few of the foreigners spread through the area, making arrangements for buying large quantities of supplies for the army. Chathamites began preparing for an inundation of troops.

The Frenchmen constructed the outdoor bakery in just a few days, and it was large enough to produce 3,000 loaves of bread a day. The fires were lit and the pleasant scent of baking bread wafted through the village. An invading army could not be far behind. On August 19, Washington sent three regiments to guard "the heights between Chatham and Springfield," east of the bakery. The men were warned to "take every precaution against a surprise." They also had orders to assist the bakery staff.

As the ovens baked the bread, British General Henry Clinton had to believe that a mighty assault on New York City was only days away. On attack day, combined French and American armies would strike at New York City, supported by a French fleet that would enter New York harbor and bombard the city.

French and American forces began their move southward from King's Ferry in New York State on August 25. Two American wings headed for Springfield and Chatham; one of them dragged the ominous attack boats. The two French sections moved inland toward Morristown. Washington arrived in Chatham on August 27 (some sources say August 28) and left two days later.

On August 27 The *New York Mercury* reported that at least 6,000 soldiers were in Chatham "and their greatest distance from Staten Island is no more than nine miles." Forces moved in and out of Chatham and Morristown, heading toward Somerset Court House, Princeton and Trenton. Most of the men were well across the Delaware River before Clinton knew the awful truth: he had been hoodwinked again by an elaborate American hoax, so neatly executed that for a brief time the Americans and French were as confused as the British.

Research by the Chatham Historical Society led to this artist's conception of twelve of the ovens built at Chatham in August 1781. The bakery was used to deceive the British into believing a strike at New York was imminent.

Chapter Twenty-four

The WAR *is* OVER — ALMOST

Shortly before 2 a.m. on October 22, five days after the surrender at Yorktown, a post rider entered the streets of Philadelphia, seeking the President of Congress, Thomas McKean. He bore an unofficial message: "Lord Cornwallis surrendered the garrison at York to General Washington the 17th of October."

Two days later, Lieutenant Colonel Tench Tilghman, a trusted aide, brought Washington's personal and official report of the triumph. Congress felt inclined to reward Tilghman for his expenses, but there was not a cent in the national treasury. Elias Boudinot reported on the solution: "The members of Congress, and I was one, each paid a dollar to accomplish it."

One month and three days later, on Sunday, November 25, word of the Yorktown surrender reached England. Despite the fact he had lost two major armies in America (at Saratoga and Yorktown), King George declared he hoped no one thought Yorktown "makes the smallest alteration in those principles of my conduct which have directed me in past time."

His Majesty was boasting in the face of difficulties piling up around the world for the far-flung British Empire. He put aside French victories in the West Indies, the English loss of Minorca in the Mediteranean, the siege of Gibraltar, a revolt in India, rumblings of trouble in Ireland, and the mighty French armies across the English Channel.

More than anything, the King seemed to be ignorant of the hundreds of miles of coastline between Boston and Savannah and the seemingly endless land rolling westward from the Atlantic Ocean. In such a land, the Continentals could retreat into the forests

In areas close to discharge points, soldiers paraded home in this joyous fashion.

and fight on as long as was necessary. The immensity of the New World had always been a matter of mystery for British royalty.

True enough, the war had not ended on the banks of the York River, although military operations virtually ceased. Washington's only immediate chance to inflict further damage after Yorktown was at Charleston, where Greene had cornered the large British force.

The commander in chief urged Admiral de Grasse to join him in a joint attack on Charleston after Yorktown, but the French admiral, already overdue to return to the West Indies, had to refuse. General Arthur St. Clair and the Pennsylvania, Maryland, and Virginia forces were sent southward to bolster Greene in his winter siege.

Rochambeau's French army was to remain near Yorktown on indefinite assignment, while Washington sent the rest of his army northward to winter quarters along the Hudson River and in New Jersey. Traveling with only a small retinue, the general paused on his way north to spend another week at Mount Vernon — only his second visit since leaving home. Then, accompanied by Martha, Washington set out for Philadelphia, where he spent fifteen busy weeks formulating plans for a possible 1782 campaign before setting out for Newburgh, New York, where winter quarters would be established in case Clinton

The Last Hurrah

The Battle of Yorktown obviously did not end the American Revolution. The South was far from conquered but neither was it ever likely to be the base for a total British triumph. In the North, the game of believing General Clinton might make some kind of decisive move — into New Jersey or northward on the Hudson River — had to be played to the end.

Washington settled down in Newburgh for the winter following Yorktown. His major forces were nearby to protect the Hudson River, Clinton's dream objective ever since he had become second in command in New York.

But Morristown and Jockey Hollow could not be left defenseless, lest Clinton pour his troops westward across the Hudson River. In late October, Washington ordered Major General Benjamin Lincoln to dispatch troops into New Jersey and New York. The New Jersey troops were to be encamped "somewhere in the vicinity of Morristown."

Thus the New Jersey Brigade moved into already-ghostly Jockey Hollow for the winter. The brigade had been here before. After the Pompton mutiny the previous January, it was sent to occupy the huts previously occupied by Connecticut regiments.

Strangely, however, during the winter of 1781-82, the brigade apparently occupied a new area. There is evidence that the troops lived in huts, but whether the structures were moved from older sites or built from scratch is not known.

made another attempt to seize the Hudson River.

Most of the nation, especially the army's officers and men, felt the war had ended. Rumors were rife that the citizens of London had petitioned King George to end the war, but Washington recited "an old and true maxim that to make a good peace, you ought to be well prepared to carry on the war."

The encampment woes of the Continental Army persisted as the Continentals faced still another winter with scare food, tattered uniforms, little or no money, and foot soldiers and their officers impatient with the slow progress toward a binding peace.

Washington did not reach the Newburgh encampment until March 31, 1782. The New Jersey Brigade's four regiments returned to occupy huts in Jockey Hollow. Its roster at full strength numbered 1,440 men, but there is little reason to believe that there were anywhere near that many men in the camp.

Cornwallis reached New York on parole in mid-November. His relationship with Sir Henry Clinton, never amicable, worsened. Each sought to fix the blame on the other for the Yorktown defeat. Cornwallis returned to England in January 1782 to be hailed in

Benson Lossing drew this depiction of Loyalists being welcomed in England, based on an allegorical painting by Benjamin West. Under Brittania's shield is the Crown of Great Britain. Closest to the Crown, wearing a large wig, is Sir William Pepperell, an English friend of Loyalists. Directly behind him is William Franklin, New Jersey's last colonial governor. An Indian holds one hand out to hail Brittania and points with the other to war-created widows and children. Various symbols of law, religion and friendship are in the clouds. West, the painter, and his wife are in the right bottom corner. West lived in England from 1763 until his death in London in 1820.

London as a conquering hero rather than a defeated general. The King praised him for his patriotism.

Recalled in May 1782, the bumbling, neurotic Clinton was at a great disadvantage in his verbal battle with Cornwallis. He left New York in a fury, filled with his usual self-pity and bombastic excuses for his failures. In England he began a long, violent public controversy with Lord Cornwallis concerning who was to blame for the failure of the southern campaign. Cornwallis had the upper edge; Clinton's career neared an end in a smoldering self pity.

Sir Guy Carleton replaced Clinton in May. He brought with him from England strong awareness of peace on a not distant horizon. Carleton sent Washington a letter on August 4 announcing that a peace conference had opened in Paris, where America would be offered her independence.

Carleton began evacuating Savannah and Charleston. British troops sailed from Savannah in July. The stalemate at Charleston continued until December, when Greene's troops entered the evacuated city as the last of the British forces went aboard ships ready to sail.

Peace negotiations dragged on in Paris, with Washington and Congress always several weeks behind in awareness of what was gong on because of the slowness of sailing ships. Great Britain did not formally proclaim the cessation of hostilities until February 4, 1783.

As the peacemakers sought final agreement, a drama with international implications played out in Chatham, six miles east of Morristown. There, nineteen-year-old British Captain Charles Asgill awaited hanging without having committed any crime other than being in the wrong place at the wrong time.

Asgill's troubles dated to March 24, 1782, when Monmouth County Tories captured American Captain Joseph Huddy and charged him with killing a Monmouth Tory. He was tried by a group of Loyalists, found guilty, and hanged despite clear evidence that he had been a prisoner aboard a guard ship, the *Britannia*, when the Tory was killed. Captain Richard Lippincott led the executioners.

Washington reviewed the case and demanded that the British send Lippincott to the Americans for judgment. If that were not done, an imprisoned British captain would be selected by lot for a revenge hanging. Asgill was chosen on the eleventh ballot. American and British officers in the room wept openly when this youngest man in the room received the assignment.

Asgill was taken to Chatham early in June and assigned an unbarred room in Colonel Elias Dayton's home. The British officer languished in the village for seven months, never knowing when he would be taken to the gallows. As the tension mounted, the case drew international attention.

Congress, eager for vengeance, refused to act on Washington's suggestion in October that Asgill be permitted to return home. It ignored direct appeals from Benjamin Franklin and the King of England to spare the captain's life, and introduced a resolution ordering Asgill's immediate execution.

The news of the approaching peace was almost lost in the growing international focus on Asgill's fate. Finally, the young captain's mother appealed in desperation to the King of France. The monarch, moved by the mother's request, ordered his prime minister to write to Washington, asking for mercy in the name of himself and his Queen. Washington forwarded the correspondence to Congress.

Congress had been heatedly debating the Asgill case for three days when the King's plea arrived. Impressed by the intense letter, Congress agreed that Captain Asgill should be released and allowed to return to England. He left Chatham on November 17, caught a ship as it was about to leave New York, and arrived in England on December 18.

Captain Charles Asgill,
his image from a program for a play written
about his death watch in Chatham.

By mid-winter 1783, provisional peace negotiations were in place. England accepted the peace document in February and it was sent westward to the United States. Congress approved the provisional treaty on April 11.

Finally, the army's remaining men at Newburgh were told that a binding treaty had been signed on April 19, 1783 — eight years to the day after the war's opening shots at Concord and Lexington The war officially was over. The United States of America had become a reality in the world community.

Joseph Plumb Martin received his discharge papers on June 11, 1783, when "The old man [their captain] came into our room and handed us our discharges, or rather, furloughs." Martin found "the happiness I should experience upon such a day was not realized." He wrote movingly of the thoughts that raced through his mind that day:

We had lived together as a family of brothers for some years, setting aside some little family squabbles, like most other families. We had shared with each other the hardships, danger and suffering incident in a soldiers life, had sympathized with each other in troubles and in sickness; had assisted in bearing each other's burdens, or strove to make them lighter by council and advice; had endeavored to conceal each other's faults, or make them appear in as good a light as they would bear....

In short, the soldiers, each in his particular circle of acquaintance, were a strict and faithful band of brothers.

"We were young men and had warm hearts," wrote Martin. "I question if there was a corps in the army that parted with more regret than ours did, the New Englanders in particular. Ah! It was a serious time!".

General Henry Knox led a select corps of American troops into New York City on November 25, 1783, entering in traditional fashion as the last of the British boarded their transports. Washington followed, accompanied by New York State Governor Clinton and their respective attendants.

Washington spent the dwindling days in farewells to the enlisted men and to their officers. On December 22, he returned his commission to Congress, convened in Annapolis, and headed for Mount Vernon a mere fifty miles distant. He would be home for Christmas — for the first time in eight years.

The war was over.

But there is one more chapter to tell — the slow evolution to the final salvation: creation at Morristown of the first National Historical Park in the United States. It took about 150 years to bring that about.

GLORIOUS NEWS.

PROVIDÉCE, October 25, 1781.

Three o'Clock, P. M.

THIS MOMENT an EXPRESS arrived at his Honour the Deputy-Governor's, from Col. Chriftopher Olney, Commandant on Rhode-Ifland, announcing the important Intelligence of the Surrender of Lord Cornwallis and his Army, an Account of which was printed This Morning at Newport, and is as follows, viz.

Newport, October 25, 1781.

YESTERDAY afternoon arrived in this Harbour Capt. Lovett, of the Schooner Adventure, from York-River, in Chefapeak-Bay (which he left the 20th Inftant) and brought us the glorious News of the Surrender of Lord CORNWALLIS and his Army Prifoners of War to the allied Army, under the Command of our illuftrious General, and the French Fleet, under the Command of his Excellency the Count de GRASSE.

A Ceffation of Arms took Place on Thurfday the 18th Inftant, in Confequence of Propofals from Lord Cornwallis for a Capitulation. His Lordfhip propofed a Ceffation of Twenty-four Hours, but Two only were granted by His Excellency General WASHINGTON. The Articles were completed the fame Day, and the next Day the allied Army took Poffeffion of York-Town.

By this glorious Conqueft, NINE THOUSAND of the Enemy, including Seamen, fell into our Hands, with an immenfe Quantity of Warlike Stores, a forty Gun Ship, a Frigate, an armed Veffel, and about One Hundred Sail of Tranfports.

This broadside, issued in Providence, Rhode Island, on October 25 — a week after the surrender at Yorktown— told the "glorious news" of the decisive victory. The announcement was typical of broadsides that appeared a week or so after Cornwallis capitulated. The Providence printer's haste to spread the news caused him to forget the "n" in Providence. He added the missing letter by hand.

Chapter Twenty-five

SAVING *a* NATIONAL HERITAGE

Tempe Wick, the youngest of five Wick children, inherited the Jockey Hollow family home and land in 1787, when she was twenty-nine years old. A year later she married William Tuttle, who had wintered in huts near the Wick home in 1782. The Tuttles moved into Morristown in 1798, renting the family home to tenants.

Tuttle served in the New Jersey Brigade, the last military unit to encamp in Jockey Hollow. Since the huts used by the Pennsylvania brigade the year before either had been demolished or were in poor condition, the brigade built new huts (in the standard form) "across the road from the Wick House, down the hill and to the left." It is very likely the young soldier met Miss Wick that winter.

Few people at that time placed great value on historical remembrance. As the years passed, area farmers and non-farmers alike tore down the Jockey Hollow huts for lumber, fence rails, or firewood. They saved anything else that might be useful, particularly nails and any other hardware.

Quite naturally, some of the scroungers kept a few treasured mementoes that they picked up off the ground in the hutting area — uniform buttons, coins, bullets, iron cooking utensils, bits of crockery that officers might have used, and on very rare occasions a rusted bayonet or a soot-covered ramrod. However, such cherishing of mementoes did not flourish generally until the twentieth century.

Nature completed the task of eliminating visible evidence of the camp. Decades of passing time gradually restored the oak and chestnut forests that the soldiers had felled. The falling leaves of each succeeding autumn gradually formed rich mulch in which shade-loving shrubs and ground cover prospered. Farm fields and orchards were interspersed with the woodlands, as they had been since earliest recorded time.

When the Tuttles left for the busy life of Morristown, the hardwood stumps of Jockey Hollow's once-great trees had begun the slow rot that in time would eliminate nearly all traces of the woodland where Log House City had throbbed with life and misery. Writers and fanciful historians visited through the passing decades and, as often as not, perpetuated legends and folklore or created some of their own.

In 1871, when Wick descendants sold the farm after 130 years of ownership, Jockey Hollow was once again a mature, sparsely settled forest. The Wick House was, of course, by then an historic building. Tenants occupied the house for another sixty years, despite its isolation.

Almost simultaneously with the Wick family's desire to escape the burden of their old, isolated farm and house, no matter how historic it might have been, the Ford family also tired of its family mansion. Memories of the vital months when the house was the center of the American Revolution had dimmed.

Theodosia Ford died in the homestead in 1824 at age eighty-three. Her sons, Timothy, Gabriel, and Jacob III, all had received degrees from the College of New Jersey. Timothy and Gabriel become lawyers; in 1820, Gabriel was named to the Appellate Branch of the New Jersey Supreme Court, a post he held for twenty years.

Timothy and Jacob III joined their sister Elizabeth in Charleston, South Carolina, where she had moved in 1785 after marrying William De Saussure, wealthy Charleston landowner and lawyer. Those three Fords all would live out their years in Charleston.

By 1805, the South Carolina Fords pointedly wanted no part of the mansion or of Morristown. That year, Gabriel bought the house from his siblings. One of his most pleasant interludes came in 1848, when Benson J. Lossing, the nationally-known itinerant historian, stopped at the Ford Mansion in his quest for first-hand memories of the American Revolution. Lossing found Gabriel eager to talk:

The venerable octogenarian entertained me until a late hour with many pleasing anecdotes illustrative of the social condition of the army, and of the private character of the commander in chief.

Unfortunately, Lossing recalled only a few of Ford's pleasing anecdotes when his book was published. He sketched the mansion before he left and in his caption summed up somewhat ambiguously his evaluation of the house: "…it was a fine mansion for the time."

Henry Augustus Ford, Gabriel's son, became the resident owner after his father's death in 1849. By 1870, the broad lawns and fields had lost their charm; the house had become the family's white elephant. None of Henry's seven children had any interest in living in the home, much less inheriting it.

With no family sentiment for the house or the surrounding property, Henry Ford decreed that on his death the property would be divided into lots and sold. About seven acres would be apportioned to the mansion. Everything would be sold "at public auction to the highest bidder."

The New York auctioneering firm that conducted the sale on June 25, 1873, featured both sentimentality and practicality in its fliers and advertising. It appealed first to a purchaser's possible hopes for nobility, seeking to attract "that citizen, soldier or statesman who desires to become the successor to the Father of his Country in its occupation."

Barring that, the auctioneers pointed out that the house "can be made into one of the finest hotels or fashionable resorts in the state." The site was extolled as "magnificent," in an area known for "the salubrity of its climate and its freedom from miasma."

Washington's Headquarters — a national shrine — up for public sale? In retrospect, it seems impossible, yet it was known that one very eager bidder proposed to buy the building and transform it into a boarding house.

There was some indignation among newspaper editors and journalists. A reporter for the *Newark Daily Advertiser* wrote:

We do not look upon this event with pleasure. It seems a desecration, almost a sacrilege. The decadence of the Republic may date from the time when as Americans we begin to merchandise our public places.

The *New York Evening Post* asked how the people of Morristown "can permit such a monument to go out of their hands" and the *Elizabeth Daily Herald* suggested (prophetically, as it turned out) that a group might buy the house "and hold it in reserve for its possible purchase by the state."

Most Morristown people — and the town's newspapers — were indifferent. An area newspaper poll reported that one person thought the house was "a tumble down shanty." Another scoffed that "Washington only spent a couple of nights there."

Three hundred people rode a special train out of New York and Newark for the sale on June 25. A detailed account of that day — and of the long history of the home — is the subject of *A Certain Splendid House* by James Elliott Lindsley, a lively story of the mansion, its sale, and its survival.

The bidding quickly reached $20,000. When it reached $24,100, ex-Governor Theodore Randolph, from Morristown, stepped before the crowd to declare that he, General Nathaniel Halsted, and George A. Halsey, both from the Newark area, would buy the home and about three-and-a-half acres of surrounding land for $25,000.

He poignantly expressed the wish that four persons could have made the purchase. He then electrified the crowd by declaring:

We propose to hold the property subject to the will of the State of New Jersey, which can have it at any time for the same amount of money.

William VanVleck Lidgerwood of Morristown responded to Randolph's wish for a quartet of buyers, declaring that he had intended to bid $25,000 for the house but would willingly become a fourth partner. Such uproarious applause greeted Lidgerwood's response that no further bidding was possible. Another bidder later told a reporter that he would have gone to $28,000 if the enthusiasm had been less.

The buyers intended to preserve the building as a museum, hoping, without success, that the State of New Jersey might buy it. Nine months after the auction, on March 20, 1874, Randolph and his associates incorporated the Washington Association to administer the house.

Association trustees could sell up to 500 shares of Washington Association stock, at $100 per share. Women could buy shares but could not attend meetings or vote. When a woman died, her shares had to go to a male descendant. Those restrictions were abolished in 1946; nearly sixty years later, a woman (Barbara Mitnick) could — and did — even become president of the association.

If any share, male or female, were not claimed within five years after a shareholder's death, it would revert to the State of New Jersey; in time the state became the major shareholder and would play a major role in the eventual disposition of the house.

The state agreed to give the association $2,500 annually, a reasonable sum for the 19th century. But that state aid, plus interest on investments of share money, had to stretch over each annual association budget. In return for the state aid, the association agreed to keep the house "open to the public, free of charge, at all proper times."

Starting in 1887, the association sponsored an annual lecture by a distinguished historian on topics related to the American Revolution or to George Washington. Those lectures, published annually, constitute one of the group's major contributions to history. The roster of lecturers includes many distinguished state and national historians.

The building was for many years open twelve hours daily, every day except Sunday. Admission was free. A single male employee, who lived in a wing of the house, kept the house clean, mowed the lawn, washed the windows and guided visitors through the site. His multitude of tasks gave him little time for spirited, detailed tours of the old mansion.

Exhibits in "The Headquarters," as it came to be known, might kindly have been termed eclectic, although haphazard might have been a better adjective, despite the value of the materials given to or bought by the association. The association accepted almost

CONTAINING A FINE COLLECTION OF REVOLUTIONARY ARMS.

THE ARMORY, WASHINGTON HEADQUARTERS, MORRISTOWN, N. J.

CONTAINING A FINE COLLECTION OF COLONIAL CHINA, SHOWING OLD COLONIAL DISHES.

THE PANTRY, WASHINGTON'S HEADQUARTERS, MORRISTOWN, N. J.

THE MAIN HALL, WASHINGTON'S HEADQUARTERS.

With a very limited staff and a small budget, the Washington Association could do little more than live up to its reputation as "Morristown's attic." Valuable artifacts (left) shown here were neatly displayed in the Ford Mansion but the impression was of dull clutter rather than intriguing interpretation. Even the magnificent front hall (above) was crowded with furniture.

every gift; for years the Ford Mansion was known as "Morristown's Attic."

However, the founding of the Washington Association, its ready acquisition of artifacts, and the maintenance of the mansion provided the stability and firm footing on which the mansion and Jockey Hollow would become a national historical park nearly eight decades later.

At the time of the association's founding, there was scant local interest in the American Revolution or in history in general. Twelve years after the auction of the Ford Mansion, Morristown permitted its other "Washington's headquarters" to vanish. The Arnold Tavern on North Park Place, where Washington had his home and offices in the winter and spring of 1777, was slated for razing in 1886.

By then, the old tavern had become home to two stores on the first floor, Adams & Fairchild, grocers, and P. H. Hoffman & Son, clothiers. The Hoffmans wanted to erect a brick building on the Arnold site to better typify the Morristown that wealthy people in the area preferred. It was said that more millionaires could be found within a radius of

He Saved Jockey Hollow

Lloyd Waddel Smith was eleven years old in 1881 when his father, George Washington Smith, was forced by economic setbacks to sell his 220-acre estate in what was then Chatham Township, about four miles east of Morristown. Young Smith promised his mother he would someday earn enough to buy back the estate.

He worked to help pay his way through Philips Academy in Andover, Massachusetts, and worked his way through both Yale and Harvard Law School. He bought back the estate in 1907, one year before his mother died, and named it Harvale Farm to honor his two university alma maters. By then, his town had incorporated as Florham Park Borough.

Smith's fortune grew rapidly in his New York brokerage firm, but when he retired in 1931 he began to play the role of a fair-to-middling farmer. He drove an old Lincoln touring car, wore old clothes and sold his farm's produce from a stand in front of his mansion.

He assembled without fanfare a huge collection of Washington manuscripts and artifacts and a great deal of valuable Revolutionary War materials. He maintained the valuable collections in Boxwood Hall, his name for the family home.

Fortunately for posterity, he began quietly buying land in Jockey Hollow, at a time when a major real estate project also was assembling land for a posh private village of large homes. Smith ultimately acquired a thousand acres of property, spending about $250,000. His donation of that land to the National Park Service made the Morristown National Historical Park more than a dream. Without the land, there probably would have been no preservation in Jockey Hollow.

When he died in 1955, he gave his precious library to the Morristown National Historical Park. His collections will be featured in the new library annex being built as an extension of the existing park museum.

---

three miles of Morristown than anywhere else in the nation. They were a powerful influence, but their interests lay more in ostentatious dwellings and expensive entertainment than in historical preservation.

Julia Keese Colles "saved" The Arnold Tavern by having it hauled down Market Street to a location on Mt. Kemble Avenue, nearly a half mile south of the town green. She hoped to remodel the once-important building into a larger hotel, but, when that idea was abandoned, the relocated tavern became the first home of All Souls Hospital. A much larger hospital was built across the street; the ramshackle "headquarters" declined and finally was damaged so badly in a 1918 fire that it had to be demolished. No one seemed to care.

More than 10,000 people flowed across the lawn of the Ford Mansion, closed Morris Street, and stretched far beyond on July 4, 1933, when the mansion, Jockey Hollow, and Fort Nonsense were transferred officially to the National Park Service. A firing squad from the Morristown American Legion opened the ceremonies with a rifle salute.

The Wick House lived on, although considerably neglected. Its survival was not because it was an historical property but essentially because it was out of sight and out of mind as part of the thousand-acre property that New York broker Luther Kountze had assembled for an area he called "Delbarton" to honor his three children (the first three letters of the names of each son, DeLancey and Barclay, and ton from the last letters in his daughter Helen's middle name, Livingston).

While Kountze erected his mansion closer to the northern part of his property, his land stretched outward through much of Jockey Hollow, and included the Wick House. DeLancey Kountze offered the Washington Association the building and some land in 1921. Association members felt their small treasury could not sustain it. Later, the Morristown DAR also declined to accept the house because of the expense involved.

There matters stood throughout the 1920s, a time of great national prosperity and small governmental budgets, municipal, state, and federal alike. Prosperity and the ever-increasing numbers of automobiles stretched the Washington Association beyond its limits as the 1920s neared their end: too many people wanted to visit Washington's Headquarters.

More than 31,000 visitors knocked on the front door of the mansion in 1930 — on the average, about 100 persons each day. The association valiantly sought to accommodate them, with too few guides, no system for scheduling visits, scant money for modernizing exhibits, and limited funds for adequate security.

In addition to the difficulties in handling visitors, there was also the constant cost of maintaining an old building — leaks in the roof, peeling paint, keeping the floors clean on rainy and muddy days, heating problems, and cleaning or replacement of windows.

The sudden collapse of the New York Stock Exchange in October 1929 spread panic and economic disaster throughout the land. Many wealthy association members could no longer contribute even small gifts to make up deficits. The association's limited portfolio of investments languished, although it did not vanish. In a nation plunging into the Great Depression, historical concerns were not high on lists of things most necessary.

At the end of the 1920s, in a most unlikely economic climate, Morristown Mayor Clyde Potts and former Mayor W. Parsons Todd, a self-effacing local philanthropist, began a movement to insure protection of, and visibility for, Morristown's vital Revolutionary War heritage.

Potts initially harbored the illusion that the State of New Jersey might incorporate the Ford Mansion and whatever remained of Jockey Hollow into the state park system. As the state dallied, a consensus emerged that Morristown and Jockey Hollow deserved national attention.

It was almost too late.

In 1929, a syndicate of powerful New York financiers with little regard for historical importance formed the Jockey Hollow Associates. They acquired substantial land in the encampment area and had plans drawn for a posh real estate development.

The proposed rich man's playground would feature expensive homes bordering golf links and bridle paths, bringing a luxurious country club atmosphere to the land where men had endured a bitter existence in the winter of 1779-80. Little of Jockey Hollow's history would remain except in the name of the development.

Morristown owned the Fort Nonsense land and a few hundred acres in its Jockey Hollow aqueduct company but it needed far more Jockey Hollow acres if its historic aspirations were to have any credibility. Potts appointed a commission to seek ways and means to acquire Jockey Hollow property with as little expense as possible. His choice for the commission chair, Lloyd Smith, was a masterstroke.

Smith was one of the so-called "quiet millionaires," a New York City banker who lived in Florham Park, about four miles east of Morristown. His interest in George Washington and the American Revolution included a huge private library of 12,000 books, 30,000 manuscripts (many of them rare), and more than 100 artifacts directly linked to Washington. The priceless collection was maintained in his large Florham Park home.

A commission with Smith as chair was almost certain of sustained effort. He bought about 1,000 acres of Jockey Hollow property for $250,000 – taken from his own pocket — and made it available to the project. Smith's purchase included 700 acres owned by the Jockey Hollow Associates. It was said that only "an appeal to their patriotism" prompted them to sell the land.

Equally important, however, was a letter that Redmond Cross, a member of the Jockey Hollow Associates, dispatched to Arthur Demaray, an assistant director of the park service, suggesting that the agency might be interested in acquiring land in Jockey Hollow and Morristown. It reached the desk of Horace Albright, director of the National Park Service. Albright answered that he was "tremendously interested in this whole historical field."

Albright had a strong ulterior motive. He had just begun a campaign to create national areas to protect and promote historic sites, mainly in Eastern states, where legislators were not as enthusiastic about the National Park Service as were western legislators, in whose states lay the majority of national parks. Acquiring, developing, and preserving the great natural areas of the West had always been the chief mission of the National Park Service. Albright hoped to win eastern support by acquiring and developing historical areas. The Morristown proposal dovetailed with his plans.

At about the time Smith's gift was revealed, the voters of Morristown agreed at the November 1930 election to donate the town's acquired land (essentially the Smith purchases) to the federal government. Slightly more than 1,300 acres — plus the Wick House and the Ford Mansion — were ready for donation to either the State of New Jersey or the National Park Service.

The Jockey Hollow land was critical, of course, and although its earthen fort was long gone, Fort Nonsense added an important dimension to the proposed park. The only intangible was the Washington Association.

Albright visited Morristown in October 1932 and proposed that a joint maintenance agreement be worked out with the Washington Association to insure that local influence was not lost. His assistant, former Congressman Louis C. Cramton, said it would be unthinkable to create a park agreement that did not include the association. Conversation with association leaders led to a revised bill that insured construction of a fireproof library and museum to house the association's collections.

The bill to create the America's first National Historical Park moved quickly through

The Arnold Tavern, Washington's 1777 winter headquarters in Morristown, faced the Morristown Green. Its lower floor was converted into two stores, with apartments above.

both houses of Congress and was signed into law by President Herbert Hoover on March 3, 1933, as one of his last actions as President of the United States. The next day, Franklin D. Roosevelt moved into the Oval Office.

It is important to point out that the park service had acquired other historical areas previously, but Morristown was the first to be designated as a national historical park.

Despite careful discussions before Hoover's signing, the bill had a potentially disastrous flaw: Washington Association members had never been asked to ratify formally the transfer of association property to the federal government. Without the Ford Mansion, the park would be far less significant.

Three committed association trustees — Frank Bergen, Lloyd Smith, and Henry C. Pitney, Jr. — set out to win membership support for the transfer. Pitney wrote as the quest began that unless a great majority of the stockholders approved, "the plan of a national historical park authorized by the recent act of Congress must fail."

The trio knew that they would be dealing with some stockholders angered because the bill might have appeared to take the Washington Association for granted. They also had to convince stockholders that the association's treasury would not be part of the deal,

In 1886, plans to raze the former Arnold Tavern were averted when Julia Keyes Colles "saved" the building. She had it towed about a half mile south on Mt. Kemble Avenue, hoping to convert the tavern into a hotel. When that hope faded, the building became All Souls Hospital. All Souls later built a large new brick hospital across the street, leaving the historic tavern to fall into ruin. After it was partially destroyed in a 1918 fire, the remainder was torn down.

that the association would have a visible role in administering the new park, and that current employees, particularly venerated guides Minnie Hotchkiss and Mary Scott, would not be fired.

Votes or proxies had to be returned by May 8, 1933. That day, 270 (out of 470) living members voted to include the association and its property holdings in the national park. The vote did not mean that 200 members opposed the action; many could not be found or submitted invalid ballots. It was moot: the governor and treasurer of the State of New Jersey cast the state's 288 shares for the project.

The formal dedication of Morristown National Historical Park on July 4, 1933, catapulted Morristown's crucial role in the American Revolution into national attention. More than 10,000 people overflowed the lawns of the Ford Mansion on what the *Morristown*

Daily Record called a "gorgeous" day. A bevy of carrier pigeons, freed to carry word of the dedication to Fort Monmouth, rose into the azure blue sky and headed south toward the fort. From there, the message was telegraphed to the White House.

A return telegram from Roosevelt expressed the hope that the nation's first National Historical Park would "serve as a fountain of inspiration for the entire country."

Governor A. Harry Moore took care to declare (with considerable exaggeration) that "five eighths of the American Revolution was fought in New Jersey," and Secretary of the Interior Harold A. Ickes formally welcomed Morristown into the National Park Service family.

Loyd Smith, whose contributions of time, money, and patience might have been the greatest gifts of all, used about one minute to present the deeds for the Jockey Hollow holdings to the park service.

On February 22, 1934 — more than seven months after the dedication — association President Frank Bergen faced the association in the annual meeting in the Ford Mansion. He assured members that the mansion would be "maintained perpetually," that the Washington Association would play a cooperative role in supervising the mansion, and that the group's treasury of $50,227.13 was properly invested and beyond the reach of federal bureaucrats.

He closed with a declaration that has rung clearly through the decades of the lasting relationship between the association, the National Park Service, and the people of America:

Although we have parted with the paper title to this property, we are still joint tenants with 130,000,000 other American citizens.

As the Great Depression settled more deeply across a gloomy, economically ill nation, President Roosevelt unleashed a vigorous program of federal aid to battle the depression and to take unemployed people off the streets. Some of that federal aid quickly moved the new national park toward reality.

One of the New Deal's "alphabet agencies," the Civilian Conversation Corps (CCC), began toiling in the park on May 25, 1933, nearly six weeks before the dedication. They were young, unemployed men whose skills ranged from physical prowess to basic historical and archaeological competency.

The young CCC men fanned out through the forest that had been neglected for nearly 150 years. They cleaned out trees felled by age, disease and hurricanes. They removed limbs, twigs, and other debris from the forest floor. As they worked their way through the woodland, they laid out walking trails. Later they fashioned shingles out of fine chestnut trunks and limbs.

Morristown's first park superintendent was Elbert Cox, who gracefully eased concerns of the Washington Association leaders and oversaw construction of the museum promised in the agreement with the Washington Association. Ground was broken in early April 1936. The Public Works Administration (PWA), another federal government agency, allocated $200,000 for the building on the rear portion of the Ford Mansion property. Noted New York architect John Russell Pope designed the building.

By ground breaking time, fifteen persons were at work on interior plans for the museum, including preserving and classifying collections and arranging for manuscript displays. Park officials were eager to get the association's collection out of the mansion so they could proceed with plans for restoring the mansion interior to its appearance and use when Washington and his aides occupied the building as the Continental Army headquarters.

When plans were formulated for the museum, the estimated cost was $140,000. On dedication day, February 22, 1937, the total announced outlay was $139,140.70. Two wings in the original plan had been deleted to bring the cost within budget. The museum was opened to the public in February 1938.

Cox was succeeded in 1938 by Herbert E. Kahler, who served only one year before giving way to Dr. Francis S. Ronalds, a dignified, scholarly leader who served as superintendent for twenty-nine years. Ronalds established a high level of scholarship in his highly effective administration.

Ronalds scored a major coup in the early 1950s when he persuaded Lloyd Smith to donate his huge, extremely valuable collection of books, manuscripts, and artifacts to the park service. Construction of a library wing to the museum in 1957 provided space to house the voluminous contribution. Smith included the gift in his will and it became effective when he died in 1955.

Ronalds was bolstered in his long stay by Melvin Weig, the historian and archivist who kept the threads of Morristown's Revolutionary War history ever to the fore. Weig wrote the first (and still-used) handbook for the park. He succeeded Ronalds as superintendent. Since then, ten superintendents have served the park, none of them for more that five years.

Park attendance increased each year; 76,544 visitors were registered between February and June in 1941. World War II put an end to active construction in the park and severely affected the budget and attendance.

Post war attendance began to climb in 1946. The American traveling public fully caught on to the importance of the Morristown Park during the 1976 Bicentennial observation of the Revolution when more than 900,000 people — an average of about 2,500 a day, from the U.S. and abroad — visited the park. The Bicentennial brought major changes; a visitor center was built in Jockey Hollow and the museum was totally upgraded

Tempe Wick's Enduring Fable

There is no Morristown story more enduring, or more endearing than the one that tells of the brave and uniquely resourceful young Tempe Wick hiding her horse in her bedroom to keep it from being stolen.

Sadly, from the viewpoint of most visitors who visit the Wick reception area seeking more information on Tempe and her horse, the story is not true. The only things that can be proved are that there was a Tempe Wick, that she lived with her family in Jockey Hollow, and that she had a horse that Continental soldiers may have tried to steal as they prepared for a mutiny on January 1, 1781.

The basic legend says Tempe was stopped by American soldiers as she was riding home through Jockey Hollow; she allegedly beat off the assailants with her whip before galloping home to hide her horse, for up to three weeks, by some accounts.

The first known account of the story, written by the Reverend Joseph Tuttle, appeared in June 1871 in *The Historical Magazine* — ninety years after the incident allegedly took place and forty-nine years after Tempe's death. Since then, the tale has appeared in countless newspaper and magazine stories and in at least two popular books for children. The "facts" vary wildly — from the date and time of the incident, how long the steed was in Tempe's bedroom, whether it stood up in the room, was forced to kneel, or was even hidden under the bed.

The "official" story since the National Park Service acquired the Wick House in 1933 has always been that the episode is false, that there never were any hoof prints on the bedroom floor, and the possibility a horse was kept in a bedroom for even a day without becoming odoriferously offensive is almost nil.

In July 1935 a statement by a park ranger that the Wick story was not true set off a minor tempest. An editorial in the *Morristown Daily Record* declared:

> *Cannot the park service let sleeping legends lie? Or has rehabilitation come to mean that the tenuous fabric of human fancy — myth and legend — must be sacrificed on the altar of historical accuracy? A pox on historical accuracy if it robs us of our fairy tales and misty characters out of old story books. Before we know it, the park service may tell us Tempe never lived or loved at all. And then would we legend-lovers be in a pretty pickle!*

Three weeks later, former Mayor Clyde Potts, one of the principal movers in the establishment of the Morristown National Historical Park, weighed in: "Whether or not the story is true seems to be beside the point. The fact remains people want to believe the story. And when people want to believe something, that settles it."

Is it any wonder that many visitors still want to know the story of Tempe and her hidden horse— and don't much care whether it is truth or fancy?

and modernized. The park service finally implemented its plan to revamp use of the interior of the Ford Mansion to reflect the busy Revolutionary War years when the building was crowded with Washington's offices, his aides, and many visitors.

In 2004, the Washington Association spearheaded action to enlarge and modernize the museum/library — four years before the seventy-fifth anniversary of the establishment of America's first National Historical Park.

The $8.5 million project was based on $5 million contributed by the federal government. The museum will be greatly expanded and the library will become a reality. The Smith collection of books, manuscripts and artifacts finally will become fully available. Many of the association's treasured holdings will be presented for the first time.

Thus, finally, as much as possible of the story of Morristown's vital role in the American Revolution will be available to visitors. The test must be how much of the terrible story of survival visitors take home after witnessing exhibitions and listening to park employees tell the story.

There is no way, of course, to tell the full and harrowing saga of starvation, freezing, and despair at Jockey Hollow, unless visitors walk barefoot in two feet of snow, clothed in little more than a thin shirt and ragged trousers. It would add a proper dimension, too, if visitors could go on a starvation diet for three or four days. One night in a log hut, with twelve people in a fourteen-by-sixteen foot space, with the only light and heat coming from a huge fireplace at one end, would help to make the visit unforgettable. It can't be duplicated; it must be experienced.

In this fanciful quest for a full experience, sleep must be in one of twelve bunks arranged around three walls, with straw for a mattress and a thin blanket for cover. To fantasize to the ultimate or perhaps the ridiculous, the hut would, of course, be built by visitors from trees they felled and hewed into proper size.

There is no way to know fully of an army with no funds, fighting for a bankrupt, uncaring nation, or of American soldiers so hungry that they resorted to bold thievery or compromised their desperation by deserting into Jockey Hollow's deep, dark forests.

On the other hand, neither is there any way to reproduce the heat of Monmouth or the roar of heavy artillery at Yorktown; the crackle of muskets at Lexington, or the slaughter on Bunker Hill.

Museum exhibits will provide the introduction to Morristown. Skilled park rangers/historians will provide the depth and the atmosphere. Visitors will leave Morristown aware that mere survival in the face of all odds deserves understanding.

The $7,000 Parkway

The inability of Morristown National Historical Park supporters to raise $7,000 in 1936 for a parkway linking Jockey Hollow and the town center prompted the *Morristown Daily Record* to bemoan the loss in words that are as meaningful today as they were in 1936:

> As the situation now obtains, tourists seeking historical shrines here [Morristown] leave with disjointed impressions of the national park. They are quite easily directed to Washington's Headquarters, but the thoroughfares leading to Jockey Hollow and Fort Nonsense are indefinitely designated and will be eventually inadequate for traffic volume.

The National Park Service secured a provisional Congressional grant of $200,000 for a "beautiful motor road" to link Jockey Hollow with the Ford Mansion and Fort Nonsense. The provision seemed easy enough to meet: Morristown must raise $7,000 to buy the required land.

To put the $200,000 in perspective, the Great Depression gripped the nation in 1936. Men were willing to work for $14 a week. Agencies such as the WPA and CCC already were at work building roads in other parks. The parkway was a feasible project.

Morristown supporters sent out 1,000 letters to the area's wealthiest residents, expecting a quick response. When the time for committing was reached, only a handful of pledges, totaling $1,000, had been received. The project died aborning.

The *Record* said the national park "will remain a tragically incomplete entity" without the parkway. It quoted residents who "cannot understand why Morristown has remained so blind to the possibilities. "

One of the mysteries is the failure of either Lloyd W. Smith, who purchased land in Jockey Hollow for $250, 000 and donated it to the National Park Service, or W. Parsons Todd, a Morristown supporter of the park and a generous donator to Morristown causes, did not respond as could have been expected. Both undoubtedly knew of the offer and either could have supported the parkway with ease.

The land that could have been purchased for $7,000 obviously is not available now, but if it were, the cost would be an incalculable multi-millions of dollars. Worse, the completion of Interstate Route 287 through town has divided the

MORRISTOWN NATIONAL HISTORICAL PARK

Supporters of the parkway prepared this map to show placement of the proposed new road. It would run from Jockey Hollow to a point on Washington Street, just west of the Morristown Green.

community, running adjacent to the Ford Mansion and necessitating a very complicated traffic pattern to get to or leave the headquarters property.

It might be said that for want of $7,000 a parkway was lost — somewhat akin to the more familiar line that reasoned "for want of a nail a kingdom was lost."

*"All evidence indicates that the winter
of 1790-80 at Morristown was far worse than
the corresponding months at Valley Forge. Yet one
wonders why every school child in America knows of
the gloomy camp on the Schuylkill yet so few know of
the camp at Morristown."*

Douglas Southall Freeman
Distinguished Virginia Historian
and Washington's biographer

The REASON WHY

S urvival is the fundamental story of the American Revolution, from Lexington to Long Island, from Monmouth to the weeks before Yorktown. The much-heralded battles of Trenton and Princeton, brilliant in concept and nearly flawless in execution, were mainly battles of hit-and-run. Washington's fast-moving forces fled both after stunning the Hessians in Trenton and the British in Princeton. Washington fought nearly all the war in that fashion, aiming always to keep his meager forces as intact as possible and in the process earning the reputation as a general of "defeat and retreat."

Nothing proves the theme of survival better than Morristown, New Jersey, and its surrounding area. There, in four separate winter encampments, the American Army survived a critical smallpox epidemic at Morristown in 1777; a season of short supplies at nearby Middlebrook in 1778-79; the most brutal winter of the war in 1779-80 at Morristown and its nearby Jockey Hollow encampment; and the war's most dire mutiny at Jockey Hollow on New Year's Day 1781.

Linked to the saga of survival in Morristown is the almost total failure of national historians to recognize the vital, even compelling, importance of the Watchung Mountains, the thirty-mile-long, 600-foot-high volcanic ridges ranging about halfway between New York City and Morristown. This mighty, natural fortress proved to be impregnable and the perfect refuge for a surviving army, close enough to monitor the British but sheltered enough to insure safety.

Why, as Freeman so bluntly states, should ingoranse of this vital story be so prevalent? The purpose of this book is to present supporting evidence of Morristown's right to national historical prominence, if not eminence.

How can national historians, including the late Dr. Freeman, ironically enough, pay so little attention to the area where Washington spent two of the first five winters of the war, established a major force for a third winter in Middlebrook, and sent a major portion of his army for yet another winter?

The short answer is that survival at Morristown and Middlebrook, in the face of near-starvation, body-numbing cold and mutinous troops, is static and without drama. No troops stormed hills or were slain on bloody battlefields. No memorable cries ("Don't shoot until you see the whites of their eyes") echoed through the din and the smoke of a hundred roaring cannons. Desparate men, barefoot in the snow, nearly naked and hungry beyond imagination, stir only a passing interest 225 years later. Year after year of starving and freezing is what modern publicists would call a hard sell.

Valley Forge had basically the same situation of desperate survival in one winter, but it became the national story as the nineteenth century began, chiefly because the encampment lay so close to Philadelphia, the very cradle of liberty. Many of the stark writings of early Valley Forge folklorists-historians undoubtedly intermingled the vicious winter of 1779-80 at Morristown with what weather historians proved was a mild winter at Valley Forge. This is not to demean or lessen the horrors of Valley Forge; nothing can or should do that. Neither should the myths and improvisations of Valley Forge lessen the role of Morristown and the Watchung Mountains.

By the middle of the nineteenth century, Valley Forge had become hallowed ground. Consider a worshipful passage written by the generally respected, nomadic *Harper's Magazine* historian, Benson J. Lossing, on his initial visit to the Pennsylvania campsite in 1848. He began:

> *Valley Forge! How dear to the true worshipper at the shrine of freedom is the name of Valley Forge! There, in the midst of frost and snows, disease and destitution, Liberty erected her altar; and in all the world's history we have no record of purer devotion, holier sincerity or more pious self-sacrifice, than was there exhibited in the camp of Washington.*

Within those words might be an answer to Freeman's "reason why" question. By 1876, when the nation celebrated the 100th anniversary of the Declaration of Independence, Philadelphia's Centennial Exposition essentially represented the nation's observance of the entire war — and nearby Valley Forge was part of the "must see" for Philadelphia visitors.

On the other hand, history had taken a distinct back seat in Morristown in 1876 as the town expanded commercially around its colonial green. The green itself had been saved from being subdivided into building lots in 1816, when the original owners, the Presbyterian Church, sold the site to preservation-minded independent trustees, with the provision it be kept forever as a "public commons."

As Valley Forge ascended both in historical narratives and in folklore, the Jockey Hollow winter encampment of 1779-80 had all but disappeared. Valley Forge was well along in the process of being preserved, but nearly all evidence of Jockey Hollow's existence was gone. Nearly a century of falling autumn leaves had laid a thick covering of soil over the hut areas. Tall oak and chestnut trees grew beside the nearly rotted stumps of trees chopped down to build the soldier huts of 1780.

The Henry Wick house, the center of the Jockey Hollow area, was neglected and the Wick farm was about to be swallowed up in one of the huge estates being assembled in the Morristown area, The importance of the house and the surrounding Jockey Hollow was remembered only by an occasional history buff who wandered into the area and wrote myth-ridden, hearsay accounts of the encampment.

Worse, the Ford Mansion, where Washington had spent the winter of 1779-80, had narrowly escaped conversion into a boarding house. It was put up for sale at a public auction in 1873. Four men, disturbed by the shame of a prime national historic site on the verge of being sold for a prosaic use, combined to buy the mansion for $25,000. The quartet hoped to sell the house and property to the state for the price they had paid. The state did not bite. Instead, the four men formed the Washington Association to keep history's flickering flame alive. Unforeseen at the time, this would be crucial to the ultimate saving of the Morristown encampment.

The Morristown National Historical Park was created on March 1, 1933. Dedication of the park, on July 4, 1933, drew more than 10,000 people to the scene.

Now about 200,000 to 300,000 visitors come to Morristown each year to see and hear the Morristown and Jockey Hollow story. In the bicentennial year of 1976, 900,000 people from every state and many foreign countries swarmed into Morristown to further their knowledge of the American Revolution.

Park rangers and historians continue to tell the story with accuracy and with enthusiasm. The thousands of visitors listen avidly, then, at day's end, leave. There is little incentive for them to linger in Morristown. There are no moderately priced motels or hotels in the area where family groups can stay. There is no major reception center, such as that at privately owned Williamsburg. No local stores specialize in Morristown souvenirs; there is no bookstore in town.

The answer to Freeman's question about why Valley Forge far surpasses Morristown in national attention mostly lies in a simple answer: Morristown doesn't seem to care, any more than town fathers cared when the Ford Mansion was up for auction in 1873. Little attention is given the vast business potential of bringing a Revolutionary War tourist business to town. The National Park gets little more than lip service from politicians.

Freeman's declaration that "every school child in America" knows of Valley Forge is as true in Morristown as it is elsewhere. Texts by national publishing firms make little effort to depict the drama and despair of 10,000 ragged, hungry soldiers freezing on Morristown's doorstep.

Few Morristown area elementary school teachers participate in the day-long seminars for teachers, offered by the park service several times each year. High school history classes from Morristown and the surrounding area seldom visit either the Ford Mansion or Jockey Hollow. Revered "teachable moments" slip sadly away. Thus, the "gloomy camp on the Schuylkill" becomes the Revolutionary War image that most Morristown school children and their teachers share with the rest of the nation's educational community.

What a shame.

ACKNOWLEDGMENTS

This book owes its existence to Eric Olsen and Tom Winslow, two experienced and knowledgeable ranger historians at Morristown National Historical Park. For a long time Tom has encouraged me to write the book, and the necessary research literally could not have been accomplished without the generosity of Eric in opening to me his extensive files. Eric's files took on critical importance because within a week of my beginning research the park's celebrated library was closed for extensive alterations and additions to the park museum-library.

Norman B. Tomlinson, Jr., of Morristown, manifested great interest in this book and considerably aided its publication with a generous grant.

I am equally in debt to Andrew Bobeck, whose skills in preparing and sharpening the illustrations made them a proper addition to the book.

Tim Cutler contributed several of his Digital Antiquaria publications pertaining to Morristown's role in the American Revolution.

The New Jersey division of the Morristown-Morris Township Free Public Library was generous in letting me use its extensive materials and illustrations. Equally helpful was the New Jersey division of the Newark Public Library.

Ruth La Clair gave the text a careful reading as the manuscript was being written, and I am especially appreciative for the skills of Perdita Buchan, who edited the text, and Leslee Ganss, who designed the book.

ILLUSTRATIONS
and CREDITS

All of the illustrations in this book are many years removed from the war, in the sense that nearly all of the drawings and paintings were executed seventy-five or more years after the war, or are current photographs taken late in the twentieth century.

All Revolutionary War images are the artist's interpretation, especially the magnificent paintings of *Washington Crossing the Delaware* and the stirring *George Washington at the Battle of Monmouth,* both painted in Berlin during the early 1850s by the German artist Emanuel Leutze. John Trumball's scenes at Trenton and Princeton were painted long after each battle. *New Jersey and the American Revolution,* edited by Barbara J. Mitnick, (2005) contains a chapter on art during the Revolution.

The most comprehensive Revolutionary War illustrator was Benson J. Lossing, whose *Field-Book of the American Revolution* contains hundreds of pen and ink illustrations and includes fairly accurate maps of battles and locations. Lossing's work was all done on-the-scene; he traveled thousands of miles in the late 1840s and early 1850s to visit nearly every Revolutionary War site. He did not glorify or change his drawings to suit popular tastes of the day.

As the nineteenth century waned, the romanticized works of highly capable illustrators, led by the artist Howard Pyle, and including Felix O. C. Darley and the prolific, if lesser known, Alonzo Chappel, glorified the war and its episodes. Yet their sketches and paintings serve to give a sense of a war fought close-range by dedicated, if often fancifully depicted, soldiers.

FRONT: pp. 8,11, Andy Bobeck; pg. 12, New Jersey Historical Society; pg. 16, Andy Bobock.

CHAPTER 1: pg. 18,19, Dover Publications; pg. 22, *New Jersey — A Mirror on America;* pg.23, *Field-book of the American Revolution;* pp. 24, 25, 28. Joint Free Public Library of Morristown and Morris Township; pg. 29, collection of the author.

CHAPTER 2: pp. 31,32, 33, Joint Free Public Library of Morristown and Morris Township; pg. 35, Newark Public Library; pg. 38, New York Public Library; pg. 40, Dover Publications; pp. 44, 47, Morristown National Historic Park.

CHAPTER 3: pg. 49, *Field-book of the American Revolution;* pg. 53, Dover Publications; pg. 58, Monmouth Historical Society; pp. 59, 61, 62, 63, Dover Publications.

CHAPTER 4: pg. 65, *Historical Collections of the State of New Jersey;* pg. 66, *The Revolutionary Scene in America;* pg. 67, Bil Canfield; pg. 71, *Field-book of the American Revolution;* pg. 75, Morristown National Historic Park; pg. 77, *Field-book of the American Revolution.*

CHAPTER 5: pg. 78, Newark Public Library; pg 80, Dover Publications; pg. 82, Joint Free Public Library of Morristown and Morris Township; pp. 85, 87, Dover Publications.

CHAPTER 6: pg. 91, Dover Publications; pg. 93, 96, 98, Morristown National Historic Park.

CHAPTER 7: pg. 100, 103, 107, Dover Publications; 113, *Field-book of the American Revolution.*

CHAPTER 8: pg. 117, *Field-book of the American Revolution*; pg. 119, 124, Dover Publications; pg. 125, Newark Public Library

CHAPTER 9: pg. 128, Newark Public Library; pg. 129, Bil Canfield; pg. 132, Dover Publications; pp. 138, Andy Bobeck; 139, Morristown National Historic Park.

CHAPTER 10: pg. 141, Dover Publications; pg. 142, *Field-book of the American Revolution;* pg. 144, Joint Free Public Library of Morristown and Morris Township; pg. 150, Andy Bobeck; pg. 151, Morristown National Historic Park.

CHAPTER 11: pg. 155, Dover Publications; pg. 158, *Field-book of the American Revolution*; pg. 160, Independence National Historic Park, Philadelphia; pg. 161, *Field-book of the American Revolution.*

CHAPTER 12: pg. 163, Dover Publications; pg. 166, Newark Public Library; pg. 167, Dover Publications; pg 171, *Field-book of the American Revolution.*

CHAPTER 13: pp. 175, 176, Dover Publications; pg. 181, *Field-book of the American Revolution*; pp. 182, 189, Dover Publications.

CHAPTER 14: pg. 191, *Field-book of the American Revolution;* pg. 192, Dover Publications; pp. 195, 196, *Field-book of the American Revolution*; pp. 200, 201, Chatham Historical Society.

CHAPTER 15: pg. 203, *Field-book of the American Revolution*; pg. 204, Joint Free Public Library of Morristown and Morris Township; pp. 207, 208, 211, Dover Publications; pg. 214, *Secret History of the American Revolution.*

CHAPTER 16: pg. 217, Morristown National Historic Park; pp. 219, 223, Dover Publications; pg. 225, *Field-book of the American Revolution*; pg. 226, Thomas Winslow Collection.

CHAPTER 17: pg. 229, Dover Publications; pg. 232, Morristown National Historic Park; pg. 235, Dover Publications.

CHAPTER 18: pg. 237, Dover Publications; pg. 240, Newark Public Library; pg. 244, Andy Bobeck; pg. 247, Chatham Historical Society.

CHAPTER 19: pg. 249, New Jersey Historical Society; pg. 250, *Field-book of the American Revolution;* pp. 253, 257, Dover Publications.

CHAPTER 20: pg. 259, *Historical Collections of the State of New Jersey;* pg. 261, Dover Publications; pg 262, Newark Public Library; pg. 268, Dover Publications.

CHAPTER 21: pp. 272, 274, 275, 277, 279, 280, 281, Dover Publications.

CHAPTER 22: pg 285, Morristown National Historic Park; pg. 293, Dover Publications.

CHAPTER 23: pg. 295, Library of Congress; pg 296, Dover Publications; pg. 297, *Field-book of the American Revolution;* pp. 298, 301, Dover Publications; pg. 303, *Field-book of the American Revolution*; pp. 304, 305, Dover Publications; pg. 307, Chatham Historical Society.

CHAPTER 24: pg. 309, Dover Publications; pg. 311, *Field-book of the American Revolution;* pg. 313, Chatham Historical Society; pg. 315, Dover Publications.

CHAPTER 25: pp. 320, 321, Thomas Winslow Collection; pg. 323, Newark Public Library; pp. 326, 327, Thomas Winslow Collection; pg. 333 *Morristown Daily Record.*

BIBLIOGRAPHY

Anderson, John R. *Shepard Kollock: Editor for Freedom,* Chatham, N.J., The Chatham Historical Society, 1975.

Barber, John W., and Howe, Henry, *Historical Collections of the State of New Jersey.* Newark, N. J., Benjamin Olds, 1844.

Bakeless, John. *Turncoats, Traitors & Heroes.* New York, Da CapoPress, 1959.

Boatner, Mark M. *Encyclopedia of the American Revolution.* Mechanicsburg, Pa., 1994.

Carp, J. Wayne. *To Starve the Army at Pleasure.* Chapel Hill, N.C., University of North Carolina Press, 1984.

Fenn, Elizabeth A. *Pox Americana: The Great Smallpox Epidemic of 1775-82.* Hill and Wang (division of Farrar, Strauss and Giroux), 2001.

Fischer, David Hackett. *Washington's Crossing.* New York, Oxford University Press, 2004.

Fleming, Thomas. *The Forgotten Victory: The Battle for New Jersey.* New York, Reader's Digest Press, 1973.

_____ . *Liberty!* New York, Penguin Putnam Inc., 1997.

Flexner, James Thomas. *The Young Hamilton.* Boston, Little, Brown and Company, 1978.

Freeman, Douglas Southall. *Washington* (An abridgement of Freeman's seven-volume *George Washington*). New York, Simon and Schuster, 1968.

History of Morris County, New Jersey. New York, W.W. Munsell & Company, 1882.

Kummel, Henry B. *The Geology of New Jersey* (Bulletin 50). Trenton, N.J. Department of Conservation and Development. 1940.

Lefkowitz, Arthur S. *George Washington's Indispensable Men.* Mechanicsburg, Pa., Stackpole Books, 2003.

Lossing, Benson J. *Field-Book of the American Revolution.* New York, Harper and Brothers, 1850-52.

Lindsley, James Elliott. *A Certain Splendid House.* Morristown, N.J., The Washington Association, 2000.

Ludlam, David. *Early American Winters, 1604-1829.* Boston, American Meteorological Society, 1966.

Martin, James Kirby, and Lender, Mark Edward. *A Respectable Army: The Military Origins of the Republic, 1763-1789.* Harlan Davidson, Inc. 1982.

Martin, Joseph Plumb. *Private Yankee Doodle,* edited by George F. Scheer. New York, Little, Brown & Company, 1962. (Popular Library Edition), 1963.

Mayer, Holly A. *Belonging to the Army.* Columbia, University of South Carolina Press.

Mitnick, Barbara J. *New Jersey in the American Revolution.* New Brunswick, N.J., Rutgers University Press, 2005.

Pancake, John S. *The Year of the Hangman.* University of Alabama Press, 1977.

Papers of William Livingston, Vols. III and IV, edited by Carl Prince. Trenton, The New Jersey Historical Commission, 1979

Prince, Carl E., Middlebrook. *The American Eagle's Nest.* Somerville, N.J., Somerset Press Inc., 1958.

Randall, Willard Sterene. *Benedict Arnold: Patriot and Traitor.* New York, William Morrow and Company, Inc. 1990.

Royster, Charles. *A Revolutionary People at War.* New York, W.W. Norton & Company, originally published by the University of North Carolina Press, 1979.

Scheer, George F. and Rankin, Hugh F. *Rebels & Redcoats.* New York, The World Publishing Company, 1957. Paperback Edition, The Da Capo Press, 1987.

Smith, Page. *A New Age Now Begins* (two volumes). New York, McGraw Hill Publishing Company, 1976.

Smith, Samuel Stelle. *Winter at Morristown, 1779-80: The Darkest Hour.* Monmouth Beach, N.J., Philip Freneau Press, 1979.

Thacher, James. *Military Journal of the American Revolution.* Gansevoory, N.Y., Corner House Historical Publications, 1998.

Thayer, Theodore. *Colonial and Revolutionary Morris County.* Morristown, N.J., Morris County Heritage Commission, 1975.

_____. *Nathanael Greene, Strategist of the American Revolution.* New York, Twayne Publishers, 1960.

Vanderpoel, Ambrose Ely. *History of Chatham, N.J.* Chatham, N.J., The Chatham Historical Society, 1959.

Van Doren, Carl. *Mutiny in January.* New York, The Viking Press, Inc., 1943.

_____. *Secret History of the American Revolution.* New York, The Viking Press, Inc. 1941.

Weig, Melvin. *A Military Capital of the American Revolution.* Washington, D.C., National Park Service, 1950.

Wertenbaker, Thomas Jefferson. *Father Knickerbocker Rebels,* New York, Charles Scribner's Sons, 1948.

INDEX

ABOUT *the* AUTHOR

John T. Cunningham has long been known as "New Jersey's popular historian," a title bestowed upon him by the New Jersey Historical Commission. His prolific contributions to state history in his books, magazine articles, documentary films and talks demonstrate that he knows, writes and talks about his native state from experience and diligent research.

This is his fiftieth book. His first, *This is New Jersey*, published in 1953, has never gone out of print. Well known in the state's schools, his extensive program of New Jersey studies features the noted text, *You, New Jersey and The World.*

One of the founders of the New Jersey Historical Commission, he has served as its chair, and was also president of the New Jersey Historical Society. Rutgers University, in bestowing an honorary degree on Mr. Cunningham, called him "Mr. Jersey." The *New York Times* said: "He helped to give New Jersey legitimacy."

With years of experience as a reporter on a major New Jersey newspaper, Mr. Cunningham considers himself to be a historian who approaches his writing with a journalist's quest for truth combined with a style accessible to all readers.

Cormorant Publishing — an imprint of Down The Shore Publishing — specializes in books, calendars, cards and videos about New Jersey and the Shore. For a free catalog of all our titles or to be included on our mailing list, just send us a request:

Cormorant Books
Down The Shore Publishing
Box 100, West Creek, NJ 08092

info@down-the-shore.com

www.down-the-shore.com

Down The Shore Publishing is committed to preserving ancient forests and natural resources. We elected to print *The Uncertain Revolution* on 50% post consumer recycled paper, processed chlorine free. As a result, for this printing, we have saved:

28 Trees (40' tall and 6-8" diameter)
11,925 Gallons of Wastewater
4,796 Kilowatt Hours of Electricity
1,314 Pounds of Solid Waste
2,582 Pounds of Greenhouse Gases

Down The Shore Publishing made this paper choice because our printer, Thomson-Shore, Inc., is a member of Green Press Initiative, a nonprofit program dedicated to supporting authors, publishers, and suppliers in their efforts to reduce their use of fiber obtained from endangered forests.

For more information, visit www.greenpressinitiative.org